THE
POWER
of TWO

Secrets

to a

Strong &

Loving

Marriage

SUSAN HEITLER, PH.D.

New Harbinger Publications, Inc.

Publisher's Note

This publication is designed to provide accurate and authoritative information in regard to the subject matter covered. It is sold with the understanding that the publisher is not engaged in rendering psychological, financial, legal, or other professional services. If expert assistance or counseling is needed, the services of a competent professional should be sought.

Distributed in Canada by Raincoast Books

Copyright © 1997 by Susan Heitler
New Harbinger Publications, Inc.
5674 Shattuck Avenue
Oakland, CA 94609

Book design by Heather Landers, Robert Frear Graphic Design
Cover design by Shelby Designs & Illustrates
Cover Illustration by Daniel Singer

Library of Congress Catalog Card Number: 96-071151

ISBN-10 1-57224-059-8
ISBN-13 978-1-57224-059-9

New Harbinger Publication's website address: www.newharbinger.com

13   12   11

25   24   23   22   21   20   19   18   17

FSC
Mixed Sources
Product group from well-managed
forests and other controlled sources
Cert no. SW-COC-002283
www.fsc.org
© 1996 Forest Stewardship Council

To the couples with whom I have worked as a marriage therapist, thank you for teaching me. Your struggles and triumphs in learning to live together more lovingly have nourished the understandings in this book.

And to my husband Bruce, my loving soulmate.

Table of Contents

List of Tables

Acknowledgments

Many individuals in so many different ways have participated in creating this book. I warmly thank you all. In addition, I want to add special thanks to the people listed below whose specific contributions particularly improved this book.

First and foremost, I feel enormously indebted to the many generous couples from my clinical practice who have agreed to allow their stories to be told so that others might learn from their growth. For reasons of confidentiality their names have been changed in the text, and I am not listing them here, but my profoundest appreciation goes out to them.

Family members sat together and brainstormed until they yielded the book's title: Norma Degen, Dorothy and Emmett Heitler, Sara Heitler, Amy Klapper, Becky Heitler Lubin, Fay Shwayder, and (*tah dah!*) Lisa Klapper, the winner of the title derby.

Jerry Hultin's incisive commentary helped me early on to clarify what to keep, what to augment, and how to partition the book's chapters. Noblette Danks reminded me that I am a teacher at heart. Mary Wells's advice to give examples has enlivened every page. Eric and Aimee Murphy brought to my attention the perspective of Ecclesiastes on marriage.

My colleague and fellow author Barbara Ellman's ideas on historical changes in marital relationships clarified the underpinnings of this book; her editorial suggestions spurred essential rewriting. Rachel Zucker and my nephew, Josh Goren, reorganized and redrafted Part I, reaching out helping hands when I was sinking in the swirl of too much writing yet to do. My colleague, Barbara Geller, and my secretaries, Janet Olson and Teresa Chavez, advised me on design decisions and fed me with ongoing enthusiasm that kept my energies up. My parents, Harold and Mary McCrensky, stood by me. Their editorial suggestions have improved every chapter and their chicken soup kept me going.

Matt McKay, Kirk Johnson, Gayle Zanca, and Lauren Docket of New Harbinger have been a first-class team. Here in Denver, John Boak and Dave Ludwig added invaluable graphics expertise.

Paula Singer's photographic artistry significantly enhances this book. I am proud that she is my sister and that this is our second book together. Her son, my nephew Dan Singer, graphically captured the essence of togetherness in his cover drawing.

How do people write books without adult children to help them? Abby efficiently, effectively, and insightfully handled the library research. Sara worked with me in drafting an essential early chapter; her writing skills upgraded my own. Jesse sharpened the introduction; I rely upon his clarity of vision and solid judgment. Jacob brings humor to all of us and sagacity beyond his years.

Finding the person you choose to marry may be the single most important event in a person's life. For discovering Bruce for me, I eternally thank my dear friend Dori Kaplan. Without her contribution I would never have experienced the understandings in this book.

Lastly and most lovingly, I thank my husband Bruce, my collaborator in testing the secrets written herein. In our more than twenty-five years together in marriage, his wisdom, laughter, love, and learning have figured profoundly in my own personal experience of the blessings of the power of two.

Other Titles by Susan Heitler, Ph.D.

Books
David Decides About Thumbsucking
From Conflict to Resolution

Audiotapes
Anxiety: Friend or Foe?
Conflict Resolution for Couples
Depression, A Disorder of Power
Working with Couples in Conflict

Videotape
The Angry Couple: Conflict-Focused Treatment

Introduction

I believe in marriage. Marriage opens the doors to many of life's most rewarding blessings, from sharing coffee in the morning to sharing a bed at night. In my opinion marriage is one of life's ultimate privileges and the core structure of a stable society.

What exactly is marriage? Legally it is a partnership contract. Emotionally, marriage commits you to comingling your lives—side by side, hand in hand, heart to heart. When you agree to marry, you commit to joining forces for purposes of housing, finances, children, sex, leisure, fostering each other's realizations as individuals, digesting disappointments, celebrating triumphs—together writing the music of your lives.

Whom is this book for?

Looking at the manuscript for this book, one of my sons, a senior in college, enthusiastically suggested calling it *What We Really Needed to Learn in Sex Ed*. He wanted to share it with his roommates and friends. "Relationships are a huge part of what makes our lives great or miserable, and we're clueless about them," he said. "For all our education, no one has said a word to us about how to do the couple thing. Anyone can do sex. We're fine at falling in love. But keeping a good relationship, that's what we need help with."

My spunky widowed Aunt Norma concurred. She told me I should title the book *Things I'd Tell My Dead Husband If I Could Dig Him Up From the Grave*. Aunt Norma realized that although she and her feisty husband Lou had enjoyed a long and gratifying marriage, the secrets in this book could have greased the wheels and eased the inevitable jolts of living life as a couple.

This book is for anyone who is now or hopes to be married: young adults forming initial connections, couples considering marriage, troubled couples, and long-satisfied spouses who want to improve their relationship skills. Everyone, I guess, except Uncle Lou, for whom the book has arrived too late.

What is the Power of Two?

In mathematics, when you multiply a number by itself, you raise it to the power of two. As opposed to addition, where adding a number to itself merely doubles it, raising a number to the power of two causes exponential growth; for example, $10 + 10 = 20$, but $10 \times 10 = 100$.

A similar increase happens in marriage. When two individuals form a couple, their communal power becomes more than twice what they each held separately. When two become one in marriage, that union can generate the power source for a life of love, nurturance, strength, and joy.

The opposite can happen, and, sadly, often does. The immense energy unleashed when two join into a couple does not always go to create good. It can become the power to hurt. The energy of your interaction can constrict your life, demoralize you, or provoke frustration or resentment.

This book provides assistance so that the power generated by your union enhances your life. It offers guidance for avoiding the risks inherent in living as a couple and for channeling the energy of your relationship into building a lovingly shared world.

The challenges of contemporary marriage

A quick perusal of the "Marriage" listings in any anthology of quotations reveals entry after entry of dark, sarcastic, and misogynist views:

> *Marriage, if one must face the truth, is an evil, but a necessary evil.*
> —Menander (343–292 BC)

> *It happens as with cages: the birds without despair to get in, and those within despair of getting out.*
> —Montaigne (1533–1592)

> *Every woman should marry—and no man.*
> —Benjamin Disraeli (1804–1881)

These negative views certainly had some basis. For most people in past eras, marriage was an economic and social necessity. Affection and mutual emotional support were bonuses, not essentials.

In recent decades, society has come to offer both the individual and the couple more options. Marriage itself is now a choice, and love is assumed to be the largest part of the equation. In the process, however, societal changes have necessitated changes in what it means to be a couple:

- The elevation in the status of women—liberating for females—often seems threatening to men, who now must share head-of-family status with their wives rather than wielding sole authority. Sharing leadership of the family means that couples need skills for cooperative decision making.

- Because the division of labor in the household is no longer determined by gender, couples must make vastly more decisions about who does what. They must also have the agility to continually adjust and readjust their assignments as circumstances change.

- Geographical dispersal of close-knit extended families offers individuals freedom to grow beyond the constraints of their childhoods, but leaves them adrift in hard times. Couples need skills for helping each other in times of emotional distress.

- With both spouses working outside the home, time for leisure and socializing has dwindled. Playtime goes to household needs. Spouses rely on each other to be support group and recreational partner as well as lover, economic partner, and coparent.

- Although liberalized divorce laws offer relief to those caught in a destructive marriage, the contemporary ease of divorce destroys the sense of permanence matrimony used to have. Security now must come from confidence that you as a couple possess the teamwork to face life's challenges together, and from the pleasure you receive from being together.

The goal of this book is to teach the skills that can enable you to meet the challenges of contemporary marriage with maximum satisfaction.

Where do the secrets in this book come from?

The secrets to harmonious living described in these chapters have evolved from multiple sources:

- *Research* by psychologists who study marital communication patterns. Pioneering researchers such as John Gottman, Neil Jacobson, Clifford Notarius, David Olsen, and Howard Markman have clearly established that couples with solid communication skills for handling the challenges of married life fare radically better than their less skilled counterparts. Watching a young couple discuss emotionally charged issues, psychologists can predict with remarkable accuracy whether their marriage will yield happiness or distress.

- *Clinical experience.* Twenty years as a clinical psychologist specializing in treatment with couples has provided me with a unique laboratory for testing and retesting ideas about marriage happiness.

- *Theory.* My book on psychotherapy, *From Conflict to Resolution*, provides the theoretical underpinnings for this current book. I posit that conflicts, within and between people, lie at the core of emotional distress. This conceptual framework, enriched by conflict-resolution research from the realms of business, legal, and international negotiation, has led me to new ways of understanding emotional health, distress, and the ingredients of marriage success.

- *Twenty-five years of marriage.* My husband and I have had to discover many of these secrets ourselves. His insights permeate this book. We sometimes joke about how complex this business of marriage is. How do people who are not continually studying marriage manage to do it? Fortunately, the more we have learned, the more our marriage has blossomed.

How to use this book

This book is divided into three parts:

   Part I teaches the basics of communicating with your partner.

   Part II describes techniques for handling the challenges presented by conflict.

   Part III tells how to enhance a good marriage and make it truly great.

This book will work best if both you and your partner read it. This way, you can learn a shared set of skills and ideas. Like any work or play done in tandem, marriage functions best when the participants are well matched—in style, skills, and agreement about the rules of play. Getting a firm grasp of the basics in Part I is a good place to start.

Beware of trying to absorb everything in the book at once. Most readers will find that they have a lot to learn. A principle often used in therapy is to go where the energy lies. That is, as you read the Table of Contents, certain chapters may strike you as particularly relevant to something going on currently in your relationship. You can choose what seems most pressing, and explore other chapters as you feel ready.

A single, quick reading of this book hopefully will intrigue you. At the same time, implementing the book's secrets is likely to take multiple readings of the chapters where you have most to learn. You also may want to bookmark certain sections so you can refer to them quickly.

Learning skills to ride resiliently through the rougher spots in marriage requires considerable commitment. This book cannot do the job by itself. New marriage skills take study, experimenting, learning from mistakes, and enjoying successes. If you decide to invest your energies in this learning, however, you just may win the ultimate payoff—a strong marriage replete with mutual well-being, enduring respect, and joyful love.

Part I

THE BASICS OF COLLABORATIVE DIALOGUE

The main way that couples enjoy and accomplish, or disrupt, the business of living together is through exchange of words. Talking together signals that you want to share your experiences with each other, that you value each other's input, and that you care about each other. What you say and hear as you talk with each other becomes your shared world. Your teamwork in running your household depends on your ability to give and take information. Your tone of voice and words convey your attitude toward each other—liking, respect, or irritation. Connecting by talking, like sexual connecting, both expresses and consolidates your relationship.

When your dialogue feels safe, loving, and satisfying, your relationship feels like a good one. If talking together becomes dominating, tense, rude, or bruising, the relationship feels both less secure and less appealing. Moreover, since verbal interaction occurs during so much of the time you spend together, and is essential to the business of living together, how you talk to each other becomes the single best indicator of the health of your relationship.

Public peace versus battle on the home front

By the time most people are old enough to hold a job, they have developed reasonably good skills at cooperative interaction. Few adults fight with friends, neighbors, colleagues—or for that matter, anyone outside the family circle. Most of us know enough about the guidelines for civil interactions to keep our public persona friendly and cooperative.

What changes when we go home? Family life requires considerably more shared decisions than friendship does: when to come to the dinner table, how much money to spend on what, who gets to do what when. All these issues and many more need joint agreement. The more issues—many of which touch highly charged and emotionally sensitive concerns like power, money, sex, self-esteem, and personal autonomy—the more likely conflict is to erupt.

A second difference is that at work, at school, or in social situations, most people try to look their best. We know how people are supposed to behave, and we usually try to look good by those standards. When we cross the threshold to our homes, by contrast, that effort may stop. We want to relax, let our hair down, put our feet up. When the reins are loosened and we're free to do what comes naturally, what comes naturally is often a replay of what we heard in the homes we grew up in.

Now the plot thickens. Human beings are creatures of learning. Patterns we learned as children may become templates for the ways we behave as adults—and for the ways we expect our mates to behave. The young boy who kept to himself to avoid getting entangled in family battles may become an adult who spends excessive time separate from other family members, particularly when they bicker. The little girl who experienced unfair criticism as a child may become hypersensitive in adulthood, hearing blame and reacting defensively even when no criticism is intended.

We are also creatures of learning in that we are likely to repeat what we have seen others do. How our mother and father related to each other may become the model for how we as adult mates talk over life's challenges. If our parents handled conflict by fighting, we may respond to sensitive domestic situations with argument. If our parents dealt with conflict by ignoring it, then when troubling events occur, we may smother our concerns.

Unfortunately, high-level cooperative dialogue skills were fairly rare in previous generations—as they are in all too many marriages today. In addition, by continuing the marital interaction patterns of earlier generations we risk perpetuating patterns of hierarchy, patriarchy, and disconnection that do not fit the ideals of contemporary couples.

What is problematic dialogue?

Dialogue that is not collaborative can take several forms. It may be combative, competitive, chaotic, or it can err in the direction of being insufficient, cut off prematurely to avoid overt conflict. Table 1 summarizes these styles.

Poor communication habits can cause you to speak insensitively. Also, the more hurt or angry you feel, the more likely you are to start reacting to your partner as an enemy instead of as a teammate. The more habitually mates talk to each other as if they were enemies, the more hurtful, defensive, and unpleasant the relationship becomes. Nastiness can beget nastiness.

TABLE 1 Styles of Dialogue

Strategy	Collaborative	Combative	Cut off
Goal	Shared understanding	To prove who is right and who is wrong. To win by inflicting the most damage or getting the other to give up.	To avoid conflict, as conflict means unpleasant fighting.
Format	Consensus building	Debate Hurtful comments	Change the topic away from sensitive areas of difference.
Tone	Positive Friendly Productive	Adamant, attempting to persuade. Can become irritable or angry.	Underlying tension; may have false cheeriness to convey that everything is fine when it isn't.
Purpose of Listening	To hear what is right and useful in what each speaker says.	To defend against incoming information.	Listening does not occur because neither party has expressed true concerns.
Toxicity	Tact minimizes saying anything that might hurt the other.	Toxic comments are seen as legitimate.	Criticism is avoided by steering clear of controversial topics.
Attitude Toward Differences	Differences are treated respectfully, appreciated and enjoyed.	Differences are divisive, leading to argument.	Differences produce disengagement, lest discussion of them evoke conflict.

Len (sounding accusatory): *Where did the wastebasket go? Do you have to be such a compulsive cleaner that you're always emptying them and leaving them who knows where? You drive me crazy. How am I supposed to throw away the newspaper if you keep hiding the wastebaskets?!*

Life in Len's household tends to be tumultuous. Sometimes Linda, his wife, doesn't even want to greet him in the evenings, and often she dreads time with him on the weekends. Len is in fact a well-intentioned, often generous fellow, who can be very fun, but he spoils the pleasure of living together with insensitive comments.

Because the family in which Len grew up spoke in demands, accusations, and complaints, he learned to convey his concerns in unpleasant, ineffective ways. Moreover, because his wife Linda grew up in a similar family, she responds with resistance instead of trying to help him, fueling his initial irritation into full anger.

Linda (defensively): *I don't hide the wastebaskets. And I wouldn't have to clean all the time if you weren't so messy. What do you think I am, your personal maid? You have eyes. Find your own wastebasket.*

What is collaborative dialogue?

Gerald faces the same missing wastebasket dilemma as Len, but addresses his wife, Gina, in a respectful manner that makes life in their household consistently emotionally safe and good-humored.

Gerald (sounding frustrated): *Where is the wastebasket? I can't find the one we usually keep in our room, and I want to clear off my desk. Have you seen it?*

Gina (with a chuckle): *I'm sorry, Gerald. I was determined to get the house cleaned up this morning before I left for work, and I'll bet I left all the wastebaskets where I was emptying them in the kitchen. Want me to get one?*

Gina does not respond with defensiveness. She has good cooperative dialogue skills herself. And because Gerald doesn't threaten her self-esteem with hurtful comments, she easily responds in good humor. She acknowledges her mistake and generously offers help.

Collaborative dialogue, as Gina and Gerald demonstrate, enables couples to pool information, build shared insights, and come to mutually agreeable plans of action. With collaborative dialogue, couples are able to:

- enjoy spending time together
- convey information easily to one another

- function as teammates in working toward shared goals, such as earning a living, creating a lovely home, raising happy children, and contributing positively to their community

- utilize the more complex communication skills delineated in Parts II and III of this book. These shared decision making, conflict resolution, and other skills only work with consistent use of cooperative dialogue, so the stakes for thoroughly learning the basics are high.

The tone of collaborative dialogue is friendly. Even when the topic is a serious one, the tone still feels cooperative, as if you have placed your problem on a table and the two of you have sat down side by side to try to solve it. You feel that you are confronting the problem together, rather than that you are confronting each other.

Another tip-off that dialogue is collaborative is that you feel a sense of forward movement as you accumulate shared understanding. Adversarial dialogue feels repetitive. When dialogue is cooperative, with each successive comment you feel movement toward a shared plan of action.

Lastly, when dialogue is cooperative, you and your partner take turns talking and listening, with equal weight given to what each of you has to say. If, by contrast, one of you feels more dominant, something is amiss.

Within an overall climate of harmonious cooperation, irritations indicate that something is going wrong. Like the jolting in a car when it veers off the road onto a soft shoulder, bumpy tensions signal that you have slipped off the track of cooperative dialogue. In response to such a signal, each of you needs to take a look at what you are doing that may be problematic. You then can figure together out how to get back on track. To use tensions as indicators of slippage, however, it helps to have clarity about what constitutes cooperative talking, and what is out of bounds.

What lies ahead?

Len and Linda and Gina and Gerald are not real couples; they are composites of the very real couples I work with as a marriage therapist. Len and Linda exemplify the problems that lead couples to seek counseling. Gina and Gerald exemplify the warmly comfortable relationship characteristic of couples who have learned better ways of handling married life.

In the following three chapters Len and Linda and Gina and Gerald will demonstrate the principles of collaborative dialogue. With these basics, you and your partner can devote your power of two to enjoying a strong partnership and a loving household.

The mutual confidence on which all else depends can be maintained only by an open mind and a brave reliance upon free discussion.

–Judge Learned Hand

Chapter 1

Secrets to Talking

Free and open expression of thoughts and feelings is a hallmark of a healthy marriage. How you express what's on your mind, however, determines whether you and your mate will feel like teammates or like enemies. The basic principles and secrets in this chapter will help the two of you to speak your mind while remaining loving allies.

Basic 1: *Say It*

Say what's on your mind. Verbalize your concerns, fears, and desires.

Holding Back	Speaking Up
Linda feels frustrated. Len generally goes to sleep after the news on TV, but she is ready to go to sleep now. Sitting next to Len on the couch, Linda sighs loudly. Len continues to watch the news. Eventually Linda goes to bed alone, so angry she can't sleep.	*Gina:* I feel tired; I'd rather go to bed early tonight than watch the news. *Gerald:* Usually I like staying up, but the news is boring tonight. How about if I turn it off in five minutes?

When Linda wants to go to sleep, she hints and wishes, but never says what is on her mind. In contrast, Gina and Gerald understand the importance of openly speaking their thoughts. Gerald might agree to turn off the TV or might prefer another solution, but Gina's statement of what she feels and wants is essential for launching a what-to-do-next discussion.

In order for what matters to you to also matter to your mate, your preferences need to be put on the table. If something concerns you and you don't say it, your partner, like Len, will have no way of knowing what troubles or what pleases you. Similarly, if you block your desires from your own consciousness, both of you will lack essential information needed for the subtle steering—now to the left, now to the right—that keeps a relationship on track.

Open sharing builds bonds of intimacy, strengthening a sense of connection. However, saying what's on your mind requires a confidence that your concerns will be sympathetically received. Your honesty and courage need to be met with positive listening skills (as described in the next chapter). This is why it is important that both you and your partner read this book.

You can also increase the likelihood that your concerns will be listened to sympathetically by taking yourself seriously, listening to your own feelings and thoughts respectfully. If you feel that your own thoughts and feelings are legitimate, the odds that they will be heard by your partner in the same way increase. How you react to your own thoughts and feelings is something you, and only you, control. Fortunately, even though being self-critical is often a matter of habit, it is a habit you can choose to change.

 ## Really say it

Hinting, or as linguists call it, indirect communication, is a high-risk, low-gain strategy. Saying outright what you feel and want is generally more effective.

Hinting	Saying
Len: Don't you think it's hot inside? *Linda:* I think it's actually quite nice. *Len (a few minutes later, after complaining about the heat again):* I wish you were the kind of person who likes to go outside more.	*Gerald:* I'm getting claustrophobic staying at home all day. I'd like to go out for a run or take a walk. Will you join me?

Len hints instead of saying outright what he wants. Linda has no idea that he wants to go outside. When Len feels increasingly frustrated, his negative comment to Linda makes matters worse, bringing her down as well. The stakes for hinting instead of saying can be costly for both of you.

In extreme circumstances indirect communication can actually be dangerous.

Linguists have studied direct and indirect communication between pilots and copilots. By analyzing the dialogue recorded in the black boxes retrieved from plane crashes, researchers have noted that accidents are more likely to occur when talk is indirect (Tannen, 1994). If a copilot says, "Getting cold out," that's hinting. Maybe the captain will be a sensitive listener who picks up the hint, and maybe not. If the copilot says directly, "The drop in temperature may be causing ice to form on the wings. I think we'd better do another deicing before we take off. What do you think?" the odds of a terrible tragedy shrink dramatically. Sadly, this precise mistake in the pilots' dialogue led to the January 1982, Washington, D.C., crash that killed 69 of the 74 people on board the plane.

Interestingly, the relationship between pilots and copilots now is undergoing changes similar to those taking place in marriage partnerships. The pilot-copilot relationship used to be strongly hierarchical, with little information traveling from copilot to captain. Now, particularly among the younger generation of pilots, although the captain is still the final authority, a more equal relationship results in better communication. Both pilots speak their minds more directly, and both attempt more attuned listening, taking seriously each other's observations and suggestions. The result is safer airline travel for all of us.

In the business world, dealmakers who work with a competitive model of negotiations may use silence as a negotiating technique. They may consider hiding their hand and maintaining a "poker face" critical for a winning strategy. Unlike poker, however, business in fact often proceeds more effectively when businesspeople, like marriage partners, can speak directly about their interests and preferences. This openness is the first step in collaborative business negotiating, which in ongoing relationships earns more for both sides than poker-style competitive negotiating.

Men sometimes feel that "saying it," or putting their cards face up on the table, is incompatible with the traditional image of the strong, silent man. It is, because *strong* and *silent* are incompatible, at least in the project of marriage. That is, a strong spouse feels comfortable making his or her feelings and thoughts known. In marriage, silence is more often a sign of weakness, of lack of confidence, than of strength.

If you hold a romantic image of the lone gunslinger who keeps feelings and cards close to his chest, bear in mind that at the end of the movie the cowboy almost always rides into the sunset alone. Although he carries an air of romantic mystery, the silent cowboy isn't suited for life as a longtime companion.

The contemporary male values the ability to be emotional, open, and intimate along with the ability to be strong and capable. Joan Shapiro, in *Men, A Translation for Women* (1992), points out that the noncommunicative prototype of maleness has significant survival value in situations in which men need to be warriors. In war, soldiers need to do what must be done, to suffer hardship silently, without complaining. By contrast, much of modern married life requires collaboration rather than heroism, emotional support rather than physical protection from a dangerous world. For today's world, communicating is essential.

Communicating and power have a complex relationship. It is said that information is power. But is it the holding on to information or the putting forth information that is empowering? Probably both. In competitive situations holding on tightly to information may increase your power and decrease your opponent's. In personal relationships, however, the person who feels more powerful is more likely to speak forthrightly; the person who feels less powerful is more likely to hint. Speaking forthrightly is in some ways the privilege of the powerful—is a *result* of feeling powerful, of feeling that what you have to say matters. At the same time, speaking forthrightly also *causes* the speaker to feel more empowered. To the extent that you speak up in your marriage, expecting to be listened to, you will feel empowered as an equal.

Beware of wishing and wondering

Wishing your mate could read your mind is a setup for frustration for both of you—as is thinking you can read your partner's mind. The alternatives to wishing and wondering are saying and asking.

Wishing and Wondering	Saying and Asking
Len is talking about a mountain hike he is planning, while Linda gets angrier and angrier at him. She wonders if he enjoys her companionship and wishes he would say, "I sure hope you'd like to go with me this summer." But he doesn't.	*Gina (in the same situation):* I want to go hiking with you. I think I need reassurance that you would like me to join you. How do you feel about me coming along? *Gerald:* I have mixed feelings. I want your companionship. Some days, though, the climbing will be pretty steep.

Both Linda and Gina want their mate to listen to their concerns. Linda wants Len to hear her concerns without her voicing them. She then feels disappointed when Len fails the impossible test. Gina goes ahead and says to Gerald what she wants him to hear. As a result, Gerald is able to answer helpfully.

Waiting for someone to read your mind can be painfully frustrating. For example, children in their second year of life often develop habits of whining. At that age they are mature enough to sense what they want, but they don't yet have the verbal skills to express these desires in words. (One of my patients says to his children, to teach them to speak up and ask for what they want, "You have a mouth, and it's good for more than eating.") It's much easier to be an adult. Unlike an infant or toddler, you needn't depend on the mind-reading ability of others. You have safer options. You can say what you want.

Guessing your mate's feelings and thoughts creates needless tension, trouble, and confusion. Instead, ask. Say aloud the question in your mind.

Guessing	Asking
Len, sensing that Linda doesn't want to go to his sister's wedding in Arizona, thinks: I guess Linda doesn't want to go to the wedding or she would have said something. I guess she doesn't care about me or my family. Or maybe she's insecure. That must be it. I remember she once said she felt uncomfortable around my sister. I'll bet Linda's jealous of her; that's why she doesn't want to go.	*Gerald:* How would you feel about coming with me to the wedding?
	Gina: I definitely want to go. I feel a little anxious about it, because I feel awkward around your brother's wife, but I look forward to seeing everyone else. Mostly, I want to be there to share it with you. I'm glad you asked me. Sometimes I have a hard time speaking up, especially when I really want something. Thank you for asking me. Actually, do you think we could bring the kids, too?
Linda, feeling insulted, thinks: I want so much to go to the wedding. Why isn't there a ticket here for me, too?	

As often happens with guesswork, what Len thinks is troubling Linda differs considerably from her actual concerns. He correctly perceives Linda's hesitancy, but when he guesses instead of asking the cause, his misinterpretation makes the situation worse. Len means well; he is trying to be sensitive and not to put pressure on Linda to go to the wedding if she doesn't want to. But his attempts to be sensitive backfire when he guesses instead of asking her concerns.

When Gerald asks Gina about the wedding her answer completely surprises him. Your partner is also likely to surprise you from time to time when you ask instead of wishing, wondering, or guessing.

Beware of "You know I think..."

When you believe that your spouse has previously heard you express a particular thought, you may be tempted to begin a statement with, "You know I think..." In general you will be better off just stating your thought than using the "You know I think..." format, which tends to sound critical and invites a defensive response.

"You Know I Think..."	"I Think..."
Linda: You know I think we're too strict with the children.	*Gina:* I think we're too strict with the children.
Len: I don't know that.	*Gerald:* In what ways?
Linda: Yes you do. Stop trying to be difficult.	
Len: Look, I can't read your mind.	

"You know I think..." starts a fruitless discussion about whether or not Len knows what Linda has been thinking. This digression distracts them from the topic Linda wants to discuss.

By stating her thought directly, without a "You know I think..." introduction, Gina successfully engages Gerald's curiosity and concern.

❤ Say what you want, not what you don't want

Saying what you don't want may express your concerns, but it gives little indication of what you do want. Telling someone what you don't want is like handing them a film negative instead of a color photograph. The negative has the colors that are not to be included in the picture, leaving the viewer largely in the dark about how the picture will really look. Instead of giving your mate hard-to-read negatives, offer the positive, the actual picture of what you want.

Don't Want	Do Want
Linda: I don't want to be left completely on my own with the children at your sister's wedding.	*Gina:* I would feel more comfortable at the wedding if we start off staying together as a family. Then let's take turns taking care of the children.
Len (defensively): I never leave you alone with the kids at family events! I always do my share of parenting!	*Gerald (answering happily):* Sure. Just give me a sign when you want to trade off. How about I take them first? I love showing them off.

You may find that sometimes, like Linda, you first become aware that you want something when you notice that something is bothering you. Describing this dissatisfaction has low odds of getting you what you want, and can easily lead to defensiveness from your spouse and hopeless feelings for both of you.

Fortunately, this mishap is relatively easy to prevent. If you notice yourself saying "I don't want," add afterwards what you do want or, more tactfully, what you "would prefer."

Don't Want	Would Like
I don't want a boring book.	I'd like a thrilling mystery.
I don't want a big lunch.	I'd like something light for lunch, maybe just a salad.
Don't talk to the children in that nasty way.	I'd love if you could try to explain to the children what you want instead of criticizing them. The anger in your voice scares them without helping them to understand what they need to do.
I don't like that outfit you're wearing.	That outfit is pretty casual for the restaurant we're going to. I'd feel more comfortable if you wore something a bit more dressy, especially since I'm wearing a suit.

An exercise that I do with my patients may be helpful for understanding the effectiveness of *wants* versus *don't wants*. Imagine that you are sitting in my office, and I tell you I am frustrated because you haven't given me the book I want from my bookshelf. This initial negative statement might provoke you to feel defensive, confused, and less-than-eager to help. Let's say, however, that you are feeling especially generous of spirit. You override your negative rumblings and instead offer to help me. You say, "Let me help you. I'd be glad to get the book from your shelf."

I then say to you, "Thank you. And I don't want a red or a blue book." What might your response be?

If you were in fact sitting in my office, at that point you might turn and look at my three walls lined with books. You might feel again confused—maybe even a tad annoyed or downright irritated. My *don't wants* have given you almost no clues as to what I *do* want.

"Which book *do* you want?" you might ask.
Hopefully, I would answer with a more helpful description: "I want the large white book with a green title, on the shelf just behind your chair."

Now you would be likely to feel relieved. Responding helpfully is easy, and both of us would be happy.

♥ Make requests, not complaints

Complaints focus on the past, creating hopelessness, because the past cannot be changed. Requests specify what you would like. They focus on future behaviors, suggesting ways to improve on the present.

Complaints sometimes are disguised as questions. If you hear "Why can't you...?" or "Why don't you...?" be on the alert. This pseudoquestion hides a complaint, something like "You should have..."

Requests include a genuine question, something like, "Are you willing to do this thing that I would like?" A request can be accepted, turned down, or negotiated: "If you could _____ then sure I can."

Complaints	Requests
Len: I get tired of broccoli every night, even if it is loaded with vitamin C.	*Gerald:* I'd like to have more of a variety of vegetables at supper, like asparagus or peas. Would that be OK with you?
Linda: The kids look messy. They look like they haven't washed their faces for three days. Why don't you help them?	*Gina:* The kids need to wash their faces. Can you help them?
Len: Your car sounds bad again. It's going to cost us more the longer you let it go. Why can't you get it fixed?	*Gerald:* Your car sounds bad again. I'm worried it will get worse if you keep driving it. I think it will save money to get it taken care of sooner rather than later. If you have a chance, can you get it checked soon?

Len's and Linda's negative comments create defensiveness and demoralization. If you complain, your mate is likely to feel similarly criticized and discouraged. While your complaint may be a heartfelt attempt to "say it," remaining negative needlessly stirs up bad feelings.

Gina's and Gerald's requests, by contrast, specify their concerns, clarifying what they *do* want. By identifying what would make you happy and what future action would please you, requests give your partner an opportunity to feel successful, to score positive points with you.

The following story illustrates the difference between the impact of *don't wants*, complaints, and the uplifting feeling when negative feelings are converted to positive requests.

> Paul complained to Pam, "We never talk with each other."
> "We're both so busy," Pam replied. "Neither of us seems to make time as a couple a priority."

Paul and Pam continued to talk about how bad it was that they never spent time together, and each began to feel increasingly demoralized. "Are we staying together just for the children?" Pam began to ask herself.

Suddenly Paul realized what he was doing. He was complaining about not spending time together instead of making a request. "What do I want?" he asked himself. Turning to Pam he said, "What I'm really trying to say is I want to have time with you."

Pam felt as if a cloud had suddenly lifted. The space surrounding her and Paul seemed clearer, brighter. She felt pleased that Paul wanted to share time with her. At the same time she realized that she had been avoiding being alone with Paul. "I'm feeling so fragile. I don't want to be hurt," she said. "I've been afraid of spending too much time together for fear I'll be criticized."

Paul was able to hold on to the realization that don't wants do not lead to solutions. "What do you want?" he asked his wife.

Pam had to struggle to clarify a positive image of the kind of shared time she would want. "I want to be able to talk together in a quiet way, in a tone that's safe from fighting. That's why I've been avoiding talking. I'd love more connecting time with you. I'd even get up an hour earlier every morning to keep you company while you exercise if you'd like, if I were sure we would only talk quietly, with zero criticism. I want us to share our thoughts, to share what we've each been doing and thinking about, without having to worry that either of us will get angry or critical."

"That's what I want, too," Paul readily agreed.

Basic 2: *Verbalize Feelings*

Feelings offer essential information that needs to be shared with your partner.

Physical pain alerts us to physical injuries, so that when we break a bone or have a stomach ache we attend to the problem. Similarly, emotions, pleasant or unpleasant, direct our attention to circumstances of import. If we had no feelings we would not know which situations in our lives are beneficial. The joy we feel, for instance, when we see a sunrise reminds us of the importance of taking time to enjoy nature's beauties. Without feelings we would not know when a situation is boring, and we therefore might not take measures to make it more interesting. Without fear and anger we would not know when to extricate ourselves from a situation that is potentially harmful.

At the same time, however, we need to take our feelings as a starting point for thinking; otherwise feelings can produce automatic responses that do not serve us well. Feelings, thoughts, and actions are triplets, all of which need to work in concert. When you note a feeling, you need to think about it in order to hear the message it is sending you. Used in this way, feelings become keys to awareness of underlying concerns, fears, and preferences. Using information from both the thought and the feeling, you can determine an effective course of action.

Feelings get single-word labels

Saying "I feel" indicates that you are experiencing emotion. The first step is to focus on that emotion until you can put a label on the feeling, such as *ashamed, joyful, nervous, disgusted, uncertain,* or *amused.* For example:

- "I'm feeling *uncomfortable* about changing the plan we had set up for the weekend. I am *concerned* that our friends will be disappointed if we tell them that we can't visit them after all."

- "I'm *eager* to reach an understanding with you about what times each of us will set aside for exercise. I'm *concerned* that without a clear agreement we'll keep frustrating each other by one of us planning to exercise and the other not being home to cover the kids."

- "I'm *annoyed* at the way the newspapers get wet so many mornings before they reach our kitchen table."

- "I'm *frustrated* that we can't seem to make ends meet even since I got a raise."

- "I'm *delighted* with all the windows and brightness in this new apartment."

The ability to label feelings is a key ingredient of emotional maturity. Naming a feeling is like catching and harnessing a horse. Unharnessed, unnamed, the horse or the feeling can run wild. Caught and held, they become helpfully at your service. When both you and your partner have the ability to label and therefore talk about your feelings, your power to use feelings constructively for the benefit of you both increases.

By contrast, inability to name feelings can undermine your relationship. If you cannot talk about feelings, it becomes harder to talk about the situations giving rise to the feelings, and harder in turn to find ways to modify and improve these situations.

People often say "'I feel that...," thinking that they have conveyed a feeling, when in fact they have conveyed only a thought. On the other hand, "I feel ____..." followed by a word or phrase describing a feeling, and then adding the thought, conveys the feeling *and* the idea.

I Feel That..."	"I Feel _____ ..."
Len: I feel that we have been spending way too much money lately.	*Gerald:* I feel nervous about money. I'd like to reconsider our budget.
Linda: I feel that we're doing fine on money, especially compared with when you were unemployed.	*Gina:* I share your nervousness. At the same time I feel sick to my stomach at the thought of having to return to the really tight budget we were on when you were unemployed.
Len: I do feel that we're doing better than we were then.	*Gerald:* I sure feel thankful that we're not that bad off now.

Len and Linda omit feelings when they say "I feel that..."; they convey just their thoughts. Conveying thoughts is important, but thoughts are conveyed with increased potency when they are preceded by a description of the speaker's feeling.

Gerald and Gina label their feelings with single words or simple phrases: "nervous," "sick to my stomach," and "thankful." Thoughts alone create an arm's-length, businesslike tone. Adding feelings gives the conversation warmth and intimacy. For maximum effectiveness, first label the feeling, then verbalize the thought.

Be especially careful of "I feel that you..."

"I feel that you..." launches a statement about the other person, not self-expression of a feeling. It provokes defensiveness, because it sounds like a warning that a criticism is on its way. Once again, the solution is to express a feeling before the thought.

"I Feel That You..."	"I Feel _____ That You..."
Linda: I feel that you don't sleep enough.	*Gina:* I feel concerned that you might not be getting enough sleep.
Len: I get enough sleep.	*Gerald:* I'm not feeling tired.
Linda: I feel that you could give me the flu if you get sick.	*Gina:* I'm worried that if you get the flu I'll catch it from you.
Len (defensively): I'm careful when I'm sick to keep my flu to myself. I wish you'd stop criticizing me.	*Gerald:* I would feel bad if I got sick and then you did, too. I do appreciate your concerns, for me and for you.

By starting off with "I feel that you...," which sounds to Len like criticism, Linda misses an the opportunity to share her feelings with Len.

Sharing feelings builds intimacy. Because they name their feelings Gina and Gerald's intimate dialogue feels loving to both of them.

Verbalize, don't "act out"

Expressing your feelings in words rather than in actions reduces the chances that you will be misunderstood, enabling your partner to respond helpfully.

Acting Out Feelings	Verbalizing Feelings
In the middle of an argument Len stomps out of the kitchen, slamming the door behind him.	*Gerald:* I feel really angry. I don't want to talk about this more right now. I'm on overload.
Linda refuses to speak to Len or eat at the table with him for two days.	*Gina:* I don't like leaving things unfinished. I'd rather try to work it out. What if we talk again in ten minutes?
	Gerald: OK, but let's talk outside. I think I'll stay calmer that way. And if I'm not calmer in ten minutes, I'll want to wait longer.

Frowning, sulking or, like Len, banging doors and stomping, does succeed indirectly in conveying that there is a problem. Unfortunately, Len's success is at the cost of two days of unpleasant retaliation from Linda. Linda also acts out her angry feelings—via silence—rather than putting her emotions into words.

When you feel hurt, sad, or angry, your first impulse may be to act out your distress. Behaving in ways that dramatize sadness, hurt, or anger probably is preferable to covering up your feelings. Fortunately, however, the human power of speech gives us a more effective option. We can *say* what we feel.

By saying "I feel," naming the emotion, and then adding what the feeling is about, you open up the possibility of problem solving. One goal of verbalizing feelings is to launch a discussion that results in improving the situation.

Furthermore, putting your feelings into words enables you to convey their intensity, which tells you and your spouse how urgent the situation is. You can say "I am concerned about..." or, "I am very frustrated about..." or perhaps, "I am furious that..." Describing feelings in words enables you to communicate levels of intensity safely. Shouting to show how angry you feel is more draining for you and hurtful to your spouse than saying with feeling, "I'm just livid about..."

Sharing painful feelings verbally demonstrates both personal courage and faith in your partner. It takes courage to show your vulnerabilities, to tell your partner about the moments in which you feel hurt, injured, or upset. And open sharing of your feelings requires that you trust your partner's ability to respond with empathy and concern, not defensiveness or aggressiveness.

If your partner has not yet developed the ability to respond constructively to your moments of discomfort, then open verbalization of your feelings may not be safe. When you express hurt or upset, if your partner responds defensively instead of listening to understand you, or if your partner uses knowledge of your vulnerability to wound you, open sharing of your distress may need to wait until both of you have developed skills of empathic responding. (See Basic 6 in Chapter 2, and Chapters 7 and 11 for more on listening with empathy.)

Calm inflammatory language

The more emotionally intense your language, the more intense your partner's response is likely to be. The more emotional you both feel, the more likely it is that you will take positions on opposite sides of whatever issues you are discussing.

Emotional Overkill	Gentler Language
Len: Linda, you are driving like a maniac! You nearly killed us going around that last corner! I feel like I'm going to vomit!	*Gerald:* Gina, I'm feeling queasy. Could you drive more slowly? I'm getting pretty anxious.
Linda: You just don't trust women drivers!	*Gina:* Sorry. I'm racing because we're late. Really, though, it doesn't matter that much to me if we miss the first few minutes of the game. I can slow down.
Len: I want to go to the game, not the hospital!	
Linda (angrily): Lori has violated our trust again. Look how selfish she is. She lied to me that she'd do the dishes for sure before she picked up the phone. There she is lazing around on the telephone instead!	*Gina (explaining):* Genny's on the phone when she agreed she first was going to finish the dishes. She doesn't seem to be sticking to the rules.
Len: She's only a kid. Let her have friends. She's just a normal teenager.	*Gerald:* She gets excited when friends call and forgets that she has responsibilities to finish first. Want me to remind her?

In the first example, Len's strong language is colorful. However, as Len discovers, his strong language invites his wife to take the opposite position. He says she is driving too fast. She insists there's no problem with her driving.

Gerald tries hard to understate his discomfort with Gina's speeding. His efforts pay off. Gina slows down.

In the second example, the more Linda maximizes their daughter's faults, the more Len minimizes them. Lori ends up getting opposite messages from each of her parents.

Gina's relatively calm expression of the problem makes it easy for Gerald to respond in a matching tone, instead of its polar opposite. Their dialogue stays collaborative, and they can parent as a team.

Sometimes, instead of provoking an inflamed counterattack, emotionally expressive language from one spouse brings forth subdued responses from the other. This kind of seesaw often is well meant; each of you offers a balance for the other. However, if you harden into these polarized positions, with one of you minimizing problems and the other exaggerating them, you risk finding yourselves in a tug of war instead of solving problems productively.

> *Karen grew up in a family in which people didn't listen to each other. Consequently she never genuinely expected that her husband, Bill, would listen to her. Thinking she had to work hard to capture his attention, she expressed her concerns using a loud voice, long explanations, duplicate descriptions (saying everything twice), or extra-dramatic language.*
>
> *Karen's hyperbole, however, yielded the opposite of what she sought. Bill felt flooded. Instead of listening to his wife's waves of emotions, he would stake out his position on the opposite side of whatever issue she described, which usually meant taking the position of "It's really not a problem. No big deal."*
>
> *Subconsciously Bill was trying to neutralize Karen's overly intense emotional expressions, hoping they would thereby meet in the middle. The outcome however was just more fighting.*

Careful attention to the words you use to describe your negative feelings can increase the odds that your partner will be able to respond constructively. For instance, "I'm angry" may put your partner's defenses on full alert. "I have a problem that I wonder if you can help me with..." may be a more engaging way to start describing your emotional state.

Sometimes, of course, you are not simply troubled, you are outright furious. Strong words like angry and enraged and furious are appropriate for rare instances of extreme feeling. Saving them for these occasions makes these words all the more potent when they are used.

Kept in reserve for emergencies, strong adjectives indicate your need for an immediate response. For instance, "I'm panicked about the fact that so many of our neighbors have had their apartments broken into recently!" says to your mate that the two of you had better sit down right away to figure out how to protect yourselves.

But keep in mind that chronically strong language risks the dilemma of the boy who cried wolf. If routine situations are described as emergencies, there's no way to convey when an actual emergency is occurring.

Beware of "You make me feel..."

"You make me feel..." is an accusation, not a statement of your feelings. Compare the following pairs of phrases:

"You Make Me Feel..."	"I Feel..."
"You make me feel frustrated."	"I feel frustrated."
"You make me sad."	"I feel sad."
"You make me feel stupid."	"I feel stupid."

"You make me feel frustrated" puts the responsibility for your feelings on your listener. By contrast, "I feel frustrated" conveys that you are describing your experience, not making an accusation. Maybe your frustration is the result of being tired, hungry, or overloaded. Maybe it comes from a misunderstanding. Whatever the source, starting with the word I opens the door to exploring the dilemma that the feeling has highlighted.

"You Make Me Feel..."	"I Feel..."
Linda: You make me feel unattractive. You hardly ever compliment me. *Len:* You make me feel like a terrible husband.	*Gina:* I feel unattractive. When you hardly ever compliment me, I think I must not look good to you. *Gerald:* I'm sorry. I think you look your normal lovely self, but I've been so preoccupied with our money problems I haven't noticed much else.

When Len hears Linda's "You make me feel" he tunes in to the accusation and stops listening to her concerns. Gina meets with considerably more success by expressing her feeling directly, starting with the essential pronoun *I* instead of the accusatory "You make me feel..."

In the following example, Gerald launches a successful collaborative dialogue by expressing his feelings without the "You make me feel..." phrasing.

> *Gerald felt angry when Gina asked him to clear the table. "You make me so mad!" was his first thought.*
>
> *Instead of voicing that thought, he paused for a moment, and then told his wife, "I'm frustrated." Thinking about his feeling, he was able to add, "I feel like I did my part by cooking dinner. I thought our rule was that whoever cooks doesn't have to clean up."*
>
> *Gina, appreciating Gerald's explanation, responded with, "You're right. That is our understanding. The problem is that the baby is a mess and needs a bath, and I promised Genny that I'd help her with her math homework before it gets late and she's too tired. That means I wouldn't get to cleaning the kitchen until it's late and I'm exhausted."*
>
> *"How about," Gerald suggested, "if I do kids and you do dishes? Kitchen cleanup feels burdensome but cleaning the baby sounds fun."*
>
> *"That would be much better," Gina answered. "I'm so tired, I'll just be irritable with the kids anyway. The dishes don't know the difference if I'm tired or energetic. I would really appreciate the time alone. Thanks!"*

The phrasing "You make me feel" is based on a profound misunderstanding. One person cannot make another feel anything. If you try to make me laugh, I may respond with amusement, but I may also respond with scorn. If you try to make me feel guilty, I may respond by regarding you as manipulative, and your attempts will leave you looking all the more unattractive. When one person says or does something, their intent may be to wound, reassure, delight, or maybe just inform the other person. The listener's response comes from a combination of factors that include the comment from the speaker and also factors within the listener.

For example, Gina, feeling agitated, might say to Gerald, "Please, keep your magazines on the shelf. The living room looks such a mess! They're all over the floor."

Gerald might respond in a variety of ways.

- He might snap back, "You make me so annoyed. Stop criticizing me!" That response would imply that annoyance is the only response he could feel when hearing Gina's complaint. The happy reality is, however, that even if Gerald may not love it when his wife gets agitated, he can react to her complaints in any number of ways.

- He might calmly defend himself, "It isn't so bad. We live here. The living room is for living in, not just a showcase."

- He might chuckle comfortably, "You're right, it is a mess. I'd rather work here another hour or so though, leaving the clutter, and then pick up just before I go to bed. Is that OK for you?"
- Or he might ask with concern, "Gina, is something bothering you? Last time you got annoyed by my chaos was when you were bummed about your work. I often make a mess like this and usually you just tease me about it."

Gerald's emotional reaction is shaped by Gina's comment and tone of voice, plus the meanings he attributes to her words and tone. Those meanings come from Gerald as much as from Gina. Gerald might respond with an automatic "kid in trouble" reaction. If he is sufficiently self-confident, he might be able to retain his own reading of himself in the face of Gina's more critical reading, in which case he might view her irritability with compassion. Self-confidence can also enable him to chuckle at his foible. A sense of humor can provide him with resilience that absorbs provocation and turns it into bemusement or empathy.

In sum, one person can't make another feel bad, or good. You can intend to make your mate feel something, but how your partner reacts has as much to do with him or her as with what you have done. While what you say and do may trigger an initial gut reaction, your partner can think about that reaction and can choose from there.

There is, however, one exception. Prolonged exposure to negativity tends eventually to have a negative emotional impact. If you spend extended time with someone who radiates genuine joie de vivre, you would have to be profoundly angry, anxious, or depressed not to find the enthusiasm contagious. Similarly, if you are exposed at length to someone who relentlessly criticizes you, you are likely to find that you can only keep your morale up for so long. If you have chosen to live with a partner who is often negative or hurtful, minimizing the time you spend together and finding upbeat others to be with for rejuvenation is essential.

Basic 3: *No Trespassing*
Speaking about your partner's thoughts is out of bounds.

While it is vital that you speak your thoughts and it is helpful to ask about your partner's, speaking about your partner violates the boundary between your personal thoughts and feelings and the territory that belongs to your partner, that is, his or her personal thoughts and feelings.

Speaking About the Other	Speaking About Yourself
Len (after a movie): You liked that film I bet.	*Gerald:* I thought that movie was foolish. What did you think, Gina?
Linda: No I didn't. You don't understand my taste at all. I'm insulted that you think I liked it. You're the one who likes sappy movies.	*Gina:* It was OK, but just barely. I'd give it a C minus—great cinematography but no plot.

Len and Linda's potentially fun evening turns sour because instead of expressing their own thoughts about the movie, Len and Linda each voice what they believe are their mate's thoughts. This strategy misfires because their mind reading, like most mind reading, is inaccurate.

By expressing her thoughts, Len invades Linda's territory. Without even realizing what she is doing, Linda intuitively defends her turf. Only Linda owns the right to speak her thoughts, so she responds with a counterattack into Len's territory: "You're the one who likes sappy movies."

Speaking about your mate compromises your partner's autonomy, merging the two of you as if you were just one being. Just as countries do not like to be absorbed by their neighbors, individuals resist negation of their separate identity. Connection feels good; it augments your sense of who you are with the feeling of belonging to something larger. Invasion and merger, by contrast, feel threatening. Connecting comes at the cost of loss of self.

To understand the basic principle of who can talk about whom, picture a spotlight shining down on Gerald and Gina as they discuss a difficult dilemma. When either of them talks, he or she can speak only about the person illuminated by the spotlight. When Gerald is talking, the spotlight shines on him; when Gina replies, the spotlight switches to her. So when Gerald talks, he focuses on expressing *his* thoughts, feelings, and concerns. When Gina talks, since the spotlight is on her, she offers information about *her* thoughts, feelings, and concerns. Neither talks about the other person. If one of them wants clarification about the other, he or she can *ask* about the other person's thoughts or feelings, which switches the spotlight to the other.

Whereas *saying* your interpretations of your mate's thoughts evokes antagonism, *asking* about your partner's concerns evokes closeness. "What do you think about...?" conveys warmth and caring. It shows that you are interested in knowing your partner's views.

Trespassing	Asking Questions
Len: You're crazy to like those people so much. They bore me.	*Gina:* What do you think about our neighbors?
Linda: You don't understand. I don't particularly like talking with them either. They're neighbors, though, so they are important to connect with at least from time to time.	*Gerald:* They bore me. How about you?
	Gina: I like them well enough, and they do all live nearby. I think they are the kind of folks we could rely on in tough times. I agree, though, that we don't have much that's interesting to talk about with any of them.

Sometimes couples are observers. Instead of talking about yourselves, you may focus on an external person, event, or idea. Sharing these views builds closeness from experiencing, analyzing, and enjoying your world together. Even then, however, you each need to be careful to express only your own views, not to speak for one another.

Speaking for the Other	Expressing Your Own Thoughts
Linda: I know you hate the rain, but I think it's kind of pretty.	*Gina:* Sure is gray out today. I love it.
Len: I do not hate rain. I'm just kind of down today. I wish you didn't always misunderstand me.	*Gerald:* I thought that was my gloom-colored glasses. In fact, the mist is quite mysterious. If we were in the countryside, I would probably think it was beautiful.
	Gina: I was going to say that you are probably too depressed to enjoy the rain, but then I realized that would have been trespassing.

Note that when individuals express their views about something in the world, the subject of the sentence is either *I* or what they are talking about (the movie, the weather). Every time they share their personal reactions to life's events in this way, their self-disclosure allows their partner to join in their private world, enabling them to enjoy life as a team.

Speaking with *I* as the subject propels conversations forward. People are less likely to get defensive if there is no trespassing. Starting out with the pronoun *I* keeps you safely on the turf of self-disclosure. On sensitive topics especially, talking in "*I*-mode" keeps dialogue constructive, so that defining problems leads to finding solutions.

You Statements	I Statements
Len: You should help me with the vacuuming. *Linda:* Can't you see that I'm already frantic with getting my own work done before our friends arrive? *Len:* You have no sympathy for how tired I am, no appreciation for how hard I've been working this week! *Linda:* You think I've been sitting on a beach?!	*Gerald:* I can't seem to mobilize myself to get anything done today. I know it's my week for vacuuming. I'm so low energy. *Gina:* With people coming over for dinner tonight, I'm not thrilled about the living room rug looking like ten teenagers partied on it last night. I knew when I asked people over a month ago I might regret it. *Gerald:* All I want to do is sleep. I appreciate that you want the house to look nice. I just can't picture how to get from here to there... I know, I could blast the radio. Will that overwhelm you? *Gina:* That would work for me. Truthfully, I'm pretty tired, too. I could use some funky, get-it-in-gear music.

Change crossovers to insights

As explained above, talking for another person, or telling them what they should do, crosses into the other person's personal territory much as walking uninvited into someone else's yard is trespassing. While such "crossovers" are easy to slip into, the cost in antagonistic responses is expensive. Remember instead to *talk about yourself or ask about your partner.*

Each time you notice that you are crossing over—talking about your partner instead of expressing something about your self—if you switch the focus back to your own thoughts and feelings you will develop skills of insight.

Crossovers	Insights
Len: You don't really want me to come when you visit your parents.	*Gerald:* I feel uncomfortable with your parents. I feel like a fifth wheel.
Linda: You don't understand me!	*Gina:* That's a shame. I'd like us to feel like one big, happy family.
Len (insisting): You think I'm a burden.	
Linda: I do not! How could you misunderstand me so badly?	*Gerald:* I feel like there is one big, happy family, and I'm watching through the window instead of being inside.

Len and Linda devote their attention to guessing each other's thoughts and feelings, and then spend even more energy defending those guesses, leaving little or no opportunity to say what they themselves want.

Gerald and Gina speak their own thoughts and feelings or ask for their partner's, avoiding needless antagonisms and gaining understanding.

For the following real-life couple, pervasive crossovers almost led to divorce. Victoria and Austin each focused perpetually on trying to get the other to act differently. They both needed to refocus their considerable intelligence on themselves. With insight, self-expression, and looking at what they themselves could change, their lives began to turn around.

Victoria complained about Austin's compulsive eating. He could sit at the kitchen table, dip his hand in the cereal box, and stay at it until the box was empty. She also complained about how much time and money he was spending on stock speculation.

What Victoria didn't do was focus on her own feelings. If she had, she might have been able to see the extent to which she was becoming appropriately frightened. If, instead of trying to get Austin to act differently, she had looked at what different action she might take to alleviate her fears, she would have separated their finances, making the considerable income that she earned inaccessible to Austin. Austin might then have been able to heed her fright, understand her action, and decide to change what he was doing. Instead, while she was complaining, Victoria was inadvertently subsidizing Austin's continued stock-market gambling.

Austin was indulging in the stock market the way he indulged in the cereal box. He was dipping into the family's savings and investing it in high-risk stocks with little attention to the actual costs. Playing the market had become an addiction.

When Victoria complained, using crossovers instead of I statements to express her thoughts and feelings, Austin became defensive. He returned

TABLE 2   Crossovers: Five Forms of Verbal Trespassing

Type of Crossover	Example	Positive Alternatives
Mind Reading Guessing your partner's thoughts	You think that movie was dumb.	*Ask:* Did you think that movie was dumb?
Emotion Reading Guessing your partner's feelings	You're too tired to go out now. You're angry.	*Ask:* Are you too tired to go out now? Are you feeling angry? *Speak of yourself:* I'm getting tired and irritable.
Labeling Attributing qualities to your partner	You are mean and selfish.	*Refrain from negative generalizing and name-calling. Speak of yourself, or ask a question:* I'm uncomfortable with the way were talking. I'd like to try discussing it tomorrow. Is that OK with you?
Criticizing Talking negatively about what your partner does or has done	You leave your clothes strewn around the house. You put too much salt in the soup.	*Use When you... I...:* When you leave clothes strewn around the house I feel agitated. I get nervous about the clutter. *Speak of yourself:* I like less salt.
Advising and Commanding Telling your partner what to do	Put on a sweater; it's cold out. Don't eat that; it's too fattening.	*Speak of your concern and/or ask a question:* It's cold out. Do you want a sweater? Would you please close the windows before you leave? Do you want to eat that? It's high in fat.

volleys of complaints back at her: "You're just obsessed with watching your weight, that's why you don't like me to enjoy a little cereal in the evenings." Or, "What do you know about investing?" Issues that genuinely needed to get discussed were sidetracked into unproductive fighting, undermining their good feelings about themselves and toward each other, and derailing problem solving.

Why did Victoria stay focused on Austin? She certainly had just cause for wanting him to change his investments, which were losing so much of their money. And his cereal binges were causing him to put on weight. At the same time, staying focused on Austin to some extent subconsciously enabled Victoria to avoid her strong feelings of desperation. Locking her focus on Austin let Victoria maintain the fiction that everything was basically fine in her life, with a storybook household of a handsome dad, a lovely mom, and two beautiful and happy children. Meanwhile, the reality was that Austin's gambling was emptying their savings, committing them to disastrous loans, devoting his career energies to watching the stock market instead of earning a living, and destroying their financial security.

Victoria's hyperfocus on Austin eventually precipitated a crisis. With Victoria at him so incessantly about what he was doing, should be doing, ought to consider doing, Austin felt increasingly smothered. Unable to express his feelings, he kept "taking it," escaping into his addiction, which in turn kept Victoria churning in anger and spewing out crossovers. Finally, Austin felt so smothered he had to break free, and he moved out. The good news was that once he had done so, both Austin and Victoria decided to seek help to begin to address their complex difficulties.

If, like Victoria, you speak in crossovers, you lose the opportunity:

- to understand your own concerns
- to generate a compassionate response from your mate to those concerns
- to invite your mate to respond with similar personal self-revelation
- to gain insight into the problem
- to find constructive solutions to the problem at hand

Given that comments about your partner block your opportunity to gain insight and create dissension in your relationship, why would anyone speak this way? Human beings are built with their eyes pointing outward. How tempting, especially when something distresses us, to look outward, focusing on the other person instead of redirecting our attention inward.

The intimacy of marriage can breed the erroneous belief that since I know you so well, I can tell you what to do and can tell what you are thinking and feeling. To the contrary, believing you have the right to tell your partner what to do and what not to do, or that you know what your partner thinks or feels seriously erodes a couple's closeness. Crossovers replace the genuine intimacy of mutual understanding with the pseudo-closeness of merging.

Untangle spaghetti talk

"Spaghetti talk" is my term for dialogue in which expressing each other's thoughts has created confusion. If you talk about what you think your partner thinks, or what your partner thinks you think, then dialogue can get hopelessly snarled. To untangle the dialogue, speak in *I* statements, expressing only your own thoughts and feelings, or ask questions.

Spaghetti Talk	I Talk
Len: You think I don't do anything around the house.	*Gerald:* I think I do a fair share of our household chores. What do you think?
Linda (defensively): What makes you think I think you're not helpful around the house? I think that you think that I'm overly uptight about the house, and that's why you think I think that you don't do anything!	*Gina:* I agree. I think we've been splitting up the household work pretty evenly. My only request would be that you keep your clothes off the floor. I can live with how we keep the house, but your clothes on the floor bug me.

Spaghetti talk makes Linda and Len's discussion a tangle of who thinks what. They sink into the confusion, fighting each other as they try to unravel what "you think I think" and whether what "you think I think" is correct. Even trying to describe their way of talking gets confusing.

Because Gina and Gerald speak in *I* statements, whose opinions are whose never comes into question. The topic—housekeeping—remains the topic.

Verbalizing what you think your mate thinks is not only counterproductive and out-of-bounds, it's also contagious. Dialogue styles, including speaking in crossovers, tend to be mirrored. If one of you trespasses, the other is likely to do the same. Before you know it, you can end up in a spaghetti tangle.

Couples who find themselves snarled in spaghetti talk often have no idea what went wrong. Genuinely trying to talk constructively, they may puzzle over how their discussions become so frustrating.

Beware of we talk

The word *we* masks the important reality that you are two autonomous individuals who often have different thoughts and feelings. You can safely use the pronoun *we* when you talk about actions, for example, "We went to the baseball game last night," or "We have two children." Using *we* when you talk about thoughts and feelings, however, can yield needless tension.

Mistaken We Talk	Talk About Actions
Len (to his friend Bill at a barbecue): We're really excited to get a dog as soon as we move into our new place.	*Gerald (to his friend Bill at a barbecue):* I really want to get a dog when we move into our new place.
Linda (surprised and annoyed): I am not sure at all that I want a dog. In fact, this "we" doesn't want hair on the carpet or barking in the backyard.	*Gina (surprised):* You do? We'll need to talk this one over. I wouldn't be happy with hair on the carpet or barking in the backyard.

Linda felt understandably miffed when Len included her in his we statement about *his* desire to get a dog. She feared that Len would proceed with getting a dog without checking to see if in fact her views and his were similar; and she resented that Len did not seem to value her opinions enough to ask instead of assuming hers were identical to his.

By using *I* rather than overinclusive *we*, Gerald and Gina can talk without irritation about the dog idea.

Family therapists point out that one of the essentials of mental health is *individuation*. The ability to maintain clear boundaries between yourself and others enables you to individuate, to feel legitimate in having your own attitudes, beliefs, and desires, and to feel comfortable letting your partner have attitudes, beliefs, and desires that differ from yours.

Trespassing tends to emerge most readily when marriage partners lack this sense of separate identities, when their boundaries as individuals become blurred. Without individuation, differences between you and your partner feel threatening instead of refreshing. Merging, and the verbal trespassing that goes with it, causes togetherness to create friction instead of fun. This friction can gradually wear down even the most loving marriage bonds. If a couple is already near the point of ignition, the friction from crossovers, spaghetti talk, and *we* talk can cause dangerous heat, sparks, and flames of destructive anger.

When you works miracles

"*When you...* I" gives you a way to talk about what your partner is doing without trespassing. This formula is very useful, because sometimes you do need to reference what your partner has said or done in order to explain your reaction.

A *when you* has two parts, either of which can come first. One part is a clause that begins with *when you* and then describes what your partner did. The other part begins with the pronoun *I*.

In this way you can refer to your mate's actions without trespassing on his or her turf. A *when you* focuses mainly on you, not on your mate. The subject of a good *when you* is always *I*.

Two forms of *when you* statements — *In both forms, the subject is I*			
When you _____,	**I _____ .**	**I _____,**	**when you _____ .**
When you left,	I missed you.	I missed you,	when you left.
When you cried,	I felt discouraged.	I felt discouraged,	when you cried.
When you fell,	I panicked.	I panicked,	when you fell.

You Statements	*When You* Statements
Linda: You should have set the table by the time I had dinner ready.	*Gina:* When you hadn't set the table yet and dinner was ready, I began to get frantic. I had worked so hard on the soufflé. I was afraid it would fall before everyone saw its splendor.
Len: How am I supposed to know when you'll have the meal ready? We eat at a different time every night. I thought I had plenty of time. You should have told me ahead of time when you were aiming for.	*Gerald:* I'm so sorry. I was outside gardening and didn't realize how late it was. It's a good thing you called me.
Linda: I've been waiting for you for two hours. You never think about my feelings. You are so inconsiderate.	*Gina:* When you were so late coming home I felt anxious at first that something had happened to you, then mad that you hadn't called.
Len: You fell asleep when we were talking. How could you do that to me?	*Gerald:* When you fell asleep in the midst of our talking together I felt hurt.
Linda: You should be more responsible about taking your medication. You could get sick again.	*Gina:* When you miss taking your medication I worry that you'll get sick again.

When Len and Linda use *you* talk, even their attempts to soothe each other degenerate into blaming each other. By contrast, Gina's *when you* statement fills Gerald in on the impact of his not having set the table earlier. Consequently, when he hears Gina's concerns, Gerald feels empathy and appreciation.

By introducing what you say about your partner with a *when you*, your comments about him or her are stated in a subordinate clause. The main clause of the sentence has as its subject *I*. If, like most people you have forgotten the grammar you learned in school, don't worry. We don't need to understand about subordinate and main clauses to know when the subject of a sentence is *I* and when it is *you*. We all seem to be hardwired to be highly sensitive to the slightest hint of crossovers or criticism, reacting immediately with defensiveness or guilt. On the other hand, if a moment is handled with a *when you... I* statement, our reactions, like Gerald's, focus altruistically on how we can help.

With or without being able to label the grammatical construction, you sense when your mate is sharing vulnerable feelings and when instead he or she is saying something negative about you. And vice versa, of course.

Basic 4: *No Polluting*

Disparaging comments about your partner pollute the atmosphere between you.

Any message can be given neutrally, appreciatively, or toxically in a way that conveys "I don't like you," or "You're a bad person." If you say, "I see that you went to the store," your tone of voice could be matter-of-fact, indicating a purely neutral observation. Your tone of voice could be cheerful, expressing delight or satisfaction. Or your tone could express disapproval—as it might, for instance, if going to the store meant that your mate was escaping from more important obligations or was buying alcohol and cigarettes.

Toxicity can also be expressed in words that have negative connotations. If you see your partner playing with the children, you could say, "I see you having fun with the kids, enjoying them." By contrast, you could see the same scene through a darker lens, saying, "I see you messing around out there, squandering your time again." If the words you use to describe your mate and his or her actions are judgmental, your comments spew toxins that can poison your relationship.

Toxic comments needlessly antagonize your partner and can polarize the two of you so that you feel pitted against one another. Toxic comments turn the power of your relationship from loving into hurting, injuring your self-esteem and harming your marriage.

When toxic comments are delivered, the receiver will almost always tune in immediately to the hurtful portion of the communication and ignore the remaining information. Tact gets better results. If you are careful, you will find that you can virtually always say what you need to say tactfully. Tactful words convey what you want to say without contaminating your discussion with derogatory innuendos.

If you find toxicity creeping in when you are intending to be tactful, you might ask yourself why. Why do you want to attach hurtful pricks and toxins to the comments you send?

- Are you feeling powerless and wanting to injure your partner so that he or she will seem less strong against you?

- Are you upset about something that happened and using toxic barbs to even the score? If resentments are prompting your toxic messages, the chapters in Part II offer more effective strategies than toxicity for righting wrongs you feel have been done to you.

- Are you regarding what your partner does in a negative light because you are bogged down in a negative state of mind, a depressed emotional state? (Pervasive negativity is one of the hallmarks of depression.) If so, addressing the sources of your depression will offer you more relief.

- Are you speaking with toxic barbs to distract your spouse, and perhaps yourself as well, from something that embarrasses you? Facing the difficulty and discussing it together will be easier on both of you.

- Have you been tone deaf to the negative messages, tuning out the hurt they cause? If so, as my music teacher used to say, "Listen up!"

Whereas toxicity involves giving denigrating messages, tact is the art of conveying sensitive information without insult. With tact you can discuss problems in a way that maintains respect for your mate as a person. Webster's dictionary defines tact as an ability to avoid giving offense in order to win and keep goodwill. Sustaining goodwill is essential to a loving relationship.

To maintain tact it can help to bear in mind that a person's actions are not the same as the person. While we all make mistakes from time to time, we all still deserve acceptance and respect as people. For instance, you may not like it that your spouse came home late from work last night, but you still like your mate as a person. You're frustrated about something he or she did.

How can you tactfully convey distress when your partner does something you don't like? To keep focused on the action, not the person, use the *when you* formula. That way, you can detail the specific act that was a problem—without negative commentary, overgeneralization, or derogatory character descriptions. Toxic crossovers include any message that verbally or nonverbally casts your mate in a negative light.

Focus on the Person	Focus on the Action
Linda: You watch too much TV. You're addicted to it.	*Gina:* When you watch TV from dinner to bedtime I feel left out. I'd like for us to talk or do something together.
Len: You were wrong not to have gotten to the community meeting on time. You're irresponsible about time.	*Gerald:* When you arrived a half hour late to the community meeting I felt frustrated. I was afraid our concerns wouldn't get expressed, and I felt uncomfortable being there alone.
Linda: How could you have gotten so angry at our neighbor! You're mean!	*Gina:* When you lost your temper with our neighbor I felt bad for him and embarrassed for you, and for me as your mate.

Give feedback, not criticism

Feedback offers a neutral mirror that enables you to see your actions from a different perspective. It helps you make more informed choices about how to act. Feedback generally leads to positive change. By contrast, criticism is a poison dart. It creates hurt feelings, defensiveness, and wounds.

Criticism	Feedback
Linda: What do you think of this chicken?	*Gina:* What do you think of this chicken?
Len: Tasteless. The whole meal is kind of uninspired actually. You need to learn to cook with more flair.	*Gerald:* It's OK, a little toward the plain side. Maybe we can add seasoning salt. I do appreciate your having taken time to make something, though.

Len means well, but tact is not his strength. Using terms that suggest that he sees Linda in a bad light, he converts what could have been helpful feedback into hurtful criticism.

Gerald, by contrast, is very specific in his comment, referring just to the flavor of the chicken. He refrains from giving global comments that sound critical of his wife, and offers only feedback that pertains directly to the flavoring. His comment suggesting an alternative solution is constructive. And he ends supportively by placing the negative feedback within an overall positive context of appreciation.

Being able to offer and receive feedback can be helpful in marriage. Mates can be each other's best allies for growth. Viewing your partner's shortcomings compassionately is essential to this ability to help each other. Compassion can enable you to regard your partner's mistakes as misguided rather than as a sign of some terrible character flaw.

Avoid toxic crossovers

Crossover comments about your mate evoke defensiveness because they invade his or her verbal territory. Negative characterizations of your partner evoke additional defensiveness because they injure your mate's self-esteem. Toxic crossovers also usually trigger a response of anxiety, anger, or resentment. Over time, they can also breed depression.

Toxic Crossovers	Tactful, Self-Expressive Statements
Len: I can't believe how inconsiderate you are! You've been home late from work every night this week!	*Gerald:* I'm feeling neglected. I would appreciate if you could pay more attention to me.
Linda: I am not inconsiderate. You're self-centered! You think you're the only person in the world. Whenever I have work I have to do, you think I'm ignoring you.	*Gina:* I have been really busy at work. It's true that we haven't spent much time together this past week. I also am feeling out of touch with you.
Len: See, there you go again. Blaming and criticizing me instead of listening to me.	*Gerald:* I'd like to try to make time for just the two of us tonight. I hope it's not too late.
	Gina: Let's put the baby in the stroller and take a long walk together. There's a beautiful full moon.

Len, wanting to have time alone with his wife, launched his request as a nasty criticism. Linda fired back with equal unpleasantness. In contrast, by staying far from *you* statements and being certain to speak tactfully, Gerald and Gina succeed in finding a way to turn their difficult situation into an opportunity.

Many people believe that the best defense is a good offense, but neither offensive nor defensive toxic comments about your mate are likely to yield improvements in a problem situation. When their "toxicity alarm" goes off, most people react by immediately mobilizing to protect their self-esteem. Sometimes the response is purely defensive: "I am not..." or "I did not..." Usually this reply is intended to convey that they are good and well-intentioned and therefore if anyone is at fault it must be the sender of the toxic message. Or the response may fight fire with fire, returning criticism for criticism, blame for blame, insult for insult: "I only did it because *you...*"

Negative comments about your mate seldom lead to insight or to solving problems. Toxic crossovers pollute a relationship for no positive gain. Psychologist Haim Ginott (1965) focused on the needless and damaging criticism parents often give children, advising parents to focus on the behavior, not on the child's personal attributes. The same message applies to talking with your spouse. Giving *when you* feedback on actions is helpful. Criticism of the person ("You're so selfish") is toxic.

TABLE 3
Toxicity versus Tact

	Toxic	Nontoxic & Tactful
Tone of Voice and Attitude	Disapproving, judgmental, critical, nasty, snide, mean, mocking, sarcastic, angry, irritated	Neutral, playful, warm, kindly, quiet, patient, matter-of-fact, informative, firm, serious
Phrasing	You know I think/want/feel that...	I think/want/feel that...
Connotations of Words	Why did you lie to me?	Why were you reluctant to tell me?
	Your laziness infuriates me!	Your relaxed attitude frustrates me.
Toxic Crossovers	Accusation, blame, condemnation, faultfinding, insults, namecalling, reproach, ridicule, shaming, condescension	*When you* statements *I* statements

Exchange toxic crossovers for insight and compassion

The antidote to crossovers, as described earlier, is insight. An insight is a readout about yourself, an expression of your thoughts and feelings.

The antidote to toxicity is compassion, the art of viewing your mate in the best possible light. Compassion comes when we recognize our mate's underlying positive intentions and overall positive attributes. Compassion grows when we see our mate's weaknesses as areas where he or she still needs to grow and learn, or as deficits, rather than as bad traits.

Toxic Crossovers Yield Fights	Insights Plus Compassion Yield Solutions
Len: I hate going to those big family gatherings on the shore. Whenever I try to get your attention you totally ignore me. You're so self-centered, you don't even care that I'm left out. *Linda:* Well maybe if you stopped sulking, I'd want to spend time with you. Why can't you understand that I want to spend time with my family? You only think about yourself. *Len:* I think next summer you should just go by yourself.	*Gerald:* When we're at those big family gatherings at the shore, I don't know how to tell you I want your attention. I see you enjoying the chance to connect with your family, but I feel stranded—beached whale syndrome, out of my element... *Gina (hugging him):* Poor whale! Now that I know that you sometimes need me, I'll be on the lookout. Is there anything specific I could do that would help? *Gerald:* Maybe we could figure out a way to touch base. *Gina:* Let's find each other every hour or so and step away from the crowd to talk—just the two of us—for a few minutes. Do you like that idea? *Gerald:* Yes, definitely. Maybe also we can decide on a Help! signal. How about if when I come over I give you a shoulder hug—that would be a sign that says, "Floundering whale—let's connect!"

Len starts out with *I* statements, then spoils his insights when he slips into you accusations. Soon he and Linda are exchanging nasty criticisms. Instead of attempting compassion, each casts the other in a bad light, firing off insults in the fight to prove who is worse. Len ends up winning the battle with a powerful final blow by suggesting a solution that deeply wounds his wife—and himself as well. Both of them, in fact, would like Len to feel comfortable when they visit Linda's large and somewhat overwhelming family.

Gerald gives readouts of his feelings. Using insight, he describes his problem in a way that engages Gina's altruism. He describes her tendency to forget about him when her family gets together in a compassionate, best-light picture. Gina in turn is able to listen with compassion to Gerald's description of his uncomfortable feelings as the in-law. Undistracted by upsetting toxic comments, and motivated by compassion, Gerald and Gina can think creatively about Gerald's distress.

The Big Picture

In this first chapter we have identified basic principles for the use of words in a marriage and clarified secrets to implementing these principles. However, these foundations of a strong and healthy marriage—open flow of thoughts and feelings, clear personal boundaries, and consistent mutual respect—are often difficult to sustain in practice.

If you and your partner do not yet abide by these guidelines as much as you would like, you have a lot of company. Most couples can see considerable room for improvement. Learning to be good at marriage is a lifelong project.

One more secret to growing as a couple is to remember that each of you is responsible only for learning your part. Critiquing each other seldom helps and can set you both back by stirring up sensitivities.

Take pleasure in your accomplishments. Your ability to enjoy your full power of two will gradually grow with time.

Nature has given us two ears but only one mouth.
—Benjamin Disraeli, *Henrietta Temple*

It takes two to speak the truth—one to speak, and another to hear.
—Henry David Thoreau,
A Week on the Concord and Merrimack Rivers

Chapter 2

Secrets to Listening

When children take a ball outside to play, the game depends on their ability to throw and catch. Dialogue requires similar skills, being able to give and receive information: speaking and listening.

Sometimes, especially when dialogue touches on sensitive topics that evoke shame, anxiety, or defensiveness, a listener acts less like a baseball catcher than a soccer goalie. The objective in listening switches from taking in the other person's perspective to defending against it by disregarding or discrediting it. If you find yourself listening like a goalie, deflecting your partner's words from their target instead of receiving them, then you know that you and your mate have slipped from collaborative into adversarial dialogue. This chapter is aimed at helping you become an effective, cooperative listener.

Being heard is to an adult what being held is to an infant. To feel listened to is to feel valued and nurtured. With better listening, your connection as a couple will feel all the more loving, and your relationship stronger.

Basic 5: *Listen to Learn*

> Listen first for what is right, what is useful, what
> makes sense in what your partner says.

If you are listening for what is useful in what your partner says, you are listening to absorb the information. You are listening to learn.

The opposite of listening to learn is listening to reject what you are hearing. If you listen primarily for what is wrong or needs revision in what your partner says, without first listening to learn, you miss valuable information and cause antagonism.

Listening to Reject	Listening to Learn
Len: I'd like to get the grass cut today.	*Gerald:* I'd like to get the grass cut today.
Linda: The grass doesn't need cutting. It looks fine. I want to go shopping together at the mall.	*Gina:* Why?
Len: Going to the mall is a bad idea. We'll just buy more things we don't need and can't afford. Besides, I'd like to get the grass cut today.	*Gerald:* It's supposed to rain tomorrow. I'm too tired to cut it after I come home from work during the week. If we leave it for too long the yard will be a mess.
Linda: Don't do it today. Do it tomorrow. It's not all that long yet.	*Gina:* That's a problem, because I was hoping we could go shopping together today. Maybe while you do the lawn I'll cook something for dinner, and we'll just plan to stay later at the mall.
Len: I can't do it tomorrow; it's going to rain.	
Linda: It seems like everything I tell you, you tell me I'm wrong.	*Gerald:* I'd appreciate that. And then we wouldn't have to spend money at the mall for supper, either.
Len: That's just how *I* feel.	

Len and Linda often feel frustrated when they talk. Because they both listen to hear what is wrong with what the other says, neither of them feels heard. Moreover, the issues they are discussing, such as whether to mow the lawn or to go to the mall, get lost, knocked out of the discussion by the perpetual disagreement.

If your partner seems to be saying something that does not make sense to you, before pointing out what is wrong, try asking questions to clarify what is right, helpful, or interesting in what was said. *After* you have fully digested the points of agreement is the best time to add new information, concerns, or corrections to what your mate has said.

To accomplish this kind of listening, you need an open mind and genuine interest in what your mate is saying. An open mind requires a willingness to absorb information that might be different from what you originally expected. Genuine interest is based on a foundation of respect for your partner's viewpoints. Marriage entails a commitment to receive what your partner thinks, feels, values, and disapproves of with compassionate understanding. Like hugs, smiles, and sexual sharing, listening expresses love and enhances love.

Whenever you listen attentively, seeking to understand the point your partner is trying to convey, your life will be enriched by the information you have taken in. At the same time, your partnership is strengthened by the underlying message, "I value you and your concerns," that your attentive listening conveys. Listening to learn strengthens the sense of warmth, intimacy, and mutual support in a relationship. Listening is an act of love.

By contrast, insufficient listening is inherently provocative and can erode even the most affectionate of marital bonds.

Beware of *but*

The word *but* erases whatever has just been said. If you answer comments made to you with a sentence beginning with *but*, that word indicates that you are rejecting rather than receiving the information your mate has just offered you. If you receive a *but* response to something you have said, you will feel a subtle irritation that indicates the frustration of not having been heard.

But-ing Away Information	Receiving Information
Len: I hope we can have a fun summer vacation this year.	*Gerald:* I hope we can have a fun summer vacation this year.
Linda: But we always enjoy our summers.	*Gina:* Me, too, Gerald. I hope it will be as fun as the last two summers have been!

Linda's *but* works like an eraser or the backspace key on a computer keyboard; it deletes what came before it.

Using the word *but* indicates that you are listening to reject rather than to learn from what your mate is saying. Even if neither you nor your partner has heard these ideas about the word but before, you probably intuitively react with frustration whenever your mate responds to something you have said with *but*. When you feel "*but*-ed," you are likely to repeat your initial comment, as if your mate's *but* indicates a hearing problem.

Without *buts*, dialogue has momentum because you are gathering additional information each time one of you talks. Even a single *but* can cause you to feel like you are spinning your wheels.

But Creates Repetition	Receiving Information
Len: I'd like to go on some kind of adventure this summer.	*Gerald:* I'd like to go on some kind of adventure this summer.
Linda: But we had planned to go bicycling together in New England.	*Gina:* You would? I feel wary of that, especially since we had a plan for bicycling in New England that I was looking forward to.
Len: This year I'm up for adventure, for doing something daring.	
Linda: But I was counting on the time for the two of us to be alone together.	*Gerald:* Yes, and I don't want to give that up either. At the same time, I'd love to go do something dramatic. I could do it on my own though, if daring doesn't appeal to you.
Len: But I told you, this year it's really important to me to go somewhere for adventure.	
	Gina: That's a thought. I'm not big on risk-taking.

Len and Linda get stuck. Linda's *buts* indicate to Len that his input is not registering, so he keeps repeating it. After several interchanges, he is still saying the first thing he said, and Linda is doing the same. Instead of accumulating shared information each of them keeps repeating the data that the other seems not to be hearing.

If, like Linda and Len, you listen with a *but*, it's likely that you will receive a *but* in return, contradicting what you have said. Soon you both may find yourselves locking into mutual *but*-ing, with each of you pointing out what is wrong with what the other has said. Progress will stall, and tensions may escalate.

Meanwhile, in the same amount of time, Gina and Gerald accumulate several pieces of shared information. Gerald's desire for an adventure, Gina's for their shared bike trip, his willingness to adventure alone, and Gina's willingness to consider this option are all out on the table.

♡ Change *but* to *and*

The antidote to *but* is *and*. The word and suggests addition; the word *but* is more like subtraction—it takes away information. With the word *and*, or a variation with similar meaning such as "at the same time," dialogue proceeds smoothly.

But Listening	And Listening
Len: I like spending time with you but I want to take a trip by myself this vacation.	*Gerald:* I like spending time with you, and I also want to take a trip by myself this vacation.
Linda: But I like having our vacations together.	*Gina:* I treasure our vacations together and at the same time I can understand you wanting to do a daring solo adventure. Maybe we can do something together half of the vacation, and the other half I can visit my friend Janet while you do something alone.
Len: But we've spent our last ten years of vacations together.	
Linda: But I wouldn't want to give those up.	

Len and Linda often get into *but*-ing matches. A *but* from one launches them both into the pattern. Gerald and Gina, by being careful to think additively, connecting their thoughts with and rather than *but*, seldom experience the friction and tug of wars that buts create.

Because the word *but* erases what was said immediately before, it has enormous potency. No one likes to feel that what they've said has been set aside rather than digested. When someone rejects something you've said, it can feel like they are rejecting you personally.

Receiving a *but* is especially distressing when the information you were trying to convey is important to you. At these times use of the word but is almost guaranteed to have a provocative impact.

Furthermore, when *but* blocks forward movement in a dialogue and the conversation becomes repetitive, you and your mate are likely to begin to feel adversarial, talking against rather than with each other. *But* conversations easily turn into arguments.

> *Ira and Mona were one of the most argumentative couples I have seen in my practice. They had rampant* but *habits. They both felt chronically angry at each other, since virtually nothing either of them said ever seemed to be received. While their frustration was understandable to anyone who understood the negative power of* but, *it was a mystery to them. They had no idea why their attempts to talk together felt so frustrating. They just knew that, as much as they loved each other and wanted to be happily married, life together involved incessant argument with zero success at reaching shared understandings.*

♡ Practice attentive listening

Attention is like a beam of light. In attentive listening, your focus is beamed wholly on what your partner is telling you.

Inattentive Listening	Attentive Listening
Linda: I'd like to find some special way to surprise my parents for their fiftieth anniversary this June.	*Gina:* I'd like to find a special way to surprise my parents for their fiftieth anniversary this June.
Len: Umhmm. Have you seen my tackle box? I'm hoping to have a chance to fish this weekend and I can't remember where I put it. Do you think I loaned it to someone?	*Gerald:* Good idea. June is not that far away. A fiftieth anniversary is an important milestone. Hold on for a sec though, OK? I'm trying to find my tackle box. Have you seen it?
Linda: Len! I'm trying to talk to you about something important!	

Len has trouble disconnecting his thoughts from searching for the tackle box. His inattention provokes Linda's frustration. Gerald was also busy searching for the lost box when Gina spoke up about her parents' anniversary. He was able to switch his focus momentarily to the issue Gina had raised, request that they talk more later, and then return to his preoccupation.

Without realizing it, partners can easily neglect to tune in to the information flowing their way when their mate talks. You may be preoccupied with your own thoughts while your partner is speaking. Something he or she says may bring to mind a series of thoughts that take you in a direction other than where your mate is heading. You may be locked in automatic *but* reactions, habitually replacing your mate's views with your own. You may actively push aside the information your mate is giving you if you read it as threatening in some way. These listening patterns run counter to attentive listening. With attentive listening, each of you fully digests what the other says.

Let's look more at the word *digests*. Listening to the information your partner gives you is like accepting food that is offered to you. Good listeners chew, savor, and thoroughly digest comments from their partner. Less effective listeners are like finicky eaters who refuse food, leave it uneaten on their plates, or taste it and spit it out. Without the nourishment of food, people wither. Without hearing one another, partners may find that their relationship withers as well. By contrast, attentive listening fortifies the marital bond. Some people believe that sexual organs are the essentials for love. Ears may be as or more vital for sustaining a strong, healthy relationship.

While non-listening can arise from many causes, the following are some common ones.

- *Habits from home*— Listening habits from your family of origin may need to be reconsidered in adulthood. Families that teach children not to listen include:
  - argumentative families in which the adults listen poorly
  - families in which not listening protects the children from absorbing toxicity or craziness
  - families in which everyone is too busy or stressed
  - families in which one of the adults exhibits the narcissistic fallacy that "I'm the only one who counts."
- *Defensiveness*— When you feel criticized, defending yourself may feel like a higher priority than taking in more information.
- *Distraction*— Listening to someone talk while you are watching a football game on TV is likely to jam the airwaves, so that neither the TV nor the talker get heard. Similarly, any absorbing thoughts on another topic can distract from listening.
- *Processing deficits*— Some adults, as well as children with learning disabilities, have difficulty staying focused on information that they hear. Responses that seem tangential (that is, vaguely related but not exactly responsive to what was just said) can be a sign of this kind of listening difficulty.
- *Either-or, right-wrong, or mine-is-better thinking*— If you are accustomed to thinking that if your view is right, then your mate's view must be wrong, your tendency will be to disparage or ignore your partner's comment any time you also have an opinion. A competitive stance, wanting to show that your view is better, can also lead to inattentive listening. Instead, you might try listening to discover how both of you are right. If you listen seeking to piece together both observations into one overview, then your conversations will feel more satisfying to both of you.
- *An oppositional stance*— Locking into an adversarial attitude can lead to harboring chronically negative views about your partner. From this stance you may automatically disparage what you hear.

Pressing the Mute Button	Listening Attentively
Linda: I'm worried about Les. For an eleven-year-old he hangs around the house with us too much.	*Gina:* I'm worried about George. For an eleven-year-old he hangs around the house with us too much.
Len: Ummm...	*Gerald:* I've noticed that too; I do enjoy spending the time with him, but he needs friends.
Linda: What do you think about a boy who seldom goes out or talks to his friends on the phone?	*Gina:* Don't boys usually go out with the guys or call friends on the phone?
Len (looking up, startled): What was that? Les needs a new phone?	*Gerald:* Well, I think he's a little shy. Maybe we could help him with meeting friends at his new school. What if we have a barbecue and invite other families in the neighborhood with kids his age?
Linda: Yeah, right. Forget it.	

Len's polite "Ummm" only barely masks the fact that he hasn't really heard what Linda has told him. His tuning her out provokes a similar reaction in Linda. She loses interest in talking with him, which is particularly sad in this case, because their son is having problems and needs their help. Gina and Gerald, both attentive listeners, zero in together on their son's problems and as a team address options for helping him.

Listening with only half an ear while your partner is speaking, and using that time to prepare your next comments or focus on other thoughts, is like turning to your mate with a remote control and turning down the volume.

When your partner says something to you and you turn down the volume, annoyance is almost certain to be the response. The irritation signals that your relationship has suffered a disconnection. Occasional disconnections are normal. Frequent disconnections put the relationship at risk for an overall disconnection.

Listening is safer

Listening to new information, even if it sounds potentially negative, benefits you. Whether its immediate effect is reassuring or frustrating, information is almost always helpful. Information is power. Even information that you don't like is better received than pushed aside.

Pushing Aside Uncomfortable Information	Listening to Learn
Linda (after a dinner with friends): I think Scott and Sara noticed you were biting your nails during dinner and thought something was wrong.	*Gina:* During dinner, I think Jodie and Jim noticed when you were biting your nails and thought something was wrong.
Len: That's ridiculous. Everyone chews their nails once in a while. You're hypersensitive.	*Gerald:* Do you really think it was noticeable? Ugh. I hate hearing that. Nail biting is a habit I've wanted to end for the longest time. I just can't seem to kick it.

Len, like most of us, feels uncomfortable when his wife points out that he has been doing something that he feels he should not do. Rather than tolerate this discomfort and deal with the problem, Len rejects the information that Linda offers him. As so often happens when we reject uncomfortable information, Len then smoothes his ruffled ego by attacking the messenger, telling Linda that the problem is her "hypersensitivity," not his nail biting.

Gerald also feels uncomfortable hearing Gina raise the issue of his nail biting. His "Ugh. I hate hearing that," follows the principle of verbalizing feelings. Saying what he feels actually eases his discomfort and helps him then to think about the difficult habit. He may or may not succeed in ending his nail biting, but he does succeed in hearing and digesting Gina's observation.

If your mate is telling you something that you don't want to hear, reassuring yourself with the following reminders can help to keep your ears open even when the information feels uncomfortable:

- *Your behavior is not you*— Your mate can object to something you do or have done and still love you. Acknowledging mistakes opens up possibilities for learning, for doing things differently in the future.

- *The part is not the whole*— You can have actions that are problematic and still have lots of other positive traits. Uncomfortable information is easier to digest when you put it in perspective by seeing it as a small piece of a bigger you.

- *You are not expected to know everything*— Making a mistake does not make you a bad person. It makes you a normal person.

- *All of us are imperfect*— We all need to keep listening and learning, and even then we will never become perfect. Perfection is not in our makeup. All we can aim for is to keep learning.

♡ Beware of listening like a litigator

Litigators are paid to respond to an opposing lawyer's comments in a way that focuses on what might be wrong, missing, or inaccurate in what their adversary is saying. In this context, negative listening is vitally important. By contrast, if dialogue is intended to be cooperative, then listening like an adversary for what is wrong just derails the dialogue.

Listening to Disagree	Listening to Learn
Len: I've been working incredibly long hours at work. I'm more stressed out lately than I can ever remember. I feel like I never relax.	*Gerald:* I've been working incredibly long hours at work. I'm more stressed out than I can ever remember. I feel like I never relax.
Linda: You do too relax sometimes. Remember that nice afternoon we had walking in the state park last week?	*Gina:* That explains why you've been so irritable with the children. Would it help if we set aside Sunday for you to relax? We could go to the park, find a lovely spot, and take it easy.
Len: Yes, but I feel like a wire ready to pop now.	*Gerald:* Maybe that will help.

Linda homes in immediately on what seems wrong with what Len has told her. She points out an exception to what he has said, brushing aside the chance to digest the information he is sharing with her about his emotional state. Len's stress level increases because now he feels he has to defend what he has said. Because of their automatic disagreeing, both Linda and Len find that trying to explain their thoughts and feelings to each other takes enormous effort.

Gina, by contrast, actively digests the information about Gerald's stress. She applies it right away to understanding other aspects of their life, namely Gerald's recent irritability. She further uses the information to suggest a plan for the day. In response to his wife's understanding, Gerald feels relief.

Spouses need to be partners, not adversaries or opponents. Adversaries home in on the weak points of their opponent's arguments. Do you sometimes hear yourself starting out your response to what your mate has said with "I disagree" or "You're wrong"? Combative, negative listening, focused on errors and shortcomings, is divisive.

Some couples do enjoy friendly debate, much as they might enjoy playing cards or tennis. Choosing to debate for fun can be fine, provided the debate is a matter of choice, not the only way you know how to converse. Particularly when the topic you are discussing has important ramifications for your lives, however, you need to be able to talk cooperatively.

If you listen like a litigator to what your mate says, you partner will experience frustration as his or her communication is blocked from entering your shared information pool. Most importantly, listening for what you disagree with prevents you from absorbing important information that you need in order to be responsive to your partner's concerns.

Beware of listening

- for what's wrong with what your partner has said.
- to critique or show the fallacies in his or her line of thought.
- to point out the inaccuracies in his or her facts.
- to show that your view is better.

Instead, listen to learn. Listen for what is right, useful, for what makes sense in what you partner says.

What if you genuinely disagree with something your partner has said? Instead of subtraction with *but* or divisiveness with negative listening, aim for addition. Listen first for what is right, what makes sense, in the point that your mate is trying to convey to you. Once you have understood what is right and useful, *then* you can *add* your different viewpoint or question aspects of what your spouse has said. We'll talk more about additive dialogue in Chapter 3.

Beware of listening like a detective

Detectives are trained to listen for clues. Instead of taking what is said at face value, they listen for what they think is the real truth hidden underneath the speaker's overt comments.

Listening Like a Detective	Listening to Learn
Len: Look at this newspaper article. This couple with enormous wealth had a battle over their wills that ended in divorce when they were on their deathbeds!	*Gerald:* Look at this newspaper article. This couple with enormous wealth had a battle over their wills that ended in divorce when they were on their deathbeds!
Linda: Does that mean that you've been thinking about divorcing me? You're warning me that I'd better not get aggressive about your will!	*Gina:* How pathetic. Why?
	Gerald: They both had children from prior marriages. He wanted to give his fortune just to his own children, and she wanted it shared by all of them.
Len: Actually, I was just commenting how sad it is that these people got so crazy about money.	*Gina:* They needed to learn how to make shared decisions. We could have helped them.
Linda: I get the clue. I'm sure you're warning me...	

Len and Gerald both want to tell their wives about an article in the newspaper that they have found interesting. Linda's immediately suspicious response casts a pall on the moment. Gina and Gerald, whose listening styles reflect a firm foundation of mutual trust, turn the same moment into a fun occasion to pat themselves on the back.

While a suspicious attitude is essential to detective work, it blocks comfortable connecting with those we love. Reading into what your spouse says creates an undercurrent of tension. Believing what your partner tells you takes far less energy than trying to guess what he or she really thinks or wants.

Being able to take what you hear at face value, of course, depends on having a trustworthy partner. Otherwise, looking for clues and unraveling secrets may be well advised, as in the following case.

> *Patricia didn't trust Jonas. She suspected that he was visiting sexual massage parlors, but he insisted that her fears were groundless. Receipts in the car for parking lots in sex-parlor areas of town fed Patricia's disbelief in Jonas's reassurances.*
>
> *When Patricia stopped in one day at Jonas's work to drop off some papers, she found a prostitute in his office. Her mistrust had been proven right.*
>
> *Patricia and Jonas immediately sought professional help. In addition to the sexual problems, they realized that if Patricia could not trust her husband's honesty, their whole relationship was in jeopardy.*

A second version of listening like a detective is guessing what your mate feels. Fortunately there is a simple cure for this kind of mind reading. Instead of listening like a detective, ask directly. You might want to review Basic 1 in Chapter 1 on overcoming wondering and its first cousin, mind reading.

Interpreting	Asking
Len: When we went into the restaurant I could tell you were unhappy and didn't want to be there. I knew you were annoyed at me.	*Gerald:* Did you mind going to that restaurant? Were you unhappy about our last-minute decision to go there?
Linda: Wrong. I was delighted to be there because it got us out of the rain and we could sit down. I had an awful pain in my stomach, which may be why you thought I was unhappy about the restaurant. I was unhappy with the pain, but I was relieved we found a restaurant, any restaurant, that was dry and comfortable.	*Gina:* Not at all. Actually, the restaurant was a big relief for me. I had an awful stomach pain which was made worse from being cold and wet. I knew that after a few minutes in the warm restaurant I'd feel better, and I did. That's why I didn't want to burden you by mentioning it.
	Gerald: I'm sorry your stomach hurt.

By assuming that he can figure out his wife's feelings without asking what her pained facial expression and strained tone of voice meant, Len suffers needlessly, believing he has done something that has antagonized her.

Gerald sees the same indicators of emotions, but then asks his wife to interpret them for him. Gina's answer, that she had a stomach ache, relieves Gerald of his self-critical interpretations, and frees him up to commiserate with her.

Beware of listening like a judge

Judges decide who is right and who is wrong. While judgmental listening may be essential in the courtroom, it is disaster at home.

Listening to Judge	Listening to Learn
Len: You should have told me that you had a stomach ache. It's not right to keep secret important information that I need to know so I can understand you. That was definitely wrong, to leave me guessing about your unhappiness.	*Gerald:* Now I understand why you looked so unhappy. I'm sorry you were so uncomfortable. Actually, I'd rather know what's going on than be "spared the burden." So, next time you look unhappy, I won't guess about it. I'll ask you!

Len listens to evaluate his wife. Gerald listens to learn. He appreciates the information Gina gives him and makes beneficial use of it by figuring out how he can handle a similar situation more effectively next time.

Use detoxification

When your partner speaks critically, peel off the toxic tags and listen for the kernel of useful information.

Defensiveness	Detoxification
Len: I can never find my keys in the morning. I'm not going to get to work on time. Some idiot must have moved them from where I left them!	*Gerald:* I can never find my keys in the morning. I am not going to get to work on time. Some idiot must have moved them from where I left them!
Linda: No one "moved them." Anyway, you'll never find them if you don't stop freaking out like this. You get so crazy about silly things!	*Gina:* Yes, keys do have a way of disappearing at critical moments. I agree it's important for you to get to work on time. Did you check your jacket?
Len: Your criticism, Linda, is not helping me find my keys!	*Gerald:* Wait a minute. Look! They're in the front door!

Linda's defensive response to Len's "some idiot" means that she heard Len's implied criticism and took it personally. Feeling hurt, she counterattacks by criticizing Len's "freaking out."

Gina protects herself from feeling hurt by Gerald's implied blame, "some idiot," by using detoxification.

This technique involves three steps:

- First, Gina answers yes. This powerful initial word reestablishes cooperation. Yes also buys time, which Gina needs to think back calmly on what Gerald has said.

- Next she expresses what is right, what is useful, in Gerald's comment. Gina agrees that Gerald's keys did disappear and that getting to work on time is important for him.

- Now Gina is ready for the actual detoxification of the poison in Gerald's comments. To eliminate the hurtful part, Gina reiterates what he has said, replacing the negative words with more neutral ones. Gina replaces the negative language of "some idiot must have moved them" with "keys do have a way of disappearing."

Detoxification is a challenging technique that takes some practice. Once you get the idea, however, it offers excellent protection from toxic comments. For more information on detoxification skills, see Chapter 6 on receiving anger without getting into fights.

Show that you've heard

When you are listening, giving evidence that you have heard what your spouse says keeps the conversation moving forward. Without a sign from you that what was said has been heard, your mate is likely to assume that the message was not received.

Insufficient Evidence of Hearing	Good Evidence of Hearing
Linda (after the new paint on their living room walls has turned an odd shade of peach): I'd prefer to live with the new walls for month and then reevaluate the color. Right now I can't tell if the color is the problem or just that it looks different from what I'd expected. Time will help me sort it out.	*Gina:* I'd prefer to live with the new walls for month and then reevaluate the color. Right now I can't tell if the color is the problem, or just that it looks different from what I'd expected. Time will help me sort it out.
Len: The color is atrocious.	*Gerald:* How much time? I don't like the color at all.
(continued on next page)	(continued on next page)

Linda: I said that my preference is to wait and get used to it for a month.

Len: It's not peach; it's apricot.

Linda: I want to leave it for a month, to wait before we decide what to do with it.

Len (annoyed): Linda, that's the third time you've said that!

Linda (surprised): Well you don't seem to be listening to me!

Gina: My preference is to just wait for a while and see, maybe about a month. I hear that you're not pleased with the color either.

Gerald: You are so right. Do you really think you can live with it for a month? I mean it's not peach, it's over-ripe apricot.

Gina: I may be fruity, but I would like to try it for at least a few weeks. It will be expensive to redo.

Linda says three times that her preference is to wait on repainting the wall. At that point Len does acknowledge what she has said, but by then his acknowledgment bursts out in annoyance. He seems to be unaware that Linda would not have repeated her comment twice if she had had any indication that Len had heard her the first time. Meanwhile, Len's quick escalation may have happened because he too was feeling annoyed at not having received any acknowledgment about what he had said.

Gerald and Gina are quite careful to respond to what the other says. After Gina's first comment, Gerald's question "How much time?" indicates he has been tracking with Gina's comments. Gina in turn indicates she has heard Gerald's comment by saying, "I hear you're not pleased with the color either."

When a baseball lands in a catcher's mitt, a reassuring thud lets the pitcher know that the ball has been caught. Sometimes the catcher holds up his gloved hand so people can see the ball in the mitt's pocket. The verbal equivalent can be expressed in multiple ways.

- a nod of the head to show agreement
- nonverbal sounds, such as "uhhuh"
- paraphrasing the speaker's comment
- a question pertinent to what was said
- a response that builds directly on the information the speaker has given, such as, "Oh, that's like when I..."

While I was writing this section of the book, my friends Aimee and Eric stopped by. I explained the idea I was writing about. Eric's head nodded up and down as I spoke. Aimee murmured periodic appreciative umms, her sign that she was thinking about what I was saying. From these reactions I knew they were following my explanation. After I had said a few sentences, Eric

*said, "Oh you mean like...?"Again, his question indicated that he was
digesting the information I was offering.*

*When I pointed out how they were showing that they were taking in what
I was saying, Aimee and Eric both seemed surprised. Neither had been
aware of their responsive listening styles, yet their natural expressiveness
serves them well. These listening styles evoke a warm, friendly atmosphere
around them that makes it a pleasure to be in their company.*

Use strategic reiteration

If talking together is becoming repetitive, meandering, adversarial, or
overly emotional, restating what you have heard can often get the conversation back on track. Emphasizing what makes sense to you about what
you have heard offers reassurance that you have been taking seriously your
spouse's viewpoint. In addition, strategic reiteration offers an opportunity to
clarify any misunderstandings that may have been causing tensions. Strategic
means that the reiteration is for a purpose, namely, to return a conversation
that has become unfocused, repetitive, or oppositional back to forward-mov-
ing, collaborative dialogue.

There is a trick to effectively restating the main points of a full dialogue.
Begin by reiterating what your mate has said. After your partner feels understood, reiteration of the points *you* have been trying to make will be more
likely to be heard sympathetically as well.

Strategic reiteration rescues floundering conversations the way tossing a
rope with a life preserver aids someone who is floundering in the sea. Both
offer a way to keep afloat in turbulence and return safely to shore.

Frustrating, Repetitive Dialogue	Strategic Reiteration
Linda: I'm so low on energy these days. I get to work and finish what I need to do, but I don't enjoy what I'm doing.	*Gina:* I'm so low on energy these days. I get to work and finish what I need to do, but I don't enjoy what I'm doing.
Len (anxiously): I have to depend on you to handle your part of family responsibilities. I can't do everything around here myself.	*Gerald (anxiously):* I have to depend on you to handle your part of family responsibilities. I can't do everything around here myself.
Linda (frustrated): I can't seem to convey to you how dark I feel. I have so little energy or get-up-and-go.	*Gina:* I can't seem to convey to you how dark I feel. I have so little energy or get-up-and-go.
(continued on next page)	(continued on next page)

Len (impatiently): Just get up and get moving!

Linda (now angry): Don't you hear me? I feel stuck, stalled! It's not so easy as "just get up and get moving!"

Len: Why don't you quit repeating yourself, get out of bed and go do something? I'm tired of your constant complaining. It's the same thing over and over again. "I'm stuck, I'm stalled. I have no energy. Poor me!"

Gerald (realizing the conversation is getting repetitive): Sounds like you've been feeling very different from your usual energetic self. Slower, more negative. I get worried when I hear that, both for you and because I can't picture how we'd cope around here without you doing all the things you usually manage to get done each day.

Gina: Exactly. That's just how I feel.

Gerald: Have you checked with the doctor? Could it be a health problem, like thyroid, hormones, or something like that?

Gina: I've been in such a stall I didn't even think of that. I'll call for a checkup today. I'm sure it's my thyroid like I had a few years ago.

Linda feels depressed, and isn't succeeding in getting a response from Len that indicates he is hearing her. She keeps repeating herself in hopes of getting through to him. Len meanwhile, understandably anxious about how Linda's depressed mood will affect the household, keeps repeating his own fears. With each round of repeating themselves, their frustrations mount. They need a strategic reiteration.

Finally, when Len gets irritated to the point of blowing up, his response does indicate that he has been listening, but in a hurtful way. Because Len's eventual reiteration of what his wife has been saying is critical instead of compassionate, it actually reduces the chances of their finding a solution to the very real problem of Linda's depression.

Gerald reiterates as soon as he realizes that Gina is repeating her complaints. "Sounds like you've been feeling..." breaks their impasse right away and brings the discussion back to cooperative problem solving.

Repetitions and irritation emerge when people do not feel heard, or feel criticized for what they have said instead of validated. Restating what you have heard your spouse say, with an emphasis on what makes sense about it, clarifies that you have been listening.

Reiteration:

- reestablishes cooperation.
- lets the speaker know exactly what information has been entered into the shared information pool.

- prevents misunderstandings by checking whether what you heard was what the speaker meant to convey.

- conveys to your spouse that you care about the information he or she is offering, and by extension that you care about the person who offered it.

- ends wheel-spinning repetitions and gives the dialogue a feeling of forward movement

Basic 6: *Listen to Feelings*

Your partner's tone of voice, quivering chin, or sparkling smile all convey critically important information.

Emotions are messengers. Words convey facts; emotions convey the "flavor" of these facts—positive or negative, helpful or hurtful, frightening or delightful—and thereby help you to respond appropriately. The sun may be shining, but it is your emotions that motivate you to go outside and take a walk to enjoy the sunshine. Similarly, if your child is about to cross a busy street, it is your emotion of anxiety that prompts you to reach down and take her hand. Most of the time emotions are not particularly salient. They sustain a background tone, such as friendliness or seriousness, that you take for granted. But when, in the midst of a conversation, you perceive evidence of a change in feeling—a knitted brow conveying worry, a tear suggesting sadness or hurt, a grin suggesting delight—tuning into these feelings and asking about them almost always leads to breakthroughs in understanding.

Ignoring Feelings	Listening to Feelings
Len: We've been driving a long time. This looks like an OK place to stop.	*Gerald (turning to Gina):* We've been driving a long time. This looks like an OK place to stop.
Linda (sounding worried): I guess so...	*Gina (sounding worried):* I guess so...
Len: It'll be really nice to take a hot bath, climb into a soft bed, and get a good night's sleep.	*Gerald:* What's wrong, Gina?
Linda (sighing): Well, I guess you're right, Len. I guess it could be worse.	*Gina:* It's just that this motel looks so seedy. I don't know if I'm comfortable staying here.
Len: Of course it could be worse, just because there's a few letters missing from the vacancy sign and a few broken windows... We'll be fine.	*Gerald (reconsidering):* Let's drive a few more minutes and see what's ahead. If there's nothing, then we can come back here.

Linda's sensors told her that the motel would be unsavory and perhaps even unsafe. By agreeing to ignore her emotional messages, Linda and Len settled for a far less pleasant place to spend the night than what they, like Gina and Gerald, might have discovered.

To many people, and especially to men, feelings such as fear, shame, or sadness may appear threatening. To be strong dependable protectors, men in particular have learned to push aside vulnerable feelings in an effort to stride bravely on. As discussed in Chapter 1, in times of war or danger this ability to tune out feelings can be very helpful. In normal times, however, the ability to pick up on subtle emotional cues gives a couple a deep sense of closeness. Emotional attunement gives you access to essential information for understanding yourself, your partner, and the situations in which you find yourselves.

Express empathy

Empathy involves hearing your mate's descriptions of his or her feelings, taking them seriously, and responding in a helpful way. A particularly effective way of responding is to paraphrase what your partner is feeling and then add what makes sense to you about those feelings.

Minimizing Feelings	Empathizing with Feelings
Len: I hate to admit it, but I'm really mad about not getting that promotion.	*Gerald:* I hate to admit it, but I'm really mad about not getting that promotion.
Linda: Well, at least you didn't get fired.	*Gina:* I can understand that. I would have been furious. There is not a shred of doubt that you had the qualifications. They've been dangling that promotion in front of you for weeks!
Len: What do you mean, "At least I didn't get fired"? Of course I didn't get fired. That's not the point. They've been leading me on with that promotion like it was a carrot and I was a horse. Don't you understand why I'm so upset?	*Gerald:* Well, that's life I guess. By the way, what's for dinner?
Linda: Don't worry. It will work out in the long run.	
Len: What do you mean "Don't worry"! I'm furious!	

When Len comes home angry and disappointed after having been passed over for a promotion, Linda tries to help. She tries to reassure him by minimizing the problem, saying "At least you didn't get fired." She is correct that getting fired would have been worse, but she misses the point that reassurance isn't going to make Len feel better—it isn't what he needs to hear at that moment. Len needs his feelings to be heard, not changed.

In order to let go of his anger and disappointment, Len needs someone he cares for to validate his feeling, to say, "Yes. Your feeling makes sense and here's why..." By trying again to minimize his distress with "don't worry," Linda inadvertently further inflates Len's upset.

Gina focuses in immediately on what makes sense about Gerald's feeling. She adds why the feeling makes sense to her. Feeling that his anger has been communicated, Gerald experiences some relief. Instead of dwelling on not having received his promotion, he begins to accept the unpleasant new reality and move forward with his life, beginning with dinner.

Note that empathy is not the same as sympathy. Empathy does not involve feelings of pity, of feeling sorry for the other person. It means hearing accurately the message about the other person's feelings, without judging the feelings or minimizing them.

Paradoxically, more attention to feelings can decrease their intensity. The mistaken belief that minimizing a feeling will help someone feel better is very widespread—perhaps because the belief does have a grain of truth. Sometimes, delivered with adequate thoughtfulness, reassurances do help. For the most part, however, downplaying feelings makes them grow to get heard.

Interestingly, when you and your partner feel that your emotions have genuinely been heard, you will find yourselves more able to figure out a way to handle the underlying problem. When a feeling has succeeded in focusing the two of you on a problem, the feeling has done its job and can go away. In its stead remains thinking, problem solving.

For example, Gerald and Gina's story might continue:

Gerald: I'm good at looking as though nothing bothers me, but it is kind of a relief to be able to admit to you how betrayed I feel. It makes me wonder why I've been so loyal to the company all these years.

Gina: Does that mean you want to think about changing companies?

Gerald (pausing to think): I guess that's what I'm beginning to consider. That would free us up to find work closer to our families. With the children growing older, and their grand-parents too, it's probably now or never if we're going to live close enough to be a real extended family. What do you think?

Gina: Can I start packing? I'm ready to leave tonight!

By being able to talk about Gerald's feelings, Gerald and Gina are able to turn a misfortune into an opportunity.

Use Ginott's Rule: Feelings first

Haim Ginott (1965), a specialist in parent-child communications, once articulated another basic principle of responding with empathy. When a child falls down, a parent first needs to focus on the child's feelings, and only after that on the cause of the fall. Mom or Dad first needs to say "Are you OK?" Only after the feelings have been tended to is it appropriate to talk about how the fall happened. Respond to feelings first by validating them; *then* analyze the situation or give advice.

Thoughts Before Feelings	Feelings First
Len (a few days later): I'm still just seething about not getting that promotion.	*Gerald (a few days later):* I'm still just seething about not getting that promotion.
Linda: Maybe you should have been paying more attention to your competition. Your old buddy Al has had his eyes on that job for weeks. Maybe it was a mistake that you didn't deal with that. I wonder too about the way you talk to people. Sometimes I think people are turned off when you joke so much.	*Gina:* What a bummer! I'm shocked myself. I was certain you'd get it too. How infuriating!
Len (stomping off): Forget it. I don't need the third degree.	*Gerald:* I don't understand why they passed me up. Do you?

Validating why the feeling makes sense does not rule out subsequently thinking about the sources of a problem. It's a question of which comes first. Then, when you do get past the feelings to the thoughts, be sure that you add your views by using *and* or "at the same time," rather than using *but* and substituting your view for your mate's, as Gina and Gerald demonstrate.

Gerald: I think maybe it's my joking. Or that I underestimated how much Al was working behind the scenes to get the job.

Gina: At the same time, I'm almost glad you didn't get the promotion. If you had gotten it we'd be locked here for years. I want so much to be able to move closer to our families.

Gerald: I can see that. It will probably take me a while to stop being mad, but—no, *and*—I can see what you're saying. In fact, the more I think about it, that promotion would have been a trap! Homeward bound sounds better.

Listening to feelings is safe

When your spouse expresses vulnerable or negative feelings, like sadness, anxiety, or resentment, you may feel tempted to respond defensively, especially when you feel either responsible for the problem or unable to help solve it.

Emotions Can Feel Threatening	Listening Is Safe
Linda: I've been feeling anxious about money. I'm not certain that we'll have enough to pay all our bills this month.	*Gina:* I've been feeling anxious about money. I'm not certain that we'll have enough to pay all our bills this month.
Len: Look, I'm working as hard as I can! What do you want me to do, work three jobs?	*Gerald:* You're right, our cash situation has been really tight lately. We were doing OK until the car gave out. Now what we earn and what we're having to spend just don't match up.
Linda: I'm not blaming you. Can you just listen to the problem, please?	

Linda's expression of anxious feelings triggers a feeling of guilt in Len. When you feel that you have done something that caused your mate to become upset, or if you don't know what to do to help, you might feel a similar urge to defend yourself. Worse, you may feel the urge to counterattack, to kick your partner when he or she is down for having brought you feelings of uneasiness.

If you hear your partner's distress as a sign that you have done something wrong, it is important to look again, to go beyond your own feelings of guilt, shame, or inadequacy, by reminding yourself to listen to your partner's feeling. When you genuinely listen to pinpoint the feeling your mate is trying to express, the next question is what makes sense about that feeling. This self-coaching can put you on the path of empathy, of *validating* your partner's feeling instead of defending against it.

In the following example, a husband's defensiveness about his part in causing upset feelings interfered with his ability to respond with empathy. Tyler, a musician in an increasingly popular band, has been married to Megan for a number of years.

"I'm sick of being married to a star," Megan said. "I want an ordinary life, with a husband who's home at night, and who isn't surrounded all the time by admiring women. It's too scary. It's too lonely."

Tyler squirmed and cast Megan a "What's wrong with you?!" look. "We have a hard time sometimes, I know, because I haven't always been perfect. I've changed a lot though. I'm home after every concert, instead of being out with the band like the other guys."

> *Megan responded furiously, "That's it! I've had it. I just want to go home to my parents. I'd rather live with them than be here alone all the time. I just want to pack up the kids and leave."*

What went wrong? Tyler heard Megan's desperation. He wanted to be helpful, but his remorse about his personal mistakes in the past kept him from hearing Megan's concerns in the present. Instead of focusing on her loneliness and fears, he became defensive and talked about himself, about his own behavior. Instead of empathizing with her feelings, he defended his self-esteem.

Megan wasn't looking for a confession or even for promises from Tyler that he would change. What she wanted was to be heard and understood by her husband. Megan longed for Tyler to say something that would indicate that he heard her frustrations and took them seriously. In their second attempt to talk about the same problem, they were far more successful.

> *Megan said, "I thought being married to a big music star was going to be exciting. Instead, I hate it."*
>
> *Tyler replied, "I can see why it's scary for you when fans, and especially the women, surround us after concerts. If I saw you surrounded by admiring guys I'd be proud of you, but I'd hate it. Is that part of what's so hard?"*
>
> *"Absolutely. And then because you have to travel so much, I have to run the house and the kids completely without you. I don't want to be a single mom. Worse, when you come home I want you to join the family, but you collapse on the couch. Then I get angry and start yelling at you, which I'm sure doesn't help either of us. I want an ordinary life!"*
>
> *"I agree about how hard it is when I come home from concert tours," Tyler said. "As much as I love my work, I can see that we haven't figured out how I can be a hero and also a normal family person. I don't know how to become part of the family when I come home, except to turn on TV and act like I live here."*
>
> *Megan responded, "I feel relieved that we understand each other. Hearing that it's hard for you, too, actually eases my feelings that I'm in this alone. I don't know what to do about it, but at least we can begin to think about what would help.*
>
> *"I have an idea. What I really would like—I hope you don't think it's stupid—really what I want when you come home is for you to pay attention to me, not the kids or the TV but to me. I'd love to have the first hug. What if when you come home I arrange a baby-sitter so we can always have at least an hour or two just for us to connect? After that I'd be much nicer."*

Being heard went a long way to dispel Megan's feelings of loneliness. Although her loneliness had multiple aspects, feeling that her husband at least understood her feelings eased the sense of being totally alone.

Unheard feelings corrode a marriage bond, dividing a couple so that they feel disconnected. By contrast, hearing each other, and in particular hearing each other's emotions, powerfully bonds two people into a couple.

Basic 7: *Use Bilateral Listening*

Bilateral listening means hearing both your own concerns and the concerns of your partner. It's like listening to a stereo system with two equally loud speakers.

One-Sided Listening	Bilateral Listening
Linda: For our anniversary this year I'd like to do something special.	*Gina:* For our anniversary this year I'd like to do something special.
Len: I'd prefer something that's not expensive. We're pretty stretched.	*Gerald:* What do you mean by special?
Linda: I'd like us to do something special to mark the day.	*Gina:* Something private, just the two of us, but different.
Len: For me it's all about money. I just can't stand the idea of spending tons of money.	*Gerald:* Private, different. And for me, I'd prefer something that's not expensive. We're pretty stretched financially. How about if we fix a romantic picnic dinner like we did on our first date? I remember we had grilled cheese and tomato sandwiches.
Linda (with a frustrated look): That's fine, Len, but can't you hear that for me it's a special day, something that I want to celebrate?	
Len (impatiently): Can't you hear that money doesn't grow on trees?	*Gina (laughing):* I bet I can do better than that now. I've learned at least a little about cooking. How about if we make it a gourmet picnic?
Linda: All you think about is money.	

Linda is concerned about making their anniversary private and special. Len's concern is money. Unfortunately neither of them hears the other's concerns as loudly as his or her own. Sadly, their *self-centered listening* results in a tug of war about whose concerns matter. Had they used bilateral listening, they would have discovered, as Gina and Gerald do, that their concerns can dovetail quite nicely.

The ability to hear both your own and your partner's perspectives pays off especially when you need consensus on a plan of action. Gina and Gerald exemplify this skill. Anything important to one of them becomes, by definition, important to the other. In this way they signal to one another "I care about you." Solutions that work for them as a couple usually prove better for each of them as individuals as well.

If I had to pick one skill that best predicts whether couples have what it takes to enjoy marriage together, bilateral listening would be it.

Beware of excessive altruism

Altruism is a laudable attitude, but it can be overdone. Taking care of others heralds the beginning of maturity. At the same time, taking care of others to the detriment of your own needs becomes excessive altruism.

Bilateral listening is tricky to sustain. Be careful to listen equally to what your partner wants and to your own preferences. You can err either by selfishly listening only to yourself, or with excessive altruism, by listening only to your partner's concerns.

Excessive Altruism	Bilateral Listening
Len: I want to go to an action movie tonight.	*Gerald:* I want to go to an action movie tonight.
Linda: OK, if that's what you want to do, that's fine with me. (While she thinks, "What I'd really like to see is a love story, so I'll be able to sleep OK afterwards.")	*Gina:* I'm worried that I'll have trouble sleeping.
	Gerald: What if we go to an early show. Would that help?
	Gina: Probably not. What if we rent an action video instead? Then you can watch it and I'll sit by you but read my book. I'm in the middle of a terrific love story.

Taking both her own and her husband's concerns into account proves difficult for Linda. As a result their decisions end up with a winner and a loser. Because Gina and Gerald routinely expect to have both their concerns taken into account, they end up with decisions that please them both. Neither of them has erred either on the side of excessive altruism, nor in the direction of selfishness. *Both* is their magic word.

Balance the volumes

To prevent excessive altruism, increase the volume on your inner thoughts and feelings. Tune in to your quiet inner voices, amplifying them enough so that you can hear your concerns, fears, preferences, and desires. Remember, you need to take these voices seriously if you want your partner to take them seriously. To prevent selfishness, turn down the volume on your internal voice and listen more attentively to you partner's concerns.

Tuning Out	Tuning In
Len (reluctantly): If I help you do cooking and cleaning maybe we could host a small anniversary party.	*Gerald:* Sitting down by the river, a quiet picnic together sounds great. Memorable, yet no expenses.
Linda: OK, that would be fine. (*Thinking to herself,* "Hmm ... if we celebrate at home, Len's going to want to invite all his buddies over. That's not how I wanted to celebrate at all. I want it to be just me and Len.")	*Gina:* Let's do it. Except, well, a little voice in me is saying, oh no, by simplifying that much, you're neglecting your friends.
Len (after a few minutes): It'll be great. We can have a barbecue, and I'll invite Dave, Steve, Joey and Mike.	*Gerald:* Let's talk about who we would really want to celebrate our anniversary with. Maybe after the picnic they could join us at home for cider and donuts.
Linda (disappointed): Oh Len! That completely misses the point!	*Gina:* I definitely want Jodie and Jim to be involved in some way. They did introduce us.
Len (confused): Wait a minute. I thought you said it would be fine.	*Gerald:* For sure. And Dennis, Scott, Jack, and Mark. Gotta have my buddies!
	Gina: As long as we have our private picnic first, that would be great! I am glad I mentioned it.

By not heeding her quiet voice telling her what she wanted for their anniversary celebration, Linda ends up having to squelch a plan that Len has been thinking they had mutually determined. Stating her preferences as they occurred to her would have prevented both Len's disappointment and her own. Meanwhile Len heard only his own voice.

Gina and Gerald voice and hear their concerns with equal volume. They keep modifying their plan until it feels just right. Where Len and Linda, by not paying enough attention to balancing their voices, end up creating negative feelings, Gina and Gerald generate increasing enthusiasm, enjoying the creative process of making plans together.

Beware of bullying

Bullying occurs when one person insists on getting his or her own way, overriding the concerns of the other. You let yourself be bullied when you give up something that is important to you instead of verbalizing your concerns so that they are included in the solution. And you become likely to bully if you have not sufficiently learned the art of bilateral listening.

Bullying	Bilateral Listening
Linda: Let's take local roads instead of the highway to save time.	*Gina:* Let's take local roads instead of the highway to save time.
Len: Are you kidding? Only a fool would take the local roads. The highway is the only way we can get there on time.	*Gerald:* I was planning to take the highway. Which roads did you have in mind? Maybe you know something I don't.

Len bullies Linda into doing what he wants by denigrating her suggestion. He makes no attempt to hear what makes sense about it, or to hear Linda's underlying concerns. While Gerald, like Len, has a different opinion on the best route to take, Gerald listens with respect to Gina instead of insisting on his way.

Denigrating your spouse's viewpoint, as Len does, is one bullying method. Statements beginning "Only a fool would say" or "Obviously the best way would be to," or "No one in his right mind would think" exemplify bulling. A raised voice, contemptuous tone, and implied threats are also bullying tactics. Whether accomplished by discrediting or overpowering, bullying is a costly way to get what you want. It depends on making your partner give up on his or her concerns, whereas to be loving is to take seriously the concerns of the one you love.

Bullying is not always intentional. You may believe you are just trying to convince the other person do things the way you are sure would be best. However, convincing often means asking the other to give up on his or her viewpoint and rely on yours. While convincing is more socially acceptable than overt bullying, like bullying, convincing blocks out the other's viewpoint. The ideal is for both of you to take into account both perspectives.

Sometimes, accomplishing bilateral listening necessitates standing your ground rather than letting your ideas and contributions evaporate. If you express a concern and it doesn't seem to be getting heard, do you cave in? You might try offering a fuller explanation.

Giving Up	Standing Your Ground
Linda: OK, Len, you're probably right. Let's take the highway.	*Gina:* I took Jefferson Street last week and I cut fifteen minutes off the usual time. Jodie says she takes Washington and it can be even faster.

Bullying and its subtle cousin, convincing, take two players, one who is overly insistent and another who gives up too easily.

The Power of Two

The power of two implies that the two people in a marriage both have power. Power in a marriage is the ability to get what you want. When your partner listens to you, and vice versa, you empower each other.

In marriages in which talking is competitive or adversarial, dominating your mate rather than mutual empowerment gets you what you want. Power equals control over rather than empowerment with. The less you listen to your partner the more forcefully you may be able to insist on getting your own way.

By contrast, in a cooperative marriage, empowerment comes from hearing and being heard. The more bilaterally you listen, the better you will become at creating plans of action that please you both. Listening enables you to maximize your power of two.

In later chapters, particularly Chapters 4, 8, and 9, we will look at the details of how to use bilateral listening to get what both of you want.

Notes

Chapter 3
Secrets to Dialogue

Picture two soccer players with a ball that they are kicking as they run the length of a field. They may take turns gently kicking the ball back and forth as they move forward. One player may dribble the ball most of the way, the other running alongside. One could kick the ball at the other, intending hurt rather than play. One could choose to aim the ball in a different direction, veering away from the direction the two of them had been traveling. Actually, there are infinite variations in how the two runners and the ball might interact—the tone between them, how they pace themselves, how they share the ball, and what path they run.

Similarly, when you and your spouse converse, you create patterns as you share the conversational ball. You may enjoy frequent back-and-forth interaction, taking equal turns talking and listening. One person may do most of the talking. You may feel tensions if each of you wants to head in a different direction as you talk. You may be playful, or you could become hostile. Your conversations can travel a straight line, like players heading for a goal, or they can meander here and there. By noticing how much you talk, how much your partner talks, the emotional tone, and how what each of you says connects, contradicts, or diverges from what the other has just said, you may recognize patterns in your dialogue.

As you begin to be able to visualize your conversations in this way, you will probably notice that the structure or pattern of how you and your mate interweave talking and listening varies depending on the purpose of the conversation. In a casual chat, for instance, a monologue in which one of you tells an extended anecdote and the other mainly listens may be amusing. Another form of casual conversation may feel more like a game of Ping-Pong than like bringing a soccer ball down the field. You say something brief about your day; your partner comments on something that happened in his or her day. You comment with more from yours, and so on, as the two of you take turns briefly sharing the day's dilemmas, frustrations, and successes.

At other times talking may have a specific problem-solving objective. A serious issue may need discussion or a decision may need to be made. For these more goal-oriented discussions, the shape of your dialogue can be vital to your success in meeting your objective. This chapter offers some secrets that can help you intertwine your talking and listening more successfully.

Basic 8: *Braid Your Dialogue*

> Skilled dialogue partners braid their dialogue, intertwining their perspectives into a single, mutually created understanding. In this way they build a consensus as they talk.

Dialogue on important issues can create frustration if you are talking oppositionally, rebutting each other like soccer players kicking the ball *at* instead of *with* each other. If your contributions feel disconnected, with each of you following separate lines of thought and paying scant attention to your partner's, you may also feel tensions.

Oppositional	Parallel	Braided
Linda: I'd like to go on a family trip this weekend.	*Linda:* I'd like to go on a family trip this weekend.	*Gina:* I'd like to go on a family trip this weekend.
Len: We can't do that. We have too many chores to get done at home.	*Len:* I can't seem to get this faucet to stop dripping.	*Gerald:* That sounds appealing. I'm just concerned about when I'll get house repairs done.
Linda: You're too conscientious. It's been so long since we've just had fun together.	*Linda:* We could drive to the mountains and maybe camp out and do some fishing.	*Gina:* I appreciate that you're so conscientious. At the same time, we need fun time too.
Len: You're being irresponsible about the house. It's filled with projects that need to be taken care of.	*Len:* I wonder if I've stripped the threads on the screw.	*Gerald:* How about if I work on Saturday morning while you pack? And let's hire our neighbor's fix-it man for the rest. He's not very expensive.
Linda: All you do is work. Workaholic all week, and workaholic at home.	*Linda:* Summer's almost over and we haven't been out of the city.	
	Len: Where's my wrench?	

When couples talk in opposition to each other whatever one says the other shows what's wrong with it. Oppositional dialogue feels frustrating, goes nowhere, and generates unpleasant friction.

Parallel dialogue, in which each person pursues his or her own line of thought with minimal interconnection, generates less unpleasantness but leaves partners feeling essentially disconnected. In their parallel dialogue, Len thinks aloud about the faucet he is trying to fix; Linda focuses on wanting to take a family trip to the mountains over the coming weekend. While they do not overtly disagree, their separate lines of thinking prevent their comments from intersecting. At some point one of them will probably need the other's full attention, probably Linda, who needs Len's assent to accomplish the family trip. She will need to be artful to find a way to attract Len's full attention without the two of them becoming oppositional.

Gina and Gerald braid their dialogue by alternating speaking and listening. Because each speaker's contribution is a response to the other's comments, both of them experience the satisfaction of being heard and taken seriously.

Braided dialogue involves

- listening attentively while your spouse is speaking,

- digesting that information aloud,

- then adding something from your own viewpoint on that topic while your partner takes the attentive listening role.

Respond with "Yes, ... and ..."

When a conversation begins to feel tense or repetitive, odds are you are slipping into either oppositional or parallel talk, which usually means that one or both of you have ceased to use attentive listening. "Yes...and..." indicates to your mate that you are bringing back your skills of attentive listening, and invites your spouse to do the same. If you both succeed, you will soon be braiding your conversation again.

To use this technique, start with the word *yes*. You can say *yes* before you even know what you will agree with. The *yes* starts a cooperative direction.

Taking the next step may require real thought. Identify something that your partner has just said that you can agree with, and reiterate it aloud to make clear that you have digested your mate's contribution.

Only then are you ready to add your own view. Starting your viewpoint with the word *and*, emphasizing this word as you say it, underscores that you are adding to, not replacing, your mate's comments.

Especially when dialogue is on a sensitive subject, starting with *yes* and digesting your partner's statement aloud before adding your own views ensures that your dialogue will feel interconnected.

"But..."	"Yes... and..."
Linda: Having such a large house discourages me from housecleaning. It takes too long.	*Gina:* Having such a large house discourages me from housecleaning. It takes too long.
Len: But the spaciousness is so refreshing compared to the tiny house I grew up in.	*Gerald:* Yes, it is a lot to clean. And at the same time I really appreciate the spaciousness.

Linda and Len react in different ways to their house. While having different opinions is completely normal for a couple, Len and Linda feel in opposition to each other when Len's response to his wife's option is "But...". If he gives no validating response to his wife's opinion, instead just setting forth his own, their opinions feel like they are pulling in opposite directions.

Gerald and Gina have the same two differing reactions to their home. By starting off with *yes* and saying first what he makes sense to him about Gina's view, that their house does take a lot to clean, Gerald sets a pattern that invites Gina in turn to agree with his view. With this pattern, Gerald and Gina steadily build a shared consensus that includes both opinions.

When your mate says something that contrasts with what you believe or want, the tendency is to point out what's wrong with what he or she has said with a *but.* If instead you can first listen for what makes sense, what is useful, and digest that aloud, you are on your way to braided dialogue.

Yes and responses require, and create, integrative thinking. By contrast, *but* is the tip of the iceberg indicating either/or thinking. Len and Linda think in terms of either/or, your way or my way, winner and loser, right and wrong. Since neither person wants to be deemed wrong or to have his or her opinions treated as irrelevant, both continuously defend their own position. Each of them listens to one side only, because to listen to the other would mean forfeiting their own view.

Couples whose dialogue skills are normally quite good may still slip into unproductive *yes but* dialogue patterns from time to time.

This slippage is especially likely to occur if:

• the topic is inherently sensitive

• emotions are running high

• one spouse says something that feels threatening to the other

• one spouse feels that his or her last point was not heard

In any of these cases, once one of you responds with a *but,* the risks go up that the other will follow suit. The dialogue risks becoming oppositional, with each of you just repeating your own points. Your voices may rise in frustration. Without *yes and* listening, braided dialogue unravels.

Pool your concerns

With bilateral listening and braided dialogue, you and your partner will find that as you discuss a topic, you will accumulate a shared information pool. You will find that mutual decisions will flow relatively easily from this shared source of information.

Separate Information	Shared Information
Linda: I don't really enjoy large dinner parties. I'd rather connect with a few people at a time.	*Gina:* I don't really enjoy large dinner parties. I'd rather connect with a few people at a time.
Len: I have to do dinner parties, though, for this job.	*Gerald:* I also prefer having just a few friends over at a time. At the same time, for this job I need to entertain.
Linda: I don't want to. I'm uncomfortable cooking for so many people.	*Gina:* I guess dinner parties aren't social life, they're work. The other part I don't like is the cooking. I'm uncomfortable preparing dinner for so many people.
Len: Well that's part of this job. This is the kind of job where the wife is assumed as a hostess.	
Linda: I'm not so sure I like it.	*Gerald:* If we need to do a dinner party, we can take them out to eat.
Len: I love it. Status. A job with a car. Lots of travel. Fancy dinner parties.	*Gina:* That's so smart.
Linda: Wait a minute. Didn't you hear me? I'm not interested in hosting.	

Len and Linda are having difficulty coping with their living circumstances. Linda relates her concerns, Len relates his, but neither of them indicates that they are hearing their partner's concerns. As a result, their conversation ends up with both of them having clarified only their own preferences and worries. Worse, the two sets of concerns seem to conflict.

As Gina and Gerald talk, all their input goes into one pool of "our" concerns. Because they both value each other's concerns as much as their own, the dialogue flows easily toward mutually agreeable plans of action.

Good listeners interrupt

In contrast to what you were probably taught as a child, interruptions can be considerate. Interrupting can actually help a dialogue stay on track. Happily married couples in fact interrupt each other more frequently than distressed couples (Margolin and Wampold, 1981). When and how you interrupt is what matters.

Helpful interruptions:

- reiterate what your partner is saying
- check that you are correctly hearing your partner
- ask a question in order to clarify something you didn't fully understand

These kinds of interruptions assure both you and your mate that attentive listening and braided dialogue are occurring.

Too Much Information	Helpful Interruptions
Linda (coming in the door out of breath): Len, you won't believe what just happened to me! I went over to the car dealership to get the car fixed, and that slimeball Nick gives me the wrong quote on the car repairs. He said it was three hundred dollars! Can you believe that? I had an oil change and the tires rotated, that's it! So I said, "I'm sorry, that can't be right, there must be some mistake." Then he gives me this look where he wiggles his eyebrows and says, "All right, sexy lady, calm down. I'll take care of you little lady." Sexy lady! Where does he get off talking to me like that! I mean really. Thank heavens Karen from down the street was there and told him he'd better watch his mouth.	*Gina:* Gerald, you won't believe what just happened to me! I went over to the car dealership to get the car fixed, and that slimeball Nick gives me the wrong quote on the car repairs. He said it was three hundred dollars! Can you believe that? I had an oil change and the tires rotated, that's it! So I said, "I'm sorry that can't be right, there must be some mistake." Then...
	Gerald: Good for you Gina. How did he react?
	Gina: He gave me this look where he wiggles his eyebrows, and he says, "All right, sexy lady, calm down. I'll take care of you, little lady." Sexy lady! Where does he get off talking to me like that! I mean really..."
Len: How much did you say he was charging you?	*Gerald (interrupting again):* Wait a second, Gina. You're telling me Nick called you "sexy lady"?
Linda: Len! Didn't you hear the rest of what I said?	*Gina:* Yes. Thank goodness Karen from down the street was there. She told Nick he'd better watch his mouth!
Len: I'm sorry. I was trying to figure out if that price was fair or not.	

Len is trying to follow his wife's lengthy monologue, but he gets distracted thinking about an earlier point she made and loses the train of what she is saying. Usually, someone who is telling a high-energy story, as Linda was, will keep listeners entranced, but because of his concerns about money, Len fixates on the large expense it sounds like their car is going to require. If he had asked for clarification earlier, his interruption might have kept speaker and listener together. As it turns out, Len's attention is still stuck on this earlier point when Linda arrives at the upsetting part of her story. Linda feels unprotected and uncared for by Len, who in fact *would* have cared, if he had heard.

Interrupting to make a different point, rather than to clarify or digest what your partner has said, is likely to disrupt rather than facilitate the dialogue. But interrupting as Gerald does, to digest what Gina has said, is helpful. His interruptions signal that he cares about what his wife is telling him, and enables listener and speaker to stay synchronized.

The following incident occurred to newlyweds who were too polite, that is, who hadn't learned to interrupt when one of them was talking too long. The husband gave more data than his wife could absorb.

> *"Cindy, I just don't know what to do about my dogs," Charles began. "I went to visit them today. The neighbors by my old house love them, and seem to be taking good care of them. But I felt just terrible when I got out of the car and they ran to the fence barking so frantically. When I went into the yard they jumped all over me, just frantic. I felt so guilty that it's been several days since I've been there to walk them. I know it overwhelms you when I bring them here to visit. Their tails do swish all over, and their hair does get on all the furniture. Retrievers are like that, full of enthusiasm and love and gushing all over me and you and the house. And retrievers are what I have and have had forever. They're so much a part of who I am. They've been my most reliable friends for so many years. Like that time they were with me when..."*

While occasionally this kind of extensive emotional venting can offer relief, in Charles's case the longer he talks, the more problems develop.

- The longer he talks the more emotionally agitated he becomes.

- He gradually begins to speak both his and his wife's sides of the conversation, instead of asking Cindy for her reaction or giving her time to speak up.

- He assumes that he knows his wife's concerns, which is only partially true. He would be better off letting Cindy speak for herself.

- The longer he talks, the more difficult it becomes for him to bring his monologue to a conclusion. He begins to forget the point he was trying to make. He also fears that he's had no feedback from his wife because she doesn't understand his point. Subconsciously, he concludes that he'd better keep talking to explain further.

- After the first few sentences, Cindy gives up on trying to remember all the points she wanted to respond to. There is major data loss, both of Charles's concerns and of the responses to his concerns that Cindy had wanted to share.

By contrast, if Cindy were able to offer Charles constructive interruptions, their dialogue would have felt productive instead of frustrating. It might have sounded like this:

> *"Cindy, I just don't know what to do about my dogs," Charles began. "I went to visit them today. The neighbors by my old house love them, and seem to be taking good care of them. But I felt just terrible when I got out of the car and they ran to the fence barking so frantically. When I went into the yard they jumped all over me, just frantic. I felt so guilty that it's been several days since I've been there to walk them."*
>
> *"What has the problem been that you haven't been walking them every day like you usually do?" Cindy interrupted to ask.*
>
> *"The weather has been so cold, I didn't want to risk getting sick again like I did last winter."*

Even a single interruption converts the conversation from a monologue into a dialogue.

> *"And why do you feel guilty if you miss the cold days, since they have such a big yard there to run around in?" Cindy asked, genuinely not understanding her husband's distress.*
>
> *"Actually, Cindy, that's a hard question. I'm not so sure myself. They don't need me to walk them. It's more a promise I made to myself. I think it has to do with the dog my parents made me leave behind when I was a little boy. I promised myself then that I would never abandon another dog in my life. That dog was my only friend. My parents were so harsh, and we didn't live near other kids. When we moved and I had to leave my dog behind I went into what I can see now was a really deep depression."*

By contrast with his anxiously meandering, lengthy monologue, this conversation, guided by Cindy's interruptions and questions, stays focused and leads to productive insights.

 ## Slower is faster

The more complex or emotionally sensitive the discussion, the more helpful it is to take short, regular conversational steps—rather than leaps or sprints—and to make sure you're both on the same path as you go along. Specifying in detail what you have heard, which is not necessary in more casual conversations, prevents time-consuming and emotionally expensive misunderstandings.

Faster Invites Misunderstandings	Slower Is Faster
Len: I'm angry at my brother. He hasn't called once or returned my calls since we visited him last summer. We had such a good time when we were there. Especially when it was just the two of us, just hanging out like we used to when we were kids.	*Gerald:* I'm angry at my brother. He hasn't called once or returned my calls since we visited him last summer. We had such a good time when we were there. Especially when it was just the two of us, just hanging out like we used to when we were kids.
Linda: It's that wife of his. She's always bickering about money, who paid for what, how expensive everything is. And she's always putting him down. He needs to get rid of that woman.	*Gina:* I'm confused. If you had a great time together, why do you think he hasn't called?
	Gerald: We did have a little argument as I was leaving. I told him I thought he should stand up for himself with his wife. That he should speak his opinions more often and not let himself get bullied. I like Darcy but she's so mean to him sometimes.
Len: Linda, that's taking it way too far. Marcy has been good for Sam in a lot of ways. And she put us up in her home for two weeks. Give the woman a break.	
Linda: I'm entitled to my opinion. You can think what you want, and I get to think what I want to think.	*Gina:* Darcy is difficult sometimes, and he doesn't stand up to her. At the same time, what's important to you is your relationship with your brother. Is there another way to reach him besides by phone?

Len and Linda move right along, adding information so quickly that they lose the point of the conversation. Len is genuinely worried about his relationship with his brother, but instead of uncovering what caused the upset between them, Len and Linda get distracted into a debate about their rights to their own opinions.

Gina and Gerald succeed in uncovering the source of the split between the brothers because their dialogue moves slowly, with frequent questions and reiterations that enable Gina to think over each of Gerald's comments. Moving slowly also enables them to keep the main focus of their discussion in mind: Gerald's relationship with his brother.

In real life, few dialogues need to involve such slow-moving, careful repetition of each other's comments as Gina and Gerald used in this example.

The topic of Gerald's brother and sister-in-law was an exceptionally distressing and confusing one for Gerald. For you, other topics are likely to need special care.

There is no single best way to pace dialogue. Quick pacing buoys up the energy level in a conversation. Slower pacing allows people time to digest each other's comments. Energy level and listening are both valuable aspects of conversation.

Keep reiterations specific

When couples first attempt to braid their dialogue, they often give overly global pseudo-reiterations. "I hear you" or "I understand" does not usually accomplish the goals of reiteration. Specifying the details of what you hear is what makes a reiteration useful.

Global Reiteration	Reiterating Specific Details
Len: I really want to get a new camera. I've wanted to pick up photography for a while, but I'm worried. Can I spend that much money not knowing for sure whether I will really stick with it?	*Gerald:* I really want a new camera. I've wanted to pick up photography for a while, but I'm worried. Can I spend that much money not knowing for sure whether I will really stick with it?
Linda: I hear what you're saying, Len. You'll be fine.	*Gina:* I knew you wanted to get a camera, and that you've been holding back. But I hadn't understood before that it was because you were worried about the money and sticking with it.
Len (frustrated): Can't you understand that this is a difficult decision for me? Are you hearing me?	*Gerald:* I'm picturing your friend Kathy spending all that money on a sewing machine and then letting it sit in its box in the back of her hall closet. I don't want that to happen to me.
	Gina: When you start something, you generally see it through. Still, if you are uncertain, you might ask to borrow my dad's camera for a few weeks.

Global summary statements such as Linda's "I hear what you are saying" generally do not suffice in emotionally sensitive discussions. Occasional "I hear you" statements can augment goodwill, but they do not verify that what has been spoken has been accurately understood.

Reiterating specifics as Gina does with Gerald enables them to keep sight of the significant issues and find a helpful solution to each concern. By contrast, if a conversation is just for casually passing time, no reiterations are usually necessary.

Basic 9: *Use the Four Ss*

Effective dialogue generally has four important characteristics: symmetry, short segments, specifics, and summary.

Sustain symmetry

Symmetry, in dialogue, refers to the balance of how much each partner talks. Is each one getting equal airtime, speaking approximately equal amounts? When one partner does most of the talking, this asymmetry, or lack of balance, tends to become annoying to one or both of them. The silent partner typically tires of only listening, while the talker can feel overburdened. Usually, both would prefer more give and take.

Unequal Airtime	Symmetrical Airtime
Linda: I want to be sure to go to the grocery store tonight. Even though I'm getting tired, I'd rather go tonight than get up in the morning and discover there's no milk. I have a number of things to get there. And I do want to tell you the latest developments in my office. I couldn't believe that my boss keeps taking Allison's side when we disagree about whose accounts are whose. Oh, and by the way, did you get the dry cleaning on your way home today? *Len:* No. *Linda:* Oh no! My good silk blouse is there and without it...	*Gina:* I need to get to the grocery store tonight; we need milk. *Gerald:* Is it essential? *Gina:* I like it for breakfast, and while I'm there I could use a few other things as well. *Gerald:* I've been thinking about your office, since mine has also been in turmoil lately. We've expanded so fast, no one's sure who is in charge of what. *Gina:* Sounds a lot like the mess with Brenda in my office over whose accounts are whose.

Different rates of speech and levels of volumes can make symmetry harder to maintain. The faster or louder partner can easily begin taking up more airtime than he or she intended. The slower or quieter one may, like Len, have trouble getting the floor.

Differing family or cultural expectations of how long to wait before speaking can also interfere with symmetry. In some families, particularly large ones, children may learn very young to launch forth in the mini-moment just before the previous speaker finishes talking. Without this ability they would seldom be heard. In other families, manners require a polite pause between one speaker and the next. Just as some typists put two spaces after the period at the end of a sentence, these families expect several moments of silence to indicated completion before the next person speaks up.

Symmetry is hardest to maintain when partners have different rates of speech and different expectations of when to speak up. Slow talkers who wait for a long, polite pause may inadvertently train their faster-talking mate to continue on and on. The fast talker, thinking that the slower one has nothing to say, talks on to help out, lest his or her mate be embarrassed at having no comment. Fortunately, open discussion about rates of speech and family or cultural expectations can enable couples to figure out how their dialogue can stay comfortably symmetrical.

A more insidious kind of asymmetry occurs when one partner's opinions count more than the other's. Your input may carry more sway because your style of expression is more vigorous, or your viewpoint may tend to get lost because you express yourself more tentatively. Or the asymmetry may occur because one of you is a better listener. If either your or your mate's views fairly consistently predominate or evaporate, modifying the pattern will be helpful.

> *Paul and Pam, married twelve years, spoke more or less equal amounts, but Paul seemed always to set the agenda. Pam felt like a rubber stamp for what he said, not a separate person with information and ideas to add.*
>
> *Paul and Pam both came from families where the parents had favorites. In Paul's family, everyone listened when the favorite child spoke up. The others had to fight for airtime and listeners. The result was that the favored child developed a dominating personality, with very little ability to hear others' needs. The favorite expected to be the center of attention.*
>
> *Paul, who had been a less favored child and always had to struggle for the floor, found a wife, Pam, with a quiet voice that he could easily speak above. When she spoke up, he would either point out what was wrong with the point she had made or simply make another point, at a higher energy level. Pam's point would then be lost. Paul meant well; he had no idea how asymmetrical their input to discussions had become. Their dialogue felt normal to him because it replayed the patterns from his family's dinner-table conversations. Pam, however, struggled with depression from her inability to maintain a sense of personal power in her marriage.*

Pam's father had commanded center stage all through her upbringing, so Paul's dominance felt normal to Pam. On the other hand, Pam's chronic depression was a concern for both of them. In therapy, Pam learned to expect to be heard and to stand up for her views if they were ignored or contradicted. Paul realized that he had been disregarding his wife's input much as his family members had his (and as his father had also ignored his mother's input). As they changed the patterns of their dialogue to achieve greater symmetry of attention, Pam's depression lifted.

Pam and Paul's growth into a more symmetrical relationship led to a further realization. They noticed that their teenage children were continuing the patterns they were trying to grow beyond. Their son's voice dominated family dinner conversations. The feelings their daughter had long lamented, of feeling less favored, suddenly made sense to them. The whole family needed to begin monitoring for symmetry and respectful listening.

Speak in short segments

Short segments refers to how much is said at one time. In effective dialogue, each speaker generally offers brief comments rather than trying to say too much at once.

Listening, as said earlier, is a lot like eating. To take in what you hear, small bites work better than large chunks. To keep the bits small enough, either the speaker needs to pause regularly, expecting to take turns talking and listening, or the listener needs to interrupt.

Long Monologue	Short Segments
Len (after a business dinner party): I made my usual stupid jokes. I was wondering myself whether I was a bit overbearing. I hope you didn't feel bad when no one laughed at my jokes. I felt a little embarrassed. Those folks were tough. They are so formal. Getting a laugh from one of them takes major effort. I thought for a while I should take a pulse to make sure they weren't dead. I still kind of enjoyed myself, but not nearly as much as when our friends come over and we laugh so much together.	*Gerald (after a business dinner party):* I joke around too much. Now I'm worried they think I'm overbearing. *Gina:* Do you know where that idea might come from? Sally and Jeff told me they think you're very funny. They aren't the kind of people who laugh out loud often. I thought you were an incredible success. *Gerald:* Maybe that's why I feel so awkward around them. They're so formal. When our friends come to dinner we laugh all night. I guess I'm just not used to Sally and Jeff's reserve. I had to work hard to get laughs from them!

As we have seen before, long monologues like Len's lose data. A listener can only pick up one or two points at a time, and can respond to only one. All but the first of the many points Len makes go by the wayside.

Long monologues also drain the energy from a conversation. Although occasional storytelling can be interesting, for the most part, briefer comments with frequent interchanges back and forth stimulate a higher energy level.

To keep your speech segments short, aim to make just one point each time you speak. Let your mate respond to that one, and then add your next point. Short segments make for more intricately intertwined dialogue.

Share specifics

Specifics means details. Details become especially vital when you are trying to solve problems jointly. To make a shared decision, resolve a conflict, or clean up after an upset, specific details point the way to positive outcomes. On the other hand, inundating your mate with too many details invites him or her to tune you out.

Too General	Too Much Detail	The Main Idea and Supporting Details
Len: Work was good today.	*Len:* When I got to work today I started with a big mug of coffee. I felt like I needed to juice myself up before I talked with Mr. Troy, the tall fellow with the mustache that I told you speaks with a funny lisp. I was nervous about talking with him. I wonder if that's because his mustache reminds me of my father's. Also it was hot in the room and I kept thinking about how sweaty I must look. He's so wealthy. Anyway, I started out by trying to sound him out on what he thought my percentage of the deal should be. It was about ten in the morning, and I was nervous also that we wouldn't close the deal in time for my lunch meeting...	*Gerald:* I enjoyed work today. I finished my big negotiation for the White deal. I was pleased because I stood my ground on the percentage that I wanted from the sale, and Mr. Terry went along with it. That gives us twenty percent more earnings this year than I had expected.

Summarize

Summaries are seldom necessary when the purpose of conversation is amusement or filling each other in on the day's events. Summaries do, however, prove powerfully useful when you are trying to solve a specific dilemma. Summaries focus your discussion and prevent loss of information. A summary that includes all the points made by both partners conveys that you are taking each other's concerns seriously.

Summaries also propel you from one stage of conversation to the next. They help you, for instance, to progress from discussing the various aspects of a sensitive problem to beginning to generate possible solutions.

Leaving the Conversation Dangling	Summarizing
Len: I wonder what the economy is like there now.	*Gerald:* So it sounds like if I take that job offer in Ohio your main concern would be finding a neighborhood to live in that has good schools and a lot of young families that could give us the kind of close-knit neighborhood we have here. And my main concerns are whether they'll pay me enough to make the risks of leaving my current job worthwhile.
Linda: I do want a close-knit neighborhood, good schools, and a place with other young families nearby.	
Len: I sure hope they'll pay me enough to make the risks of leaving my current job worthwhile.	
Linda: So that's that.	*Gina:* You forgot our most important reason for moving! It would be great to live near our parents, our sisters and brothers, and their families.
Len: That's what? We haven't decided anything.	

Including all the concerns that both of you have expressed, as Gina and Gerald do, ensures that a summary will be effective. Summaries consolidate the information put forth thus far. If any input has been omitted, the summary gives you a second chance to be certain that it has entered your shared information pool.

Basic 10: *Use Climate Controls*

Whatever stresses and tensions a couple faces,
they can choose the climate of their relationship.

How would you describe the climate in your household? As a couple you may mostly feel comfortably warm toward each other, mainly cold, or sometimes stormy. Unlike the weather outside your windows, the climate within your marriage, like the temperature in your living room, can be controlled. One of the great benefits of the modern age is this ability to keep our homes warm in winter and cool in summer. Similarly, with contemporary understanding of emotions, whatever the stresses and tensions in your world, you and your partner still can determine the climate within your marriage.

The climate between the two of you does, of course, become more difficult to control when the conditions in your life are stressful. Relaxing together out in the sunshine on a warm summer's day, most couples would find themselves in a mellow mood. But life is not always sunny. Cooking dinner after an exhausting day with crying children when one of you is annoyed that the other has lost the checkbook and the other is upset over demeaning treatment at work—these are turbulent weather conditions. They pose serious challenges.

Throughout either calm or troubling conditions, however, you can largely control your turbulence as a couple, by using "climate controls."

- monitor for heat and speed
- use word patrol
- as the pace picks up, pause
- plan exit and reentry routines
- monitor for fatigue, hunger, illness, and overload

All these principles are based on the reality that high intensity debate does not create an environment conducive to talking about sensitive personal matters. To verbalize deeply felt concerns and feel safe expressing hurt, anxious, sad, or frustrated feelings, quiet talking is essential.

The more emotionally activated you feel, the harder it will be to keep your communications open, noninvasive, and nontoxic. The more agitated you become, the harder it will be to continue to listen for what's right and useful in what your partner says instead of tuning in to what you don't like. Assiduously staying within the basic guidelines is seldom easy when you are discussing sensitive topics, but it is your best guarantee for preventing hurtful emotional disruptions.

Monitor for heat and speed

When a conversation gets louder, faster, or angrier, the discussion is likely to spin out of control. Increases in heat and speed make it harder to maintain the basics of cooperative dialogue, just as the faster you drive, the more likely it is that you will have an accident and be injured. If you notice that your dialogue is heating or speeding up, stop. Pause, think, make the necessary adjustments, and then proceed.

Speeding Toward a Crash	Monitoring for Heat and Speed
Len: Linda you totally embarrassed me in front of my coworkers.	*Gerald:* Gina, you totally embarrassed me in front of my coworkers.
Linda: I didn't mean to embarrass you, I was just kidding around.	*Gina:* I didn't mean to embarrass you, I was just kidding around.
Len: Kidding around? That's what you call kidding around? You made them think that I'm selfish and lazy. And it's totally untrue. You said that I never help out around the house, that I watch TV all day. And what was that you called me, "Captain Len?" I can't believe you called me that while they were all listening. As if I'm the one who does the bossing around! It's this petty fantasy world you have created where you are the martyr and I'm the evil husband. Well if that's the way you want it, fine!	*Gerald:* Kidding around? That's what you call kidding around? You made them think that I'm selfish and lazy. And it's totally untrue. You said that I never help out around the house, that I watch TV all day. And what was that you called me, "Captain Gerry?" I can't believe you called me that while they were all listening. As if I'm the one who does the bossing around! It's this petty fantasy world you have created where you are the martyr and I'm the evil husband. Well if that's the way you want it, fine.
Linda (furiously): Oh, Mr. Self-Righteous! There was a lot of truth to what I was saying. If you would listen to me for just one second without your Mr. Perfect, Captain Len smirk you might learn something!	*Gina (firmly):* Hold on a minute. Let's take a breather here...
Len (yelling): There you go again, Linda, calling me names. You're such a child!	*Gerald:* Somehow this conversation has gotten out of control. I'll count to five... That's better...
	Gina: These are definitely issues we need to discuss, but more slowly. What upset you about what I said?
	Gerald (pausing to breath deeply and then continuing): The stuff about me not helping in the house was the most upsetting. Do you really believe that?

Len, already heated up, blurts out blame, launching an escalating exchange of insults. Linda's instinctive defensiveness could have been headed off if she had paused to think. Instead, with increasing heat and speed, Len and Linda continue to fling toxic words.

Gerald and Gina similarly get off on the wrong foot. Upset about Gina's comments in front of his coworkers, Gerald fires off an accusative you statement. Gina, however, notes their escalation. By observing that the conversation is careening out of control, she helps them both to pause.

By monitoring the temperature and rate of their talking, and slowing down when they note that they have exceeded safe limits, Gerald and Gina convert a potential argument into an important productive discussion.

I have seen time and again in my practice how increases in speech rate and volume predict verbal battles. Similarly, a parent preparing dinner in the kitchen can anticipate when the children, out of sight in another room, are about to get into a fight. Elevation in the pitch, volume, and intensity of their voices offers a sure warning of trouble ahead, even when the children's words are not audible. The same holds true for adult dialogue. Louder and faster generally means a fight is just around the verbal corner.

The opposite is also true. When couples are involved in productive dialogue on issues of serious significance the pacing is slow enough to allow for thoughtful digestion of new information, and the tone is quiet.

The earlier you cool down, the less difficult it will be to douse the flames, and the sooner you apply the brakes, the less likely it is that you will crash. But how do you monitor, cool down, and brake in conversation?

The question of how to bring escalating hostilities back to cooperative dialogue is addressed in greater detail in Chapters 7, 9, and 10. For now, however, several strategies can help:

- Do something sooner, rather than later. If corrective action is taken at the first hint of a nasty tone of voice, for instance, shouting will not occur.

- Make sure you stay in bounds. It's tempting to respond to your partner's errors with criticism: "You're blaming me," or "That was a *but*." It isn't, however, useful.

- Pause to think about how to get back on track: "I need to stop and think a second here."

- Listen to what is right and useful in what you hear, then reiterate.

- Summarize what each of you has said, to reinstate cooperation.

- Ask a good question that gets the discussion back on track: "So in what ways do you think we agree on this?" or "What is the main point you want me to hear?" or "What would help?"

- Explore what triggered the slippage: "We were talking so well, and then the tone changed. Let's both look back and figure out what triggered the tensions."

Realistically, from time to time emotions will still flare, and dialogue will slip into out-of-bounds speaking or ineffective listening. The good news is that curtailing escalating dialogue becomes easier as you form a clear agreement about which verbal behaviors are constructive and which are out of bounds. In the meantime, monitor for heat and speed.

Use Word Patrol

"Word Patrol" is a self-patrol. Each of you is responsible for monitoring your own speaking and listening. Table 4 details common inflammatory verbal habits, most of which have been discussed earlier.

Word Patrol, like much of this book, suggests both what to avoid, and ways to find your way out of difficulties. Two particularly helpful tactics are to shift from *we* to *I* and to change *should* to *could* or *would like*.

"We Should..."	"I Could..." "I Would Like..."
Linda (clearly troubled by a recent argument): We don't seem connected. *Len:* What should we do? *Linda:* I don't know.	*Gina:* We don't seem connected. *Gerald:* What would you like to do? What could I do that would help you feel more connected with me? *Gina:* I would like to spend a few moments each evening before we go to bed, and maybe a moment or two in the mornings when we wake up, looking directly in your eyes as we talk. That would help me to start and end each day feeling that we had a connection, a partnership.

Linda and Len's phrasing of their dilemma leads them to an impasse. Both *we* and *should* are difficult words. As discussed in Chapter 1, *we* is really two *I*s, each with different thoughts and preferences. Talking about two people as if they were one merged being adds to confusion, not clarity. Talking in terms of *should* is confusing because it implies that there is just one perspective, one right answer or course of action. Fortunately, for most dilemmas there are multiple good solutions, not just single, fixed right answers.

Gina and Gerald demonstrate some simple changes that can point the way out when *we* or *should* cause dialogue to become frustratingly blocked:

- Break the *we* down into an *I* and a *you*.
- Change *should* to *could* or *would like to*.

TABLE 4   Word Patrol

Beware of	Example	Instead Try	Example
But Yes, but...	You want a gourmet meal but I want a light supper.	And	You want a gourmet meal *and* I want a light supper.
We	We like Chinese food.	I want... What are your preferences?	I'd like Chinese food. How about you?
You think that...	You think that I don't watch how much we spend.	What do you think...? How do you feel about...?	What do you think about eating out? How do you feel about cooking?
Should	I should spend less.	Could	I could spend less, and that would put more time pressure on us to cook and shop.
You make me feel...	You make me feel guilty for wanting to eat out so often.	I feel	I feel guilty for wanting to eat out so often, and yet if I stay late at work and I'm too tired to cook, eating out really helps.
I feel that you...	I feel that you should do some of the cooking.	I feel (*one word*) when you...	I feel terrific when you do some of the cooking.
Don't you think...?	Don't you think that you could do some cooking?	Do you think...?	Do you think that you could do some cooking?
Always Never	I always am on cooking duty. You never take a turn.	Sometimes, Generally, Often, Seldom	I generally do cooking duty.
I don't want...	I don't want the full responsibility for meals.	I'd like...	I'd like to cook some of the meals, and be able to count on you or on going out two days a week.

❤ As the pace picks up, pause

Above, in the discussion of monitoring for heat and speed, a pause was recommended as a way of slowing escalation. A pause is often your last chance to prevent hurtful arguments.

> My children play a sport called Ultimate Frisbee, a fast- growing sport on college campuses. Watching one of their games, enjoying the fast-paced running and frisbee-tossing as they traversed a soccerlike playing field, I saw an event that struck me profoundly.
>
> The seven members on each team usually fan out across the field. At one point, most of the fourteen players from the two teams were converging into an intense pack of fast-pumping elbows and knees near the goal. Someone said aloud, "Time out." All play stopped immediately.
>
> "Clogging," someone announced, the term for when players are crowding in too close to each other. The players all knew what to do. They fanned out, calmly and comfortably, for safer play.
>
> "Play," someone said. With full enthusiasm the game resumed.

When couples feel themselves getting too heated up, too speeded up, and at risk for becoming angry or defensive, they need a way to call a similar time out. By calming your dialogue with a pause, the two of you can give yourselves time to think and a fresh start. Why are pauses so vital in maintaining climate control? The emotional message system in the brain reacts faster than the thinking system (see Chapter 5 for a fuller description). With emotions traveling at breakneck speed and thoughts struggling to catch up, our brains need time to allow our capacity for thoughtful reasoning to function. A pause both cools the rapidly escalating feelings and allows time for constructive thinking about the situation to emerge.

❤ Plan exit and reentry routines

Discuss together a plan for exiting quickly and safely any conversations or situations that seem to be getting too hot. Once you are in a hot situation it is too late to start discussing how to disengage.

If you individually or as a couple tend to overheat even sometimes, you need to devise your exit plan at a time when you both are in comfortable good humor. It is also helpful to practice it, the way schools practice fire drills, so that you will be able to implement your plan should the need arise. Anger can induce determination to "settle the argument" by following the other rather than letting them leave. Practice ahead of time makes pauses and exits more reliable when you really need them.

A good exit plan needs to include these elements:

- *How* the two of you will mutually disengage when the going feels potentially too hot.
- *Where* each of you will go to cool off so each of you is in a separate space physically as well as emotionally.
- *What* you will do while you are apart to soothe your anger.
- *How* and when you will reengage, so that initially you spend a period of time together being normal before you again address the problem that proved overly sensitive.
- *When* you will talk again about the sensitive topic so that disengagement does not mean giving up on discussing the issue.
- *What if—* what you will do if subsequent attempts to talk about the topic keep proving dangerous. It is helpful to have a third party you can turn to for help negotiating difficult issues: a friend you both trust; a religious advisor; or a counseling professional.

To implement your exit plan, know your own and your partner's early warning signs of danger ahead. When you see any of those signs, be sure that you heed them. Remember that using your exit system, even if the danger signal proves to be a false alarm, is far better than missing the cues and ending up in a blaze.

Monitor for fatigue, hunger, illness, and overload

Fighting is more likely to erupt when you are physiologically stressed by hunger, fatigue, illness, or too much to do. Interestingly, awareness offers the best antidote to these physiological risk factors. If you can tell your mate that you are hungry or tired, and therefore more brittle than usual, both of you are more likely to be extra careful about how you talk and listen to each other, and how you interpret each other's fussiness.

Tuning Out	Tuning In
Linda: You've got to fix that screen door. I'm going to scream if I hear it bang closed one more time.	*Gina:* I must be tired. I never like hearing that screen door bang, but I felt like screaming now with the noise.
Len: Please stop nagging me.	*Gerald:* Sorry about that. When the weather warms up I'll fix it. Meanwhile how about a nap? I could watch the kids.
Linda (suddenly shouting): Look! You're tracking in mud!	

Needless to say, the best response to fatigue is sleep; to hunger, food; and to illness, rest. For overload, stopping and looking specifically at the sources of your stress is the first step; then you can map a plan of action. When your mental and physical resources are lower than usual or already overutilized, simplify. Removing all but the essentials from your list of must dos can ease your tension.

Prevention, of course, beats cure. If you notice a pattern to spats, you can prevent many of them with simple agreements like these:

- No tough topics before dinner.
- No tough topics after ten o'clock in the evening.
- No difficult dialogues when the children need attention.
- Plan ahead, to prevent feeling rushed.
- Good news/bad news: If you have a problem to discuss, put it in the context of something nice.

Choosing a Climate

A central premise of this book is that the climate of your marriage is something that you as a couple can choose. You can decide whether disagreements will be handled by shouting or by talking. You can decide whether energies generated by differences will go to thunder and lightning or to intense but safely quiet dialogue.

You can make these decisions by default, letting whatever happens happen. Or you can choose your marriage climate explicitly by discussing together the atmosphere each of you would like for your home and committing yourselves to learning the necessary skills.

TABLE 5 Part I Review

The ABCD's– All the Basics of Collaborative Dialogue

The BASICS	Avoid	Be Sure To
1. Say It	Hinting Wondering *Don't wants*	Say aloud your concerns and preferences. Convert *don't wants* to *would likes*.
2. Verbalize Feelings	Acting out your feelings instead of using words. "You make me feel..." " I feel that you..."	Put feelings into words so they can guide you to understanding. Use "I feel..." Use "I feel (*one word*) that..."
3. No Trespassing	Crossovers– speaking about your partner's thoughts and feelings, or telling him or her what to do.	Speak your own thoughts and feelings, or ask your partner's. Use "When you... I..." to speak about something your partner has done.
4. No Toxicity	Disparaging comments towards your partner.	Give feedback with when you, not criticism. Use tact.
5. Listen to Learn	Pressing the mute button, *but,* listening for what's wrong with.	Listen attentively. Give evidence of hearing. Listen for what's useful, what makes sense, in what your partner says.
6. Listen to Feelings	Ignoring, criticizing, or brushing aside your partner's feelings.	Explore feelings. Focus first on feelings, then return to thoughts, when you see or hear evidence of emotions.
7. Bilateral Listening	Selfishness: hearing only your concerns. Excessive altruism: hearing only your partner's concerns.	Make the concerns of both of you count when you discuss opinions, decisions, or conflicts.
8. Braid Your Dialogue	Responding "Yes, but..." oppositional or parallel dialogue.	Respond "Yes,..., and..." Intertwine your perspectives, building a shared information pool as you talk.
9. Use the 4 Ss	Unequal airtime Long speeches Generalizations Leaving loose ends	Symmetry Short segments Specifics Summary
10. Use Climate Controls	Letting emotions build and getting overheated.	Monitor for heat and speed, tired or hungry, or overloaded. Use word patrol. Pause or exit when dialogue gets hot.

Part II

DEALING WITH DIFFERENCES

Married life flows like a river. Sometimes you can relax, enjoying the flow like rafters drifting on a calm sunny day in gentle waters. At other times you'll need all your wits about you as you hit the rapids. For highly skilled river rafters, the challenges of rapids provide the most exhilaration of the trip.

Marriage presents multiple kinds of rapids. In the face of these challenges, the fundamentals of talking, listening, and weaving dialogue become both more difficult and more essential. Hurt and anger at these times tell you something dangerous is happening. A situation that evokes these feelings has the potential to convert your loving alliance to antagonism.

Identifying the kind of rapids—the category of challenge—you are facing, can begin to make the challenges of married life feel more manageable. Labels are tools. Being able to name a difficulty gives initial power to you as individuals, and even more as a couple, to handle it in new ways. Each of the chapters in this part of the book names a different type of challenge.

- *Chapter 4: Fix-It Talk*— for when change would be helpful.

- *Chapter 5: Anger as a Stop Sign*— for utilizing angry feelings effectively.

- *Chapter 6: Receiving Anger Without Fighting*— for responding constructively when your spouse is angry.

- *Chapter 7: After Upsets, Clean Up Procedures*— for recovering after arguments.

- *Chapter 8: Shared Decision Making*— for reaching mutual agreement on issues large and small.

- *Chapter 9: Conflict Resolution*— for settling disagreements constructively.
- *Chapter 10: Out-of-Bounds and Fouls*— for dealing with unacceptable words and actions.

In addition to naming marriage challenges, the following chapters combine the basic communication skills into dialogue strategies specific to each challenge. Like river maps, these strategies are tools to aid your journey, to help you navigate with more certainty, ensuring a safe, satisfying, and exhilarating married life.

What's the big deal? Don't all couples fight?

All couples have disagreements, but all couples do not fight. Fighting means your communication system has broken down. When your communication skills are functioning you can talk with each other to solve your dilemmas—which is very different from fighting.

With the skills in Part I plus the strategies coming ahead in the chapters of Part II, you will find that you and your spouse can gradually learn to talk constructively about even your most sensitive differences. As you understand each other better and succeed in resolving issues you may have bickered over time and time again, little will be left to fight about.

That is not to say you won't still have occasional disagreements. No one rides the river of life in continuously perfect physical or emotional working order. Every year, at least once, you probably find that when too many germs in the air combine with a surfeit of stresses in your life, you end up with a cold or a flu. Similarly, every so often overload or circumstances may trigger misunderstandings that add up to an argument. Chronic tensions, however, are no more normal than chronic cough or fever. Your emotional well-being as a couple can be measured by how well your communications work in the face of life's daily challenges—by how seldom you find yourselves, like river rafters thrown overboard in rapids, submerged in the turbulence of fighting.

Notes

'Tis not love's going hurts my days,
But that it went in little ways.

—Edna St. Vincent Millay, "The Spring and the Fall"

Chapter 4
Fix-It Talk

Dialogue for talking over minor problems and deciding together what to do about them is what I call *fix-it talk*.

Healthy couples need to be able to glide gracefully together as they execute the complex challenges of daily life. To succeed, like ice-skating partners we admire in Olympic ice-dancing competitions, loving couples need to continually perfect their dance.

As much as skaters practice, and in spite of their extraordinary levels of skill, even the best stumble from time to time. Moments when their coordination is a bit off inevitably occur. Skaters need a comfortable process for remedying difficulties and for continuously developing new choreography.

When skaters lose their balance once in a particular part of a routine, they will probably stumble there every subsequent time they skate that routine. To eliminate the problem, they need to look closely at that moment, analyze precisely what is causing the stumble, figure out alternatives that will eliminate the problem, and then practice to make the new way automatic. At first they will have to think their way through the change, very consciously guiding themselves. After a number of repetitions, however, the new way will feel automatic, and they will be able to execute the new maneuver almost without thinking about it.

Marriage conflicts work similarly. Like moments when skaters lose their balance, moments of minor irritation convey to couples a warning that it's time to do things differently. Couples generally argue over the same minor disagreements again and again. To fix them they need quiet analysis, redecision, and then practice to reprogram the new ways into their habits.

Force-It Strategies

*Life is not so short but that there is always
time enough for courtesy.*

—Ralph Waldo Emerson, *Letters and Social Aims*

Criticism, raising your voice, blame, demands, threats, punishment, and manipulation by guilt are attempts to change a situation by forcing your mate to do something you want. Like the road to hell, these force-it strategies are paved with good intentions. While they may get the end result you think you want, the costs are high.

Force-it strategies prove costly in multiple ways. They attempt to control your spouse, instead of respectfully requesting cooperation. They tend to be negative, focusing on what you don't like rather than on your preferences. They motivate by spreading a pall of bad feeling rather than by appealing to your spouse's desire to be a considerate teammate. As crossovers, force-it strategies invite defensiveness. As toxic messages, they pollute your relationship. Most importantly, they disregard your partner's concerns.

Aaron and Donna were talented young professionals with a strong love for each other and an unfortunate expertise in the uses of force-it strategies. Like the other couples who agreed to share their trials and triumphs with you in this book, Aaron and Donna can take great pride in the commitment they made to themselves and to each other to learn to be a more effective couple. They both realized that none of their parents, all divorced, had had sufficient skills at marriage partnership, and they welcomed the opportunity to break the family patterns that had caused their parents such distress.

> *Aaron was very annoyed. Each evening at dinner Donna asked him whom he had eaten lunch with that day. Aaron heard his wife's questions as signs that she thought she had to keep checking up on him or else he would cheat on her. At first he was patient, but eventually Donna's questions led to his thinking, "I don't need a policeman! What kind of person does she think I am?" Aaron felt tempted by a number of possible force-it strategies to force his wife to stop quizzing him on his office social life:*

- Demands— *"Stop asking me who I ate lunch with!"*
- Blame— *"You're creating problems by asking me those same annoying questions every day. I've told you to stop and you still keep going."*
- Criticism— *"You're too intrusive!"*
- Threats— *"If you don't stop asking me that question, I'm going to start having affairs!"*

- Punishment— *"I'm going out drinking after work tomorrow! That's what you get for continuing to bug me like that."*

- Coercion— *"Stop talking! I told you not to ask me that and I mean it!"*

- Manipulation by guilt— *"Do I ask you that kind of question? You should trust me. You shouldn't be checking up on me every minute!"*

Any of these force-it strategies might have gained Donna's compliance, but the price in resistance and resentment would have been high. Donna might have stopped asking Aaron about his lunch arrangements, so on the surface Aaron would have succeeded in getting what he wanted. Because he had not addressed Donna's concerns, however, the distrust in their relationship would merely have gone underground. Donna would have interpreted Aaron's belligerence as hiding something, which would have fed her suspicions about his relationships with the women at work. Her increased distrust would have seeped out in subsequent snippiness and surly remarks. She would have resented having been bossed around, treated as if her concerns did not matter. No one likes being treated as a bad guy, the source of the problem. Meanwhile Aaron and Donna would have lost an opportunity to understand each other more fully and to deal with their very real and potentially relationship-destroying dilemma as a team.

In sum, force-it strategies fail on multiple grounds:

- They create an unpleasant atmosphere, replacing the happiness and safety of your relationship with feelings of tension, regret, anxiety, dissention, and distrust.

- They tend to be ineffective in fixing the problem. If, instead of demanding, you listen respectfully to your partner's point of view and add it to your own concerns, you can discover far better and longer lasting solutions.

- They create a false sense of having solved the problem. If you haven't addressed your partner's concerns, that part of the problem may still be brewing.

- They invite retribution. They invite your mate to get back at you, sooner or later, in some similarly negative way.

- Toxic words destroy love. Demanding and demeaning behaviors do not make you look very lovable. The fear and resentment they stir up corrode your mate's affection for you. Toxic words also poison love in the person who says them. The more you act critical and angry, the more you convince yourself that you dislike your spouse.

Effective fix-it talk, by contrast, solves problems without either partner dominating the other. With fix-it talk, you solve disruptions to the harmony in your home by seeking mutual understanding and finding solutions that meet the concerns of each of you.

Later in this chapter Aaron and Donna will succeed in using fix-it talk to remedy their problem. First, however, let's look at the steps involved in effective fix-it dialogue.

The Five-Step Fix-It Sequence

Effective fix-it talk starts with focusing on yourself, expands to looking at the situation and what you would like to do about it, expands further yet to add your spouse's preferences and concerns, and concludes with a solution that both of you can feel good about:

1. *Listen to your feelings*, which indicate problems and preferences.
2. *Describe the dilemma*, the situation that troubles you.
3. *Make a request*, suggesting at least one solution that would help.
4. *Listen to the response*, to understand your spouse's concerns.
5. *Devise a solution*, that works for both of you.

Your spirit in this kind of dialogue may be serious or may be playful, but it stays respectful without even traces of negative, critical, or demanding tones. That's often a challenge, and one well worth meeting. To illustrate, let's return to the first real-life example in Chapter 1—a bedtime conflict.

> *Donna and Aaron often found that they wanted to head for bed at different hours in the evening. Donna had to start work earlier the next morning and tired earlier. Aaron was a night owl who loved late-night news. They kept a TV in their study, just off their bedroom.*

Step 1: Listen to your feelings

> *Donna felt frustrated. She couldn't fall asleep. The sound of the TV irritated her. It seemed to be keeping her up. She could have smothered the frustrated feeling, telling herself, "It's the only TV he watches," or "I don't want to be selfish about this," or "It's not worth making a big deal out of—I'll fall asleep eventually."*

These self-quieting options may from time to time be wise choices. Dampening feelings often, however, causes them to amplify (as explained in

Part I). The more Donna tries to smother her frustration, the more likely that eventually it will break out in an explosion.

> *Donna could have used the opposite strategy, ruminating on how irritating the TV was until finally she leapt out of bed complaining: "Damn it! How can you blast the TV like that when you know I'm exhausted and won't be able to sleep with the noise?"*

By stoking the fire of feelings you can work up enough anger that the potency of your feelings forces you to address a problem. Dilemmas then, however, are likely to get addressed toxically, not with quiet fix-it talk.

> *Fortunately, Donna decided to listen to her feelings while they were still small, hearing her mild frustration instead of waiting for it to grow to full-scale anger or a raging fury. Her quietly irritated feeling successfully nudged her to identify the problem, which she could then begin to address.*

Step 2: Describe the dilemma

While there are a number of strategies for beginning to talk about a dilemma, what all of them have in common is Basic 3: No Trespassing. Focus on your reading of the facts of the problem, or on yourself, rather than speaking about your spouse.

- *Describe the specific problematic situation:* "The television voices carry through the walls and make it hard for me to go to sleep."

- *Verbalize your feeling and the situation:* "I'm frustrated. I'm having trouble falling asleep with the TV sounds."

If you need to reference what your partner is doing that is problematic, utilize the when you formula: "When you listen to TV in the study, I can hear it in the bedroom." This way you make yourself the subject instead of trespassing by talking about your partner, a sure invitation to defensiveness. Also, this formula enables you to define the problem in a no-fault way that includes both of you and blames neither.

Step 3: Make a request

A well-phrased request includes both what you would like and a question about how your partner would feel about that solution. That is, a good request launches bilateral listening.

- The statement of what you would like can be tactfully expressed by beginning with a phrase such as "I would prefer," "I would like," "I'd love if you could."

- Conclude with a genuine question to find out your partner's concerns: "Would that work out for you?" or "I would appreciate if you could turn the TV down even lower. Could you still hear it OK?"

Step 4: Listen to the response

Aaron sighed, "I barely can hear it now. I would like to watch the news before I go to bed. The walls must be made of paper."

Step 5: Devise a solution. A real solution to a problem is one that works for both of you.

Aaron suggested, "How about if I go downstairs and use the TV in the kitchen? I wouldn't mind grabbing a snack anyway. Thanks for telling me there was a problem. I don't mean to be keeping you up."

Donna also offered a suggestion: "When I'm standing in the study I can barely hear it either. The wall between here and the bedroom must amplify the sound. I'll try putting a pillow over my head. Let me try that, unless you want to go to the kitchen anyway."

All five steps may not be necessary for fixing every problem. Sometimes just the first, becoming aware of a problem by noticing a feeling, can lead to your doing something different, which in turn will either take care of the problem or lead to your spouse handling the situation in a new way.

Donna noticed that she felt irritated when Aaron went on cleaning binges. He raced through the house like a fast-moving snowplow, removing everything that had been out of place and leaving each room picture perfect. Having realized her irritation, she asked herself "Why does his speedy cleaning irritate me?"

Donna figured out that she feared that Aaron would move or throw out things she needed as he cleaned. With that realization, she found a large laundry basket, which she offered to Aaron for anything out of place that might be hers. Aaron was delighted with this addition to his system, and Donna's irritation with his cleaning evaporated.

Alternatively, if you complete the first two steps, noticing an uncomfortable feeling and then mentioning it, your spouse may then offer to do something different before you even need to go on to Step 3, making a request.

"I worry that my things will get thrown away when you clean."

"How about if I put anything that looks like yours in one pile on your desk?"

Preparatory thinking at each stage before you speak or act is likely to pay off. Especially if you have been in the habit of smothering your little voices that say there's a problem here—or, conversely fanning your sparks of irritation into flames of angry criticism—you may want to pause, think, and consider just how to proceed before each step. Thoughtful preparation increases accuracy in most activities, from shooting hoops on the basketball court to planning a lovely birthday celebration. The same applies to successfully negotiating the five steps of fix-it dialogue.

Changing Force-It Talk to Fix-It Talk

Inviting your mate to speak up about his or her concerns ensures that your partner will feel a part of, not pushed into, the new plan of action. Persuasion and debate may be more tempting, but asking your mate's concerns will win you more satisfaction in the long run.

When you feel irritated, it can be hard to remember that your partner has feelings and preferences too. You may have to keep reminding yourself that fix-it talk is not a matter of getting your spouse to agree to your initial request. Rather, the goal is to find a solution that works for both of you.

> Donna was tempted to blurt out to Aaron, "You should be nicer to me! I do everything the way you want. I moved to the mountains because you wanted to. I'm waiting to have kids because you don't feel ready. It's not fair that you're not nice to me when I phone you at work!"

Donna was tempted to use manipulation by guilt to force niceness from Aaron in their daily phone calls. The fact that she could recite a list of decisions that had been made by her giving up and going along with—rather than by genuine mutual choice—says that force-it strategies have been an ongoing problem. Now Donna wanted a force-it payback, her chance to insist that Aaron do what *she* wanted.

Fix-it talk enabled Aaron and Donna to address their current problem more cooperatively. Remember that fix-it talk fixes *it*, the problem, not your mate. In the following example, Aaron is not Donna's problem. The tone of their phone calls is the problem.

Step 1: Listen to your feelings.

> Donna realized that she was feeling hurt.

Step 2: Describe the dilemma, expressed as a when you.

"I felt hurt today when I called you at the office and you didn't seem to want to talk to me," Donna said.

Step 3: Make a request, expressed as "I'd prefer," and ending with a question.

"I'd prefer if you could be more enthusiastic when I call, or at least not sound irritated. What are your thoughts on that?" Donna continued.

Step 4: Listen to the response, being sure both of you understand the full range of concerns that situation raises.

Aaron responded helpfully, "I'm sorry. I don't mean to be hurting your feelings. You're right though. I do get agitated when you call and seem to want to talk. I don't want people at work having anything to do with my private home life. I don't like or trust them enough. That's why I sound impatient and cut you off. I'm afraid if I sound pleased to hear your voice you'll want to talk more."

Donna expanded on her hurt feelings: "I hear other people at my office talking with their husbands at work, which makes me want to be able to do the same with you. At the same time, given how intrusive a number of the people in your office are, I can understand your reluctance to talk. Still, I do need to touch base with you at least once toward the end of the day so we can arrange what time to meet to drive home together."

Donna's use of "at the same time" to link her description of her thoughts and feelings with evidence that she has listened to learn Aaron's concerns makes it clear that both of their concerns matter.

Step 5: Devise a solution.

Aaron agreed, and began thinking about possible solutions. "You're right. How about if I call you instead? Or better yet, since you're better at remembering to call than I am, what if we agreed that phone calls will be quick? Could we save our leisurely talking for when we're in the car heading home?"

Donna thought for a moment. "That would work for me now that I understand why you're being brusque. I used to keep you talking in hopes that you would begin to sound friendlier. Now, understanding your situation, I would be OK with keeping the calls short and friendly."

Aaron felt relieved. "If we don't talk about anything I wouldn't want the others in the office to hear, I can be friendlier. And if I know enthusiasm won't be misinterpreted as an invitation to chat, I can relax when you call."

Fix-It Talk for Touchy Topics

At the beginning of this chapter, Aaron was upset because each evening Donna would question him about whether he had lunched with one of the women in his firm. He would feel criticized and angry, and they then would spend their evenings in bitter tension. Let's look at how they succeeded in turning their argument into a constructive fix-it exploration with a surprising conclusion.

Step 1: Listen to your feelings.

Donna continued to have uneasy feelings about Aaron's relationships with the women who worked in his architectural firm. Listening to these feelings, she realized that she felt particularly uncomfortable about Liza, whom she had seen acting seductively toward Aaron at the firm's Christmas party.

Step 2: Describe the dilemma.

"I feel uneasy about your going out to lunch with Liza," Donna acknowledged to Aaron. "My woman's intuition says that she's out to seduce you. That's why I ask you each evening who you had lunch with."

Aaron thought for a moment. Although his first impulse was to feel wrongly accused, he tried to move beyond the gut feeling of defensiveness to listen to what made sense in what Donna had said. "I can see that you do feel uneasy about her," he agreed. "And I can see why. She is pretty dazzling looking, although I don't like to admit that I notice."

Step 3: Make a request.

Donna replied, "I would feel better if you didn't go to lunch alone with her, although if it's a group lunch I guess that's OK. Would that be acceptable to you?"

Step 4: Listen to the response, to understand your spouse's concerns.

"No, actually. I bristle at that idea," Aaron admitted. "The idea that you don't trust me really bothers me. That's why I get so angry when you ask me each evening about my day, and I feel like you're really asking if I ate lunch with Liza. I don't want to feel that you control who I can and can't have lunch with. Why do you think Liza bothers you so much?"

Donna thought a bit, remembering Basic 2 about talking about herself, then asking his views, rather than doing a crossover and telling him what she thought he thought. "I think that if I was still thin like when we were first married, I would have enough confidence that I wouldn't care who you ate with. But I feel so not-me since I've put on weight. And your comments about it have given me the sense that my extra pounds are a problem for you, too. Is that right?" she asked.

Aaron tried hard to stick to the positive, emphasizing his likes, not his dislikes: "I don't like to admit it, or bug you about it, but I'm a visual kind of guy. That gorgeous figure you used to have was fabulous."

"I think Liza bothers me also," Donna continued, "because I don't see that you read her advances as sexual come-ons. That worries me, because if you're naïve with a woman like that, she'll easily find a way to catch you."

Aaron blushed. "I don't like admitting that I see my business associates in a sexual way. I try to just do my work and then come home and be a good husband. I get defensive when you talk about the women, partly because all you are saying is true. I try to reassure you by acting like the sex thing isn't a big deal. The truth, though, is that my whole office is play- ing sex games. I'm getting fed up with it. Jim, the senior partner, is dating Kim on the sly; if his wife found out she'd leave him. Patrick is single, so it's more understandable, but he's courting the new secretary. The whole place reeks of sexual intrigue. I just hate it. Worse, Jim keeps arranging for me to work on projects alone with Liza. I get the feeling he's trying to trap me so I'll help him ease his own guilty conscience, or cover for him with his wife, or something crazy like that. The whole mess is very distracting."

"I am so relieved to hear you acknowledge all that. Thank you!" Donna sighed, feeling herself relax.

Step 5: Devise a solution.

Aaron continued, "Whether I eat lunch with Liza or with the man in the moon isn't really the problem. When we're working together and we're pressed for time, it's easier to order up lunch and eat as we work, or go out together for something quick. Like we discussed when we talked about your phone calls to me there—the real problem is that the firm is not a culture I want to have to deal with every day. How would you feel about my risking unemployment by looking for another job?"

Donna continued to feel enormously relieved. "Just hearing that you know that Liza and the workplace there are on a sexual track lets me feel that I don't have to keep thinking about it. If you are aware that sexual seduction is a danger, then I can forget about it. At the same time, I'm delighted with the idea of your looking into a job change. I never liked that firm, not just because of the sexual games, but also in terms of the quality of their work. You're better than they are."

Aaron interrupted, "I really appreciate your support, Donna. I'm scared though. These aren't good times for architects in this city."

Donna continued. "Whatever you decide, I support you. You know best whether to stay or leave. As for me, now that I can stop worrying for you, I feel free, more energized. I'm going to start going to the gym again. When I'm feeling upbeat, I stick with an exercise program better. I can focus on me now that I know that you are taking care of you. Thank you!"

Delaying fix-it talk invites anger or depression

If harboring feelings about something bothersome tends to make feelings grow, why do people tend to hold back from speaking up when something disturbs them?

Donna was afraid to tell Aaron that she wanted to go with him on a motorcycle ride through Nevada that Aaron and his brother were planning. She felt angrier and angrier that he had left her out. "He should be able to take a weekend trip with his brother if he wants to," she would admonish herself, but the anger kept growing, and with it a sad, depressed feeling. "I want you to include me!" she felt herself screaming inside, but to Aaron she said nothing. Fearing that her wish would soon explode in a flood of fury and tears, Donna decided to tell Aaron that she felt left out.

Fortunately, once Donna's feelings were out in the open, she and Aaron were able to have a good heart-to-heart talk. Like Donna, people may suppress their feelings for a variety of reasons:

- They mistakenly believe that it's braver to squelch their feelings.
- They have difficulty believing their feelings, though feelings don't know how to lie.
- They do not feel entitled to take their own feelings seriously.
- They hold back for fear of conflict, though often conflict becomes more inevitable the more that feelings are suppressed.
- They fear that if they say anything they will "say it wrong."
- They lack confidence in their mate's ability to hear their concerns with empathy.

Telling your feelings requires that someone hear them

Why did Donna tend to delay in speaking up about her feelings?

Donna grew up with a mother who was in perpetual distress, which taught Donna that no time was a good time to tell people your concerns. A defensive father added the message, "Don't tell me I'm doing anything wrong; I'll just get mad at you." With so much experience with adults who reacted to her feelings with anger, Donna was understandably reluctant to try to verbalize her feelings to her husband.

Unfortunately, Aaron also had a pattern of becoming angry when Donna expressed vulnerable feelings. He heard Donna's "I feel hurt" as an accusation that he'd done something wrong rather than a call for empathy. "I feel hurt" also sounded to him like a call to fix the hurt, which immediately triggered a cascade of panicky feelings. He felt swamped by cluelessness as to what he might do to help. Anticipating inadequacy, he felt shame at the belief that he would certainly fall on his face if he tried to help. This rapid onslaught of scared and helpless feelings, all embarrassing, jelled and transmuted instantly into what felt like a more acceptable response—anger at Donna for having the feelings she was sharing.

Aaron's difficulties responding sympathetically made Donna's cautiousness about expressing hurt feelings pretty sensible. Fortunately, while Donna was learning to verbalize her feelings, Aaron simultaneously was learning to respond with helpful concern rather than defensiveness.

♥ Use your full power of two

Effective fix-it talk depends on exploring both partners' perspectives. Otherwise, you risk slipping into force-it strategies.

When the problem is a simple, practical one, like the TV noise dilemma, the five fix-it steps flow quickly. For more complex situations, or problems with deeper concerns, fix-it talk requires more time.

Donna gradually identified that her desire to be included in the motorcycle trip came from three sources: She liked motorcycle journeys, she had been working very hard and felt ready for some vacation time, and watching Aaron and his brother have such fun with planning their trip triggered a realization for her of how isolated she had become from friends and family.

Aaron expressed how important the trip was for him. He and his brother had never been close before. In fact, this trip marked the first time he had ever felt full acceptance from anyone in his family.

Verbalizing their specific underlying concerns gave Donna and Aaron the information they needed to find solutions that addressed all their issues.

> Donna understood Aaron's reluctance to include her on the motorcycle trip. She agreed that adding her presence would dilute the bond the brothers were building.
>
> Aaron appreciated Donna's three concerns. They brainstormed on ways to satisfy them and came up with a creative set of solutions. They decided first that Donna would visit out-of-state cousins for the long weekend of the motorcycle trip. She was excited at the chance to reconnect with them, and their home by the beach in California would offer her a vacation as well as renewal of the relationship. In addition, Donna and Aaron would plan a motorcycle trip together for later in the summer. Most importantly for the big picture, the two of them agreed to make it a priority to build friendships in the community to which they had recently moved so Donna would feel less alone there.

Once Donna's distressed feelings had alerted Donna and Aaron to the problem, they were able to proceed smoothly with gratifying fix-it dialogue. Her problem became their problem. Their resulting mutual understanding and the "solution set" they came up with, responsive to all the concerns of each of them, pleased them both.

Receiving a Fix-It Request

Communication skills are essential when you are on the receiving end of fix-it talk. Our old friends Len and Linda and Gina and Gerald will help review those skills in the following sections.

Beware of the impulse to strike back

When your partner expresses hurt, frustration, or irritation, especially about something you have done, your immediate impulse may be to retaliate. Saying something hurtful back may even the score but it doesn't deal effectively with the difficulty.

You may feel calmer if you can remember that it is just your action, not you as a person, that is posing a problem for your spouse. Actions are not like eye color. They can easily be changed.

If calm listening is difficult for you, you might review the section on "Listening is safer" in Chapter 2. In general, however if you find yourself defending yourself by attacking the messenger, pause. Remind yourself that hearing the message will bring better long term solutions than blockading or counter-attacking.

Striking Back	Listening to Learn
Len: I felt frantic, and truthfully quite angry, when you were so late picking me up after work. Is there a way you could get there at the time we agreed on?	*Gerald:* I felt frantic, and truthfully quite angry, when you were so late picking me up after work. Is there a way you could get there at the time we agreed on?
Linda: Well, you're late, too, sometimes. In fact you're late more often than I am. And at least I apologize!	*Gina:* Well, I can see why you were frantic. I was late. I'd like to be able to leave a meeting when everyone else is staying late, but I can't seem to pull it off. I couldn't figure out how to leave gracefully, so I stayed. I felt terrible. Any suggestions on how to get out of those situations?
Len: If you apologize, I seem to be the last to hear.	

Len and Linda discover that striking back—that is, defending yourself with a strong offense—just converts a practical problem into a fight. We all experience an impulse to hurt back when someone says something negative to us. Sending a countercomplaint to even the score, however, invites your mate to strike another blow in return, augmenting the unpleasantness all around and leading further away from solving the problem.

Gina feels the same impulse to strike back, and then she overrides it. She chooses to listen to learn, to what makes sense, in what Gerald has told her. Her ability to acknowledge her part of the problem kicks in, and soon she and Gerald are working together to help her with her dilemma.

Questions transform *don't wants* to *would likes*

If your mate does sometimes offer you the negative rather than the positive, the game is not over. When you hear don't wants rather than would likes, what can you do? Ask for the information you need.

Asking "What would you prefer?" or "What would you like, what would help?" in response to a complaint can help your partner clarify the picture for both of you. These questions can move you solidly into cooperative dialogue, especially if your tone of voice sounds sympathetic. Asking for more information can help ease your partner into sharing more concerns so that both of you will be more effective at finding solutions.

Defensiveness	Asking for Input
Len: I don't want to be stuck waiting for you every afternoon.	*Gerald:* I don't want to be stuck waiting for you every afternoon.
Linda: Well, I don't like not having my own car.	*Gina:* What would help? What's your concern?
	Gerald: When you are going to be delayed, if you could give me a call some time before I leave I could use the extra time productively at my office.

By asking further questions, Gina turns Gerald's complaint into an opportunity for constructive problem solving that will prevent similar upsets in the future.

Your wish is not my command

Your partner's expression of a wish or preference is just Step 3 of a five-step process. You can respond with either yes or no. Most importantly, after hearing your partner's concerns you need to share your own so that the solution you devise works for both of you.

Your Wish Is My Command	Wishes Are Requests
Linda: I do wish you would be more enthusiastic when I go to the effort to make plans for the weekends.	*Gina:* I do wish would you be more enthusiastic when I go to the effort to make plans for the weekends.
Len: I just don't feel enthusiastic but I guess I could try.	*Gerald:* I appreciate your effort. At the same time, I've been working such long hours that going anywhere and having to talk to more people on the weekend feels like too much. I just don't feel enthusiastic.
Linda: You never get enthusiastic. It's such a bummer living with a dark cloud for a husband.	
Len: Thanks, pal. You, of course, are a barrel of sunshine.	*Gina:* What if we took a break from socializing for a few weeks? I'd be happy to sit on the couch with you, with a video or maybe music, and veg together on Saturday nights.
	Gerald: That would be a huge improvement.

How to Know When You Need Fix-It Talk

Fix-it talk is likely to come in handy when you face new situations. Entrances and exits from the family unit for instance often pose challenges. When a family changes size with a new baby, an elderly parent moves in, or a child departs for summer camp or college, you and your spouse will find that you need to renegotiate many of your ways of doing things. The division of labor that works fine for a couple before they have children may need a total rearrangement after the arrival of a baby. Likewise, a change of work hours or a shift in income may necessitate changes in your division of labor, social life, or spending patterns. New circumstances create new stumbles.

In addition, minor friction between the two of you may indicate that one of you would like the other to do things in a particular way, or to do more, or less, of something. For example:

From the "wanting things done a particular way" department

- I'd like my husband to fold the towels and T-shirts in thirds instead of down the middle when he takes the laundry out of the dryer.
- I wish my wife would help the children wash their face and hands and brush their teeth instead of shouting at them when they haven't washed up.
- I wish my husband would drop his clothes in the laundry basket instead of on the floor.
- I wish my wife would keep the balance tallied in our checkbook.

From the "wanting more of" department

- I wish my wife would show more enthusiasm for sex with me.
- I wish my husband would listen better, with more empathy, when something is bothering me.
- I wish my husband would express his feelings more openly, so that I could be more helpful when he's distressed.
- I wish my wife would tell me more often things she likes about me.

From the "less of" department

- I want less criticism.
- I want my husband to stop giving long monologues when we are out with friends.

- I wish my wife would stop devoting all her evening time to doing homework with the kids and would realize that I'm around, too.

- I wish my husband would stop pressuring me to lose weight; I'm trying, and his attempts to supervise my eating just jam my airwaves.

From the "more and less of" department

- I want my wife to show more joint ownership of our money and less reliance on me to handle everything having to do with finances.

- I want my husband to discuss financial decisions with me with less impatience when I'm slow to understand. And I want equal access to our funds, not an allowance from him as if he owns all the money.

With effective fix-it talk, you can resolve these differences between what is happening and what you would prefer to have happen.

Fix-it talk also works when you are angry

Anger tells you there's a problem. You can use fix-it talk to correct the problem, but it's best to wait a bit until you feel calm enough to think flexibly and talk cooperatively. Get past the angry feelings, and then raise the issue.

If you launch the discussion cooperatively, your spouse will feel less threatened and will be more likely to participate with a desire to help you out. Both of you will be less likely to drive off the cooperative road onto the dangerous soft shoulders of critical, complaining, demanding, or defensive ways of talking. Take the classic toothpaste example:

> Gina has just left the cap off the toothpaste for the umpteenth time. Gerald is annoyed. If Gerald addresses his dilemma at that moment, his voice is likely to sound irritated. On the one hand, the irritation would alert Gina of his growing impatience. On the other hand, his irritation would switch the dialogue into toxic coercion mode: "Put the cap back on or I'll be mad at you!" would be the implied message. In response, Gina might from then on put the cap back on the toothpaste tube. The cost, however, could be that each day from then on the toothpaste tube will evoke Gina's irritation at Gerald.

By contrast, let's see what would happen if Gerald cooled down first and then raised the issue tactfully, remembering that a request is not a demand. It's a starting point, not a final offer.

> Gina might respond, "I'd love to put the cap back, just because I know you like it that way. The problem is that I brush my teeth on automatic pilot. I never seem to be able to think about it."

Now Gerald understands his mate's perspective. With this information, the two of them as a team have a chance to come up with creative solutions.

> *"I know," Gerald might suggest. "You brush first; I'll brush right after. I always remember, so at least the cap won't be left off all day or overnight."*
>
> *"We could try it," Gina says, "Or what if we try the pump kind? It doesn't have a cap."*
>
> *"Brilliant!" Gerald grins. "I bet they invented it just for couples like us."*

Brainstorming like this turns their dilemma into fun.

Can fix-it talk solve major problems?

Fix-it talk remedies the many minor ruffles that can feel like major irritants, particularly when they recur many times. It has been said that when people are considering whether to buy a new car of the same make as their old one, the tendency is to recall the minor hassles, like a knob that kept falling off, rather than to consider less visible yet far more crucial factors like safety and fuel efficiency. In marriage, too, minor irritants repeated without remedy can detract significantly from owner satisfaction.

Every so often a problem that may have sounded like an occasion for fix-it talk turns out to be more complicated than it looked at first. If the two of you deadlock on a problem, then additional measures may become necessary. Chapter 9 on conflict resolution offers ideas on managing those times.

At other times, major issues, such as infidelity or substance abuse, call into question your basic marriage contract. Even these potential deal-breakers may respond to fix-it talk. Certainly the fix-it formula offers you a way to start addressing the issue.

Deal-breakers generally, however, need additional techniques beyond fix-it talk for healing to occur. Chapter 10 focuses on ways to deal with major mishaps. Counseling also can be a positive option in these situations.

How Much Fix-It Talk?

Skaters, like all athletes, need a balance between time devoted to improving their skills and time devoted to enjoying their sport. Most serious athletes devote considerable time to improving their performance. At the same time, just as all work and no play makes Johnny a dull boy, all practice and no freeskating would take the enjoyment out of what they do.

Fix-it talk, like skating practice, takes considerable energy. Looking diagnostically at difficulties and coming up with creative new solutions takes time and precise self-control. Like skaters, most married couples initially find they need frequent sessions of fix-it talk to be able to enjoy most of their time together smoothly. Fortunately though, with fix-it talk skills you are likely to need less and less fix-it talk over time.

. If you find yourselves involved in frequent fix-it work, either you may be adjusting to changed circumstances or something problematic may be going on. If one of you is investing your energy in running the other's life, for instance, too much fix-it talk may indicate that you need to reclarify whose life is whose. In general, the more you each let your mate do things his or her way, appreciating rather than supervising your partner's contributions, the more contented you will both feel.

Some couples schedule periodic marriage meetings, the way you might schedule administrative meetings at work or practice sessions for an athletic team. Setting aside a regular time weekly or monthly can create a comfortable context for identifying and dealing with situations that need fix-it rearrangements. These can be enjoyable times that include a hike in the sunshine or a night on the town as part of the routine. Marriages flourish with the fullest and most robust power of two when your occasional fix-it talk is embedded in a broad array of positive times together.

If anger is not restrained it is frequently more hurtful to us than the injury which provokes it.

—Seneca

Chapter 5

Anger as a Stop Sign

Anger feels like a green light. Anger indicates that your body's chemical plant is shifting into a higher gear, producing chemicals to charge you up. Epinephrine, norepinephrine, cortisol, and for men, testosterone course rapidly through the bloodstream, giving a sensation of power and readying you to attack. Speech speeds up; speaking volume increases. Your attention focuses on the threat, on what someone is doing that provokes you.

Given its energizing feeling, how can anger be a stop sign? Anger is a sign of some kind of difficulty. To keep your marriage safe, strong, and loving, you need to learn that when either of you feels angry, the best strategy is to *stop*. Stopping enables you to figure out what the difficulty is and what you might do to take care of it. When anger gives you a feeling of urgency, maturity is the ability to delay acting, to give yourself time to think.

Anger springs up via a more rapid neurological route than the mental processing of thoughtfully reasoned responses. For example, if you feel stung by criticism from your mate, your anger superhighway might convey the message and respond with an aggressive retort before your thinking brain is able to evaluate the comment. By contrast, if you are able to inhibit the impulse to strike back immediately, after another moment you might react quite a bit more calmly. You might chalk the remark up to your partner being hungry or overwhelmed by the noise of the children playing. With this fuller understanding, instead of angrily snapping back, you might respond with a more tactful plan of action, such as after dinner, on your quiet walk together, asking what that comment was about.

In sum, angry feelings, like stop signs, alert you to problems. Putting on the brakes enables your thinking to catch up with your feelings. Zooming forward at stop signs can be dangerous. Looking about you to gather more understanding before you proceed is generally a far better strategy.

The Nature of Anger

Anger arises when something you value feels threatened. No matter how healthy your marriage, you will inevitably, from time to time, read your spouse as saying or doing something that appears to challenge one of your values (trust, closeness, reliability, safety, fairness) or your valuables (your time, your money, your self-esteem). Feelings of anger erupt especially readily when getting what you value involves getting someone else, in this case your mate, to do what you want. Anger and controlling others go hand in hand.

More intensely angry feelings convey greater urgency. They tell you that a problem requires your immediate attention. Intense anger turns the stop sign into something more like the wail of an ambulance siren. Full-scale anger turns up the volume to be sure that you pay attention now. The anger alarm warns you that someone is doing something that you don't like—or not doing something you want them to do. At the same time anger grabs the attention of those you feel mad at, forcing them to listen to you.

The intensity of your anger, however, can give you inaccurate readings of the seriousness of a problem. This inaccuracy occurs because stress has a cumulative effect. When your physiological system experiences one minor irritant and then another in close succession, it doesn't realize that the second irritant was equally small.

For example, if you are irritated because your new shoes are getting wet in a rainstorm, and then as you are walking along your mate inadvertently bumps into you, your reaction is likely to be disproportionate. Because two doses of anger chemicals have been spilled into your system, your anger level reacts as if the second problem was of double the seriousness of the first. Your mate, of course, probably doesn't know about your shoes; he or she is just receiving what seems like a strong response to a minor mistake. Unless you understand the cumulative effects of anger, you may conclude that your partner's error was egregious because your anger *feels* so strong. In fact, however, your strong anger says more about the physiology of anger than it does about your spouse or how problematic the bumping was. If your spouse then says something that hurts your feelings, such as, "That was uncalled for," this third infusion of anger chemicals could trigger a major explosion.

The cumulative intensity of anger poses particular risks when dialogue turns into argument. Each successive angry comment can ratchet up the level of anger. As your anger escalates, at some point you may reach a critical level that psychology researcher J. Gottman (1994) refers to as "flooding," the sudden rush of explosive anger that can bring forth uncharacteristically aggressive behavior. Flooding involves a change of mental state, much like bubbles reflect a change of state (liquid to gas) when water heats up. With flooding, rational thought gives way to impulsive behavior uncontrolled by thoughts of the consequences. One of the primary purposes of disengaging from anger-inducing situations is to prevent flooding and the destruction that it can wreak.

Even moderately intense anger, a significantly lower level than flooding, causes alterations in perception and thinking. Anger propels you into an altered state of consciousness, a state as different from your normal daily humor as a drug high is from a nondrugged state. In this altered state, the way you view the world changes. Your ability to hear others' concerns diminishes; your ability to take in new information narrows. You begin to feel determined to get what you want at any price. Alas, taking action from this feeling can be expensive. Charging forward in anger, or even dealing with difficulties with quiet irritation, mostly makes trouble.

Kate and Tanner, an affectionate and immediately likeable couple, realized that anger was causing major havoc in their relationship. They first experienced Tanner's capacity for intense anger early in their marriage.

> *Kate remembered the first time she ever saw her husband erupt in full-scale anger. Roundly pregnant, she was trying to drive a golf cart. Her many nieces and nephews were having great fun all trying to pile on to the cart at once, when, with the unbalanced weight of so many active bodies, the cart began to wobble.*
>
> *Tanner panicked. Envisioning the cart toppling over, his pregnant wife and as yet unborn baby getting crushed, he erupted in fury, gesticulating and shouting angrily at the children to get off immediately.*
>
> *Tanner's anger emptied the cart at once, the children's delight turning to chagrin. Still in his anger mode, Tanner started to lecture the children. Only gradually, as he realized that the danger had long been averted, did he let the children be.*
>
> *Later, Kate and Tanner talked over the incident which had given them both much to think about. The incident showed Tanner how strongly he treasured his wife and how protective he already felt toward their child. At the same time, they agreed that there had been no urgent danger. Tanner could have told the children nicely to climb down from the cart without frightening them with his anger, and he certainly did not need to lecture them. They realized how easily Tanner's anger could become excessive.*

Anger alerts you to problems. In emergency situations, whether the problem is a physical danger, a moral injustice, or an invasion of territory, anger mobilizes you for immediate action. In most marriage situations, however, there is no emergency. As you stop and think and your anger calms, you can begin gathering information and start a quiet dialogue. By contrast, if you or your spouse deal with routine life situations with angry voices, bullying insistence, or, like Tanner, excessive inflammability, you are misusing your anger.

Why Do We Act Angrily?

Anger is momentary insanity.
—Horace, *Epistolae*

To understand why you act angrily, as opposed to feeling angry and then stopping, thinking, and addressing the problem in an effective and tactful way, it can be helpful to look both in the rearview mirror and down the road ahead.

The rearview mirror shows where you've been, how your anger can stem from your upbringing as well as from events immediately preceding an anger outburst. Looking down the road ahead can help you to understand toward what purpose you allow yourself to act in anger. Both the rearview mirror and the road ahead shed light on why you sometimes act grumpy, mad, or mean.

Check the rearview mirror

Your ideas about how to treat other people came initially from what you witnessed as a child in your family.

How did your father and mother interact with each other?

Our parents provide our first models of how men are supposed to act toward women, and women toward men. If your father shouted at your mother, or your mother deprecated your father, you are at risk for repeating their behavior. Our parents' ways of handling anger are learned along with language in childhood. If your parents spoke angrily to one another, unless you make a conscious decision not to repeat their tone, this early learning can become your mode of anger response.

The content of your parents' battles also can become yours. Think about the issues you tend to complain about in your marriage. Were these issues your parents used to fight about? Having heard arguments on these topics as children seems to supersensitize us as adults to anything that sounds even remotely like what our parents used to berate each other about. It's as if our parents gave us their unfinished business, which is ours to conclude with a happier ending. We subconsciously tend to remember both the style of how our parents talked with one another and the content of their disagreements.

How did your father and mother treat you as a child?

Did your parents listen to you? Hopefully they did. Hopefully they also set limits, respectfully explaining to you when and why your behavior was inappropriate. If, however, your parents tended to speak to you abrasively, routinely hurting your feelings, lecturing you, and overdoing punishment, you may be at higher risk for excessive anger.

Parents who use excessive punishment on their children invite their children to grow up being mean to others, or victimized by others, both in childhood and in adult life. A punitive parent teaches children that when someone else is not doing what you want them to do, hurting the other can make their behavior conform to what you want, irrespective of the other's desires. In addition, parental anger and punishment increase the child's sense that the world is a dangerous place. In response, children may learn to overvalue the need to appear powerful. The extreme result can be the sadistic and paranoid personality of a Hitler, who spends a lifetime perpetuating cruelty and destruction to others after a childhood of having had to endure humiliating criticism and severe beatings.

> Warren appeared to be a kind and cultured gentleman, yet he frequently spoke with surprising nastiness to his wife. In therapy, Warren explored the kinds of situations that triggered the impulse to criticize or verbally strike her and where he had learned to act so cruelly.
>
> Warren's father had frequently berated him. A joyful and sensitive child, Warren received repeated criticism for "not being a he-man" or "for being a washrag." These onslaughts succeeded to some extent in squelching Warren's enthusiastic playfulness. He also learned to lash out, like his father, when he saw others doing something he felt they shouldn't or that he didn't want them to do. As young as six or seven, seeing another child picking his nose, Warren kicked him to get him to stop.
>
> Warren by nature was in fact a kindly soul, but his family upbringing had taught him to smother his more tender feelings. Since childhood he had been trying to look strong by verbally kicking himself and those around him. The realization that he no longer needed to play this role, and could actually get more of what he wanted in life by talking quietly, without bullying, came as a great relief.

How did you treat your parents and your siblings?

Who controlled your home growing up, the children or the parents? If you grew up ordering your parents around, throwing tantrums when they did not do what you wanted, you are likely to be at risk for throwing tantrums as an adult to get your partner to do your bidding. Were you kind to your siblings, and were they considerate of you? If you used to be mean to them, or if they in any way abused you, you will want to pay particularly close attention to be certain that your relationship with your mate does not repeat any of these early relationships.

Fortunately with today's proliferation of self-help books and audio tapes, as well as the accessibility of couple counseling, adults no longer need to be limited in their marriages to repeating what they learned as children. As I said last chapter about actions in general, angry behavior is not inborn, like eye color. It is a matter of learning and of choice.

Other childhood risk factors

A number of other childhood factors can put you at increased risk for tendencies to excessive anger. Were you either larger or smaller than other children your age? Sometimes either extreme of physical size leads children to develop patterns of using anger to bully people: large children can easily get their way by pushing other children; small boys, Napoleon-style, may compensate for their lesser size by perpetually proving how tough they are.

Temperament also can be a factor. Some children are born mild-tempered; others show belligerence from an early age. Similarly, some children show strong altruistic tendencies when very young. Even as toddlers they will offer help to another child who seems distressed. Nature, however, is not a final decree. Quick-to-anger children just need more adult modeling and teaching to learn to replace shouting and shoving with courteous talking. For most children, emotional education is vital.

Likewise, children's ability to tolerate frustration varies broadly. Some young children resiliently transition to another activity if they can't have something they want. Others insistently throw temper tantrums when they hear the word no. Again, just as more coaching is necessary for children with less natural athletic ability, emotional education is essential for those who are not naturally resilient. Without this guidance, children who insist too strongly on getting what they want without learning to consider parents', teachers', or other children's concerns can become difficult adult partners.

Severe stresses in childhood can produce neurological changes that result in a more delicate emotional system in adult life. Painful childhood experiences, such as the death of a parent, incest, or abuse, can lead to increased adult vulnerability to anger and depression in response to life's normal ups and downs. People who were emotionally or physically abused as children may develop physiological changes that cause them to more readily experience anger in adulthood.

Physiological factors can now be normalized by taking medication.

Excessive anger may diminish remarkably with use of the same medication that alleviates a tendency toward depression. Many people with a biochemical vulnerability to either depression or anger experience a new emotional resilience when they begin to take these medications.

Whether you continue anger habits learned in your childhood into your married life may depend on how aware you are of the detrimental effects of anger. If you have not yet learned that frequent anger is not healthy, you are at risk for adult anger problems.

Ultimately, whatever your rearview-mirror vulnerability factors, angry behavior is a matter of choice. Everyone experiences anger. We each then, consciously or unknowingly, make choices about what to do next.

Take a look ahead

Let's turn our attention now to the question of why—in the sense of toward what purpose—people are sometimes tempted to deal with difficulties in anger. In other words, when you let yourself get into an argument, what do you hope to accomplish?

I don't mean to imply that you consciously sit down and think, "Hmmm, I think I'll get mad so that I can..." However, people usually keep doing things that they think bring them some benefit. If you continue to speak or act in anger from time to time in your marriage, what do you believe that the anger gains for you?

The biggest reason couples in my practice give for their fighting is to settle conflicts. Other than fighting or withdrawing—which ends the skirmish but doesn't solve the problem—they don't know what to do when they feel frustrated, hurt, or irritated. Of course, fighting doesn't resolve differences, but in the heat of anger that minor reality seems to get lost.

It is an interesting fact that couples who fight, including those who resort to physical violence, tend to have less developed cooperative dialogue skills than those who don't fight (Holzworth-Monroe & Anglin, 1990; Rograd, 1988; Morman, 1979). Without dialogue skills, talking about difficulties is not an option.

Anger can serve to mask the more vulnerable feeling of shame. Many individuals are prone to feeling ashamed, often because of parental discipline techniques that punished by shaming and blaming. Sometimes shame also comes up when people make mistakes that with hindsight they regret but do not know how to rectify. In the words of Thomas Haliburton, a popular 19th century Canadian writer and astute observer of human nature, "When a man is wrong and won't admit it, he always gets angry."

TABLE 6 Alternatives to Arguing

Erroneous Beliefs that Foster Fighting	Better Options
If my feelings are hurt, I need to get mad to get back at my partner.	Say "Ouch." Offer a *when you*. Ask, "What's going on here?" Discuss the difficulty.
Fighting brings drama and excitement into the relationship.	Find athletic and other exciting activities to share. Remember that while fighting may be exhilarating for the more powerful mate, it is depressing for the less powerful one.
The passion of fighting ignites passion in sex afterwards.	Spend positive time together before your sexual time. Exercise, for example, stimulates the flow of sexual juices
Getting mad gets my partner's attention.	Try being funny. Make eye contact. Set aside a quiet time for the two of you to talk.
Raising my voice gets my partner to do what I want.	Listening to your partner's concerns makes it more likely that he or she will hear yours.
I need to show my mate who's boss.	Fighting just shows who is bossy. A good boss is respectful of others.
When I feel depressed or down on myself, anger energizes me.	Professional counseling and/or medications can treat depressed moods more effectively, with no one getting hurt.
Getting mad shows how much I care.	Anger shows how much you care about getting what you want. Listening and respect show caring love for your partner.
I don't want to be a marshmallow.	Stating your concerns without resorting to anger is a sign of personal strength.
I cant control it once I'm angry.	That is why anger is a stop sign.

The Costs of Acting in Anger

A word is dead
When it is said,
Some say.
I say it just
Begins to live
That day.

—Emily Dickinson, "Life"

For anger to be expressed safely, without leading to fights, both partners need to talk as teammates using the ABCDs from Part I. Speak without crossing into the territory of talking about the other. Stick with nontoxic language. Tune in to what is useful, what might be true, in the difficult message your partner is trying to share. If you can stay within these guidelines, then your anger can convey the seriousness of your message.

The difficulty is that the more angry you feel, the harder it becomes to follow these principles, as either speaker or listener. You are engaging in high-risk dialogue. Especially as anger escalates, a single crossover or toxic message can mark the end of helpful problem solving.

> *"I'm furious. I feel like I can never get it right. I'm trying to help you sand your deck, and all you do is complain!" Tanner shouted.*
> *Feeling criticized, Kate started defending herself. She liked pretty things. She wanted the deck to come out right. Before she had finished insisting that the problem was Tanner, not her, Tanner spun around, the electric sander in his hand. The sander landed, hard, at her feet. "Finish it yourself!" Tanner yelled.*

Anger, for many people, escalates quickly, as it does for Tanner and Kate. Cooling off and then talking is almost always a safer strategy than trying to talk when you are heated up.

Anger begets anger

Many emotionally expressive cultures consider angry words a good way to "blow off steam." While the drama of these cultures has its appeal, the reality of anger is that venting it actually fans its flames. "Blowing off steam" can easily set off explosions of rage, just as the heat from steam can cause injuries to anyone who comes too close. The more anger you express, the more anger you will feel, the longer you will remain angry afterwards, and the more angry your partner will in turn feel toward you.

The book *When Anger Hurts* (McKay, Rogers & McKay, 1989) surveys research on the idea that it's healthy to ventilate. Its conclusion: "Experimental studies consistently point out that the popular remedy for anger, ventilation, is really worse than useless. In fact, the reverse seems to be true: expressing anger tends to make you even angrier and solidifies an angry attitude." Dealing with the *problem* indicated by anger is helpful, but dealing with it in an angry way creates additional anger.

Anger leads to forcing, not fixing

Unfortunately, anger blinds you to others' concerns. As you feel increasingly irate, your underlying thought is likely to be, "I want what I want, and I don't care what you want!" If your partner doesn't agree, your anger serves to force him or her to do what you want.

As your steaming anger boils over, what you wanted initially, your original objective, may get lost. As you move from anger to rage, your objective changes. The new objective becomes to cause hurt, and in the extreme, to destroy the other.

The heat of anger vaporizes your awareness that in marriage there are two of you, both of whom have legitimate concerns. Until you find solutions that feel comfortable to both of you, one of you will always have a reason to keep raising the same issues.

Anger wounds

Angry words cause both physical and psychological damage. Their toxicity is not just metaphorical; it is all too real. The damage hurts you, your partner, and your marriage.

When you speak angrily or critically to your spouse, both of you undergo rapid physical transformations. Blood pressure and cholesterol go up; immunities go down. It is no wonder that couples who fight manifest more physical ailments such as headaches, hypertension, ulcers, and heart attacks than couples who live together more harmoniously. Unhappily married people report poorer health than happily married people of the same race, sex, and age. Researchers now are discovering that—as much and perhaps even more than obesity, lack of exercise, or poor nutrition—marital conflict can be hazardous to your body's health.

Your anger also can cause your spouse to suffer emotional disorders. Toxic words can fester in subtle but painfully long-lasting ways. They corrode self-esteem. They undermine mutual trust. They breed resentment, anxiety, sleep difficulties, and depression. Contrary to popular wisdom, while sticks and stones break bones, words can also hurt, destroying both the physical and the emotional health of the fighters.

The toxic impact of fighting can be remarkably long-lasting. One spiteful interchange can undermine weeks of positive time together. I have seen couples for whom one mean verbal fireball ignited tensions that lasted long after either of them could remember the source.

You are almost guaranteeing that your marriage will suffer if you become angry:

- frequently, in either small or large outbursts
- occasionally, but getting very mad when you do or staying angry for quite a while
- persistently, harboring subtle angry feelings that never fully go away

You may say to yourself, "Well, I'm only mad sometimes. The rest of the time I'm nice." No matter. Your good moments do not undo the harm done by angry outbursts.

Anger hurts innocent bystanders, especially children

Couples who fight may not realize how strongly their squabbles affect those around them. Do you like to visit in homes where a couple bickers? The ongoing tension sets everyone on edge.

The vast majority of children with emotional and behavioral problems have parents, married or divorced, who fight. Just as smoking predicts cancer, but not all smokers actually get cancer, children of parents who fight do sometimes escape unscathed. Depression, anxiety, school problems, eating disorders, underachieving, and delinquent behavior, however, are costs borne by children from high-conflict homes.

Moreover, angry parents teach their children that fighting is how you resolve problems. In homes where the parents fight, siblings tend to fight more with each other. The end product can be a home that's a battlefield.

Anger blocks insight

Tanner felt frantic and furious: "We have too much programmed for this summer!" he shouted, raging at his wife Kate. "There's no way I'll be able to get my work done! You invited too many people! And you planned too many trips! You should have been more realistic!"

Our eyes are pointed outward. When we are calm, we can succeed in turning our eyes inward, and can use this inner eye for insight, for seeing our own behavior. The angrier we feel, the stronger our impulse to look outward, to look for someone else to fault for our distress. Tanner exemplified the way in which anger blocks headway on the actual problem.

Instead of seeing his part in how their summer plans had gotten out of hand, or better yet focusing on adjustments he could make to improve the situation, Tanner's focus was riveted on his wife. The more he tried to pin blame on her, negatively interpreting what she had done, the more enraged he felt. Worse, in the process of criticizing and blaming, Tanner developed a distorted view of his wife, missing the chance to enjoy their life.

Anger blocks your ability to understand the problem indicated by your anger. Furthermore, the more angry you become, the more likely that you will look to blame instead of addressing and solving the problem.

Anger gives you dark glasses

Anger is the reverse of love. Love enables us to see our partner's attributes all in the most positive light. By contrast, anger actually causes you to lose the ability to see what is attractive about your spouse. The angrier you become, the less you will be able recall the aspects of your spouse that you cherish. Even after your anger has cooled, the negative views of your mate that you kept repeating to yourself when you were angry may continue to dampen your affections. In other words, anger gives you dark glasses, so that you see your partner in a negative light.

Tanner continued raging, working himself up into ever- increasing fury, "You pretend to ask me if the plans are OK, but really you didn't take me into consideration at all in making your decisions. All you care about is the things you want to do. How am I supposed to earn a living if you are book-ing all my time with your activities. You just exploit my good nature. You take advantage of my willingness to be nice to your family. You're just trying to make me furious so I'll look like the bad guy in the household. You're so conniving, manipulative, controlling!"

As your anger escalates, your interpretations of your mate's actions become increasingly negative. For instance, you may usually regard your spouse as busy. If you become angry, you may label the same productivity as self-absorbed. As you become even angrier, you may arrive at "inconsiderate workaholic." Negative labels like this may serve to justify the impulse to hurt the person you most love.

Should the harsh words that you spit out in the heat of anger be believed? There will generally be a grain of truth in every negative you see when you are angry, but this grain of truth will be enlarged out of proportion. Your angry beliefs are likely to be inaccurate interpretations of the actual facts. Kate had taken on responsibility for making the family's summer plans. Tanner's accusation that she was "conniving, manipulative, and controlling" was an excessively negative interpretation of her attempt to carry through that responsibility.

> Kate had in fact consulted Tanner about each of their plans for the summer. Then, as was their custom, she went ahead with making reservations and inviting family and friends from out of state to visit. She was open to making whatever changes might help Tanner feel more on top of his work. But the more he yelled at her, the less generous she felt. Feeling wrongly accused, Kate felt less and less willing to consider Tanner's realization that they had overbooked their summer schedule. His accusations were becoming a self-fulfilling prophecy.

Angry views of your spouse need to be reappraised after you have calmed down. Sometimes your anger proves justified. If your spouse has gambled away a chunk of savings, for instance, your anger can mobilize you to make changes to ensure the loss never happens again. On the other hand, most of the time, later consideration of an angry incident will yield a milder interpretation that is more accurate, more conducive to solving the actual problem, and less detrimental to your mutual affection than the negative views that arose when you were furious.

Anger increases projection

The angrier you become, the more likely that your view of the situation will be distorted by what psychologists call projection. Projection involves treating the person you are talking with like a movie screen. What is within you, the projector, you see in your spouse. If you have a habit of blaming, for instance, you might say to your partner, "The problem is that you think everything is *my* fault."

> Tanner accused his wife of not having been realistic in planning their summer. However, in agreeing to the plans, in spite of work agendas that he knew of but had not told Kate about, he himself had not been realistic.

By projecting, you are advertising your own shortcomings, which is quite embarrassing once you realize what you are doing—especially if your partner also understands what projection is and how it works. And, projection can be quite hurtful to a mate who does not understand the phenomenon.

To check whether you have been using projection, try this experiment: Listen back to accusations you have thought or said to your mate. Then ask yourself whether what you were thinking about your partner might actually apply to yourself. If it does, you have probably been projecting.

Projection blocks your ability to understand both your partner and yourself. Insight is far more effective in helping you to get what you want in life.

Anger ends in guilt and shame

In the moment, anger temporarily blinds us from seeing what we are doing; afterward, once the fury has subdued, you are likely to see clearly the damage that your anger has wreaked. Seeing the pain you have inflicted on the one you love may result in remorse, shame, and guilt.

> *After ranting at Kate in increasingly intense episodes over a period of weeks, Tanner suddenly felt terrible. Many times he had brought his wife to frantic tears, to the point that she had begged for mercy, crying out in genuine desperation, "What can I do?" Once he felt calmer, he knew that his raging behavior had been way out of bounds. His guilt felt crushing. Now, instead of feeling furious, he felt demoralized and ashamed.*

Anger corrodes love

Unfortunately, words propelled by even a brief surge of anger can have a long-lasting impact on your partner's feelings toward you. A lashing comment such as, "You're so controlling!" can seriously erode your partner's loving interest in what goes on in your life.

Moreover, angry people look ugly. When you are angry, your spouse is unlikely to feel loving toward your snarling face. When angry, you are not lovable. As John Webster said in *The Duchess of Malfi,* "There is not in nature/ A thing that makes a man so deform'd, so beastly,/As intemperate anger."

> *Kate began to ask herself why she was staying in the marriage. "Are the good times worth this pain? Tanner gets so frightening when he is angry, I don't want anything to do with him. And when he is normal, I find it harder to enjoy him because I keep remembering what he's like in a rage."*

Anger invites divorce

Multiple research studies now have shown that married couples who fight are at significantly higher risk for divorce. The test of a marriage's worth may be its positive times, but the best predictor of whether it will endure is the frequency of its bad moments (Newton et al., 1995; Kurdek, 1993; Markman, 1993; Notarius & Markman, 1993; Gottman, 1994).

Anger invites violence

Verbal fighting risks escalation into physical fighting. Throwing things, shoving, hitting, choking, beating, and eventually killing—each is another step on a ladder that begins with verbal violence. It's best to terminate hurtful interactions at the first rung of this ladder, with your first angry impulse.

Violent behavior tends to become worse over time. The man or woman who injures a spouse in any way, even once, is at risk not only for doing it again but for gradually increasing the extent of the violence. If you have ever become physically violent with your mate, or if your father used to get physically violent with your mother, or vice versa, you are at risk.

You may be tempted to say, "If only my partner wouldn't... I wouldn't get mad." If you hear yourself saying something like this, beware. Blaming your spouse for your rages indicates a particularly serious anger problem. *Only you* are responsible for what you do when you feel angry. Difficulty accepting this personal responsibility is a sign that you may need professional help. Nothing your mate does merits your becoming physically violent in marriage.

Anger and the power of two

In sum, the costs of dealing with problem situations from a position of anger are high indeed. The power of two in anger is the power to cause harm—to yourself, your partner, your children, your marriage. The good news, however, is that you can create positive solutions to even your most longstanding disagreements. Switching from anger to mutually respectful, problem-solving dialogue can give you new levels of respect and affection for each other, not to mention better personal physical health, emotional well-being, self-esteem, and the ability to live life joyfully together.

Using Anger for Good

Be master of thine anger.
—Confucius

You are the only person who can decide what you will do when you feel anger brewing. When you *feel* angry, if you *act* angrily, with a harsh voice and critical words, you risk all the dangers enumerated above. If you suppress your anger, you risk your anger continuing to fester into a resentment that poisons your relationship. Smoldering anger also can break out suddenly into a dangerous blaze. And smothered anger can darken your life by submerging you in depression. None of these options are good for couples either.

What can you do to turn this powerful emotion into an asset in your marriage? The strategies and tips that follow can help you. Learning to use them, like learning to use the ABCDs of Part I, will take practice, but will have definite payoffs as you see how much happier your household will feel.

Strategy 1: Stop, look, and listen

As you do on the road when you see a stop sign, stop, look, and listen.

Stop

When you feel angry, first be sure to *stop interacting*. If at all possible, remove yourself temporarily from the immediately provocative situation. Give yourself time to cool down.

Once you have begun getting angry, the more you try to talk, the more unproductive the dialogue is likely to become. The more angry you are, the more you will be likely to overreact to whatever your partner says or does next. The longer you stay in a provocative situation, the more likely you will "lose your temper," that is, switch into that altered state of mind in which you blurt out extreme negative views that hurt the person you love.

Look

As your anger cools and your automatic search-and-destroy radar turns off, you will find that you can think more constructively. At that point you can try to address the problem again.

Look to expand your understanding of the situation. When you were angry, your focus was probably fairly narrow, like tunnel vision. As your emotions cool you are likely to find that your view of the problem widens. The additional information you take in can point the way to fresh perspectives and alternative solutions.

Listen

Anger virtually always involves frustration about what your partner is or isn't doing. Your anger means that what he or she is doing doesn't fit your agenda. If, however, you add to your understanding of what you want an understanding also of your partner's concerns, this broader view can be both calming and helpful in finding new solutions. *Listen* to your spouse's concerns.

Expressing your anger constructively will be easier and more satisfying if your spouse also can listen constructively. If your spouse becomes defensive when you sound angry, even when you use only *I* and *when you* statements, you both are likely to need to calm yourselves before you will be able to talk cooperatively about the sensitive problem.

Strategy 2: Take three steps, then find a solution

When you suddenly find yourself feeling angry, and you need to deal with the problem immediately rather than first cooling down, you can use another three-step approach. In this case anger's stop sign suggests that you pause long enough to think ahead to remind yourself of the steps you will be taking:

- Name the feeling.
- Convey your concerns.
- Ask to find out the other half of the story.
- Then look for solutions.

After these steps, looking for solutions will generally flow fairly smoothly.

Runaway Anger	The Three Steps
Len: You took my laptop computer to work?! How could you have done that! I told you I would need it at home every night this week! I can't believe you did that! *(Going on and on, and getting increasingly revved up with each repetition.)* You don't ever listen to me! I couldn't have told you more clearly! *Linda (defensively):* You did not tell me I couldn't take it. You said I could. You know I wouldn't have taken it if I didn't think it was OK with you. *Len (stomping off, and slamming the door behind him):* I'm so furious!	*Gerald:* You took my laptop computer to work?! Oh no! **I'm just furious.** I don't know what I'm going to do. I **was counting on using it at home tonight.** I thought I had told you that. I have a report due on Friday and I had planned to work on it. **Why did you take it?** *Gina:* Oh! I feel so bad. I do remember now your mentioning that report. I just wasn't thinking. I was caught up in trying to pack the baby's things for daycare this morning, she was crying, and I grabbed up the computer on the way out the door. I had a letter on it I needed for work. I sure didn't mean to mess up your work plan. I'm so sorry. *Gerald:* Well, I guess that's that. I'd better chalk it up to human error. I'm mad though. I had so carefully planned my time. Now when will I get the report started? Maybe I can switch things around. I could go to work earlier tomorrow and work there. I'm exhausted tonight anyway. I wouldn't have been able to concentrate well enough to write clearly.

Anger begets more anger. Len gets himself more and more worked up. The more he blames and criticizes Linda, the more he convinces himself that his feelings are justified. Also, each reiteration freshly rewounds him, stoking his anger. Meanwhile Linda's defensiveness, intended to fend off Len's anger, just adds fuel to the fire.

:ontrast, Gina and Gerald resist the impulse to keep feeding the flames with ruminating, blaming, and escalating. They know they can feel better sooner by using the three steps. By following this pathway they quickly cool down enough to map a plan of action. Their strategy works. Gina and Gerald succeed in converting the upset into an opportunity. Gerald figures out a way to write a better report and also to improve their morning routines.

Strategy 3: Ask the three magic questions

This third strategy can be unbelievably powerful. Once you get the idea of how to do it, you will never need to get stuck in escalating anger again.

The main secret is to shift your focus from the person you are mad at to yourself—not to be angry at yourself, but to understand better what is happening both within yourself and between you and your mate.

As you refocus on yourself, the three magic questions give you "traction" so that your mental wheels stop spinning in the rut of ruminations and you return to the road of constructive thinking.

- What do I want?
- How can I get what I want without having to get my partner to change?
- Other than what my partner did or didn't do, how did the problem happen?

When you experience angry feelings that either persist or escalate that's a tip-off that it's time to use the three magic questions. Whether at that point you decide to step out temporarily of the inflammatory situation, or you think that you can stay and talk productively, the questions offer a potent technique for gaining insight into the problem that has triggered your anger. With insight, solutions become the easy part.

These questions also help to release you from repetitive angry thoughts. Saying over and over what you don't like about what your partner did makes your anger grow. Whether your angry ruminations are silent or aloud, each repetition of what you didn't like reinforces your angry stance. By contrast, the three magic questions direct your attention away from your mate and back onto yourself. They redirect your thinking from *don't wants* to *do wants*. And they redirect you from trying to control your partner to using your energy to fix the problem.

What do I want?

Ask yourself, "What do I value that feels threatened?" Or in simpler language, "What do I want?" If the answer is to get back at him, or to get her to hurt as badly as you do so she knows how you feel, you are locked in blaming or striking back. Ask yourself again, "What do I want?" to identify your concerns so that you can switch from blaming to problem solving.

Tanner realized:

- *What I want is to finish the repairs on the barn so we don't lose animals to the cold this winter.*
- *What I want is to get back a sense that I am running my life. I think I've been giving control over my time away too easily.*
- *What I want is to be able to say no to some of our out-of-town family and friends who want to come visit, or at least to be a less available host.*

How can I get what I want without having to get my spouse to change?

Another way of asking the question is, "What could I do to solve my problem and feel better?"

- *I need to figure out how I can carve out two weeks from the remaining four weeks of summer. If we work together for ten hours a day for two weeks, we can get the barn finished before Bart has to go back to school. I depend on his help. If I leave the repairs for weekends, I won't get the barn repaired before the cold weather sets in.*
- *I need to find a motel where we can have our out-of-town visitors stay in the future. With visitors in the house, it's too hard for me to keep my focus on what I need to get done.*

By looking at what you can do to rather than staying focused on changing your spouse, you will find alternatives. Options are power.

How did this happen?—other than what your mate did or didn't do.

This question will help you identify situational factors. If you need to place blame somewhere, find something other than yourself or your mate. Identify external factors—fatigue, insufficient communication, being rushed—that contributed to your difficulty. Not only will this question stop the urge to blame; it also can give you good insights into where to look to prevent recurrences.

When Tanner asked himself this question his answers surprised him.

- *It's been raining so much. I get demoralized and my temper flares when there's no sunshine for so long.*
- *The noise from visitors in the house frazzles me and I get short-tempered.*

- *I've been angry at my mother. When I'm mad at her, everything else that bothers me begins to loom larger, to get way out of proportion.*

- *Our system for planning the summer was too casual. We need in the future to sit down with a calendar and mark out all our summer plans before we commit to anything. Agreeing to them one at a time, I didn't realize how full the summer was getting.*

Remember, the anger alarm goes off in order to:

- point out a problem that needs to be addressed.
- indicate to you by the intensity of your reaction how important the problem is.
- motivate you to address the problem—to clarify both of your concerns and find responsive solutions.

"The problem" is what you want that you are having difficulty getting, not what you don't like about what your partner is doing. The three magic questions help you to clarify the true problem and resolve it to the benefit of both of you.

Additional Fight-Prevention Techniques

When angry, count ten before you speak; if very angry, an hundred.

—Thomas Jefferson, "A Decalogue of Canons, for Observation in Practical Life"

Navigating through the moments in your marriage that bring on angry feelings requires steady skills, courage, and determination to make it through safely. The following additional suggestions may help.

Take two breaths, and put your mind elsewhere

Conventional wisdom has long suggested that you count to ten when you are angry. Other people say to take a deep breath. While both have their merits, ten can seem like a long count when you are impatient for resolution, and one deep breath, while better than none, is often too short an interval to slow down an accelerating train of angry thoughts.

So, for an effective pause that allows your thinking ability to catch up with your fast-track feelings, take two deep and cleansing breaths. As you slowly draw in air and then release it, focus entirely on your breathing.

To maximize your self-soothing, make sure those are slow, deep breaths. The problem situation will still be there when you are finished. There's no need to rush. Part of the effectiveness of this strategy depends on the connection between slower breathing and a slower, calmer emotional state.

The effectiveness of this technique also lies in turning your attention away from your mate and the situation you are angry about. That's why it's so important to *focus* on your breathing. When you return and look again at the problem situation, you will be able to see it from a broader and more constructive perspective. If not, take another breather.

To intensify the helpful effects of a pause, change the topic to one that is neutral or even pleasant for several moments. The pause gives your adrenaline time to drain off and your thinking time to kick in. Changing your thoughts, in addition, can change your feelings, giving your system an extra boost of physiological soothing.

> *Tanner developed a clever distraction technique. Whenever he felt himself overheating, he would say to himself, "Think eating."*
>
> *"Oh, by the way, Kate, what time are we eating dinner tonight? I'd like to stop and do some errands on the way home if there's time." The nonsequitur shifted his mood along with his mindset.*

It is a good idea to select ahead of time, when you are not angry, some topics that would be safely nonemotional ones for you to switch to. Having these ready in your mental "back pocket" will make it easier for you to access them when you need them.

 ## Use the Twenty-Four-Hour Rule

You can save yourselves many arguments by making a twenty-four-hour rule. That is, any topic that arouses irritation in either of you gets a twenty-four-hour cooling off period before it's discussed. In the interim, most angers evaporate. Issues of consequence can be discussed the next day in more relaxed humor. Like wine, anger mellows with time.

 ## Take time out

In Chapter 3, in the discussion of climate controls, I mentioned the need to plan exit and reentry routines for when emotions get too hot. The following pages offer a brief review of the guidelines plus additional suggestions for success.

Time-Out and Reentry Checklist

Initiate time-outs when you:

- begin to feel emotionally overloaded, or sense that your mate is getting overheated
- hear yourself or your partner saying the same thing over and over or getting more insistent, and reiteration isn't helping
- hear volume or irritation rising in either of your voices
- feel any early warning signs of flooding

To initiate the time-out:

- Use a prearranged signal. Do not enter into a discussion of whether or not to call a time out. A hand signal helps you feel protected rather than rejected by the departure. You might want to use a time-out signal from a favorite sport.
- Leave to predesignated places—a separate room for each of you if you are at home—without further dialogue.
- Once there, soothe yourself. Do activities you enjoy, or resume normal activities. Reestablish a level emotional state.
- Write in a journal if you like, to clarify for yourself what happened, what the sensitivities were about, and what might be helpful for you to do differently when you discuss this topic again. List the concerns you heard your mate expressing.
- Do not ruminate on what your spouse did wrong or generalize about his or her traits.

When you reengage:

- Wait to reengage until both of you are feeling normal.
- Reengage first in ordinary activities. Discuss the topic again only after you have first experienced a period of normal time together.
- If you have reengaged before one of you is ready, give the sign and disengage again until both of you are ready.
- Be certain that your plan includes specifications for when you will return to the hot topic with cooler conflict-resolution dialogue.

Exit rules:

- No door slamming.
- No parting comments.

- Sooner is better than later.
- Focus on your exit, not on what your partner is doing or saying.
- Never block your mate from leaving, or follow after.
- Remind yourself that this is a temporary disengagement, not a permanent separation. Beware of all-or-nothing thinking.
- When the going gets hot, keep cool and exit.

Avoid needless angers

Do you feel angry often? If so you may have a case of "needless angers," my term for anger in day-to-day living situations that do not warrant getting steamed about. Save your anger for major grievances. For daily life, be nice. It gets you more of what you want, and without hurting your loved ones.

Interestingly, when children who are treating each other angrily are told, "Children, be nice," they almost always know what "nice" is. Moreover, they generally can turn off their internal anger and switch into nice mode. Adults who find themselves responding to day-to-day frustrations with needless anger may be equally surprised to discover that can they tell themselves, "Wait a minute. Be nice." The outcome turns out better than if you had ranted and raved. You won't get revenge, but you are likely to get resolution of the problem, and a far happier household.

If you have been getting irritable over minor glitches, the problem may not be what your partner does or doesn't do. The problem may be that you try to control him or her. And it probably means that you have developed an automatic habit of speaking in an irritated voice when there's something you want. Fortunately, being unpleasant is a changeable reaction pattern. Like being polite rather than rude, pleasantness is a matter of training and choice, not an inborn characteristic.

If you feel angry often, that is, more than once every few weeks or months, identifying and ending your needless angers can reduce much unpleasantness in your life and for your family.

To identify your needless angers, keep a list for a week of all the incidents to which you responded with anger. Note that I did not say "incidents that made you mad." Incidents, like people, don't make you mad. You choose or have a habit of responding with anger.

Once you have a full list, notice patterns in the situations. Do you get angry in response to minor mistakes, yours or others? Do you get angry when your spouse isn't doing what you want? Note how these needless angers could have been handled in better humor—by explaining what you wanted instead of insisting, by fixing problems instead of affixing blame, and by reminding yourself after mishaps that mistakes are for learning.

You will be well on your way to a strong and loving home if you can find ways to handle one hundred percent of your needless angers without irritation or blame.

Ask instead if interpreting

When you feel angry about something your partner has done, you may give yourself an explanation about why he or she did such a thing. If you assign negative intentions or attributes to your mate for having done this thing that bothered you, you are likely to feel angrier and angrier. You are at risk then for needless suffering. If the explanation you are giving yourself is one that casts your partner in a negative light, your interpretation most probably is a misinterpretation.

Instead of offering your own interpretations, *ask* why he or she did whatever troubled you. Then listen to learn from the answer. You may be delightfully surprised.

> *Tanner again felt himself getting angry at Kate. They had gone grocery shopping together, and she seemed to criticize his purchases on every aisle. "She's so controlling!" he said to himself. The more he thought about her comments, the angrier he felt, and the more overpowering and intrusive his wife appeared to be.*

Tanner's negative interpretation of his wife's comments as they shop together feeds a growing anger. If instead of interpreting what she is doing he asks her, the outcome becomes very different. Watch as Tanner later asks instead of interpreting. Moreover, the answer he gets leads Tanner and Kate into an important discussion of the major change coming up in their lives.

Start with a *when you*

> *Tanner turned to Kate. "I felt angry in the grocery store when you seemed to be criticizing my every purchase. I was hearing that you think I don't have enough sense to figure out for myself what we need in the house. I felt like you were being competitive with me, trying to show me that you can shop better than I can."*

Ask what your spouse was thinking, feeling, and doing

> *"Did you feel that way?" Tanner asked.*
> *Kate thought a moment. "I actually was enjoying shopping together. It made shopping an opportunity to share time together instead of a chore. I did fill you in on why certain products, like the cereal with virtually no nourishment in it, are not ones I usually buy. My experience, though, was of sharing rather than of competition. I wonder where your darker interpretation comes from?"*

"Dark is an apt word," Tanner mused aloud. "I have been feeling dark. Maybe I was attributing to you the feelings I was having. I felt kind of competitive toward you, like 'I can shop as well as she can!' And I was also downgrading myself. 'You dummy. Why didn't you read the nutritional information on the cereal box?'"

As Tanner and Kate switch from blame to self-exploration, they identify situational factors that might be precipitating the problem.

"It's almost like I'm depressed," Tanner speculated.

"Do you think it has anything to do with Bart going off to college?" Kate asked. "I miss him with his funny jokes. Are you grieving his absence, too?"

"That sounds just right, unfortunately. His going off to college feels like he's gone forever," Tanner said sadly.

"I guess we need to look at what changes to make with Bart gone." Kate said. "It's empty-nest time, but I'm actually kind of excited. We hardly even have to do grocery shopping without him at home to feed. You and I are happy with rice and beans. Instead of cooking, we could take a walk before dinner. We could go to a movie or visit friends in the evenings."

Having switched from conflict to collaborative decision-making Tanner and Kate can devote their energies to finding solutions.

"Well," Tanner said, "now that I know what my distress was triggered by, I feel more comfortable. I think I'll go sit in the living room and feel the sadness for a while. I actually like doing that. Sadness is part of life. What did Shakespeare say, something about 'parting is such sweet sorrow'? In any case, I'm relieved to be feeling sad instead of mad."

♥ Set anger ceilings

An anger ceiling is the level of anger that you allow yourself to feel, and the way in which you allow yourself to express this anger, before you take action to cool down.

Everyone instinctively sets ceilings on how angry they will feel and act before they extricate themselves from a situation. Some need only to feel slight angry rumblings. At that point they step back to think about the anger, its message, and how to deal most effectively with the provocative situation. Some people need to hear themselves speaking in an angry tone of voice before they pull back to cool down.

Some couples engage in debilitatingly angry arguing for hours on end, setting their ceiling at verbal ventilating, and staying at their ceiling levels for long times. Others allow themselves to become physical against objects—throwing dishes, punching holes in walls. The worst, of course, is to let yourself become physically violent against your mate—hitting, punching, squeezing, or choking, and in the most extreme, killing the person you love.

You determine where you will set your anger ceiling. Following the guidelines for cooperative dialogue and using this chapter's anger strategies hopefully will keep you far below your ceiling. If not, disengage.

Hold on tightly to your communication skills

Expressing anger effectively and safely requires that you be especially skillful at the communication techniques detailed in Part I. The following reminders and additional pointers merit frequent review so that you can reliably use the ABCDs to guide your dialogue whether you feel mildly piqued, seriously angry, or furious.

- *Verbalize your feeling,* and then halt any further emotional escalations as quickly as possible: "I'm mad." "I'm irritated."

- *Verbalize your concerns* so that you and your mate can begin to address the difficulty your anger has alerted you to.

- *Ask what makes sense to your partner about your concerns.* If you are tempted to continue acting angrily, it may indicate that you are not yet confident that you have successfully conveyed your distress. Rather than continuing to escalate on the presumption that you have not been heard, *ask* your mate what makes sense in what you have said. Speaking louder, as if he or she isn't hearing because of deafness, makes for less hearing, not more.

- *Maintain climate control.* If your anger is too strong to talk quietly in a problem-solving way, deescalate the intensity before you try to talk more. Use pauses and deep breathing, or distract yourself by talking briefly about something unrelated. Maintain an emotional climate in which you can be certain that you will not fall into criticism, insults, or blame, and in which your words and tone of voice will not encourage your spouse to feel defensive.

- *Use word patrol.* Be sure to talk in *I* mode. If you need to reference what your spouse did, use *when you* statements. Stay away from *should* by converting it to *could* or *would like.*

- *No crossovers.* Focus on what you have contributed to the problem and what you can do differently to fix the situation; let your mate focus on what he or she can do.

- *Listen to learn,* in order to genuinely understand your spouse's concerns and add them to your own.

- *Ask, rather than talking about your partner's thoughts and feelings* or assuming you know them. Many angry escalations begin with misinterpretations of what your mate is thinking or doing.

- *Zero toxicity.* Be especially tactful so as not to evoke defensiveness by slipping in toxic barbs.

- *Use bilateral listening.* Hearing your partner's point of view on a situation that is bothering you can have a remarkably calming effect. Remember that the point is not to bully your mate into doing what you want, but to find a solution that works for both of you. Your capacity for bilateral listening holds the key to a successful outcome.

- *Take time out.* If you continue to feel angry and you sense that you may not be able to stay within these guidelines, *exit immediately.* Leave well before the situation goes beyond what you can handle.

Deciding to Change

If you often express your desires as irritable comments, use anger to get what you want, or experience intense anger, you have a serious challenge ahead.

How can you change anger habits? Interestingly, the initial steps are the same as for changing any counterproductive habit, whether it's smoking, tardiness, messiness, or, in this case, excessive anger:

- *Understand the negative consequences.* Who have you hurt with your anger (including yourself)?

- *Make a clear decision.* Make a commitment to yourself that acting hurtfully in anger will be for you like eating worms. It is on your list of things that are *simply not done.*

- *Become aware when you feel anger.* The hardest part of change is awareness. Just as you can drive for hours without ever being aware of your foot on the gas pedal, you can speak in an irritated tone, bully people by saying hurtful comments, or control people with the implied threat "and if you don't I'll get mad at you"—all without ever being aware that you have been expressing anger.

  You can override your automatic pilot if you listen closely to your tone of voice and to the niceness or nastiness of what you are saying. If you catch the old critical voice and comments coming out, a quick apology and then a second draft will likely be appreciated by the person you are talking with. Eventually, you will find that you can catch yourself before you start to talk, quiet the irritability, and then proceed in a tactful and respectful way.

- *Notice patterns of when angers occur.* Do you tend to anger easily before meals? When you are tired or overloaded? When talking with particular family members? When you are hurrying? When you are talking about particular topics?

- *Remind yourself that you are not authorized to say what your partner* should *do.* Seeing the world in terms of *should* is a setup for rapid anger reactions. Telling your spouse what he or she *should* be doing is out of bounds. You can voice what you would like, then listen respectfully to your partner's concerns and preferences. *Shoulds* are bullying, not partnering.

- *Keep reminding yourself of the basic dialogue rules.* Talk about yourself, or ask about the other, but never tell the other person what he or she is feeling, thinking, or doing. Along with trying to make your spouse do what you want, anger most often comes from crossovers, from guessing or telling instead of asking your partner what he or she thinks, feels, or might do.

- *Look for solutions to the situations that are the subjects of recurring arguments.* Identify recurring topics that you typically react to with anger. As you notice that certain topics tend to lead to feelings of irritation, remember that most couples fight over the same few issues again and again. Instead of continuing this fruitless pattern, sit down together.

- *Use fix-it talk to come to new, mutually agreeable options for handling these situations.* The chapters coming up on shared decision making and on conflict resolution will further augment your toolbox for settling these disputes. The best antidotes to argument are cooperative discussion and new solutions.

Signs that say "Get help"

Expressing, or receiving, anger taxes your sense of well-being. If you find that you are doing either one very often, something is amiss.

The signs that you as a couple could benefit from professional help with the anger in your relationship do not have to be extreme. In fact, the less extreme your anger problem, the more likely that professional help can rapidly make a major difference.

The following conditions suggest a significant anger problem. Professional help from a marriage counselor or clinical psychologist who specializes in work with couples could help you to ease the strains.

- chronic irritability
- frequent anger outbursts
- frequent fighting
- physical violence of any type: threatening, shaking, pushing, hitting, choking, squeezing, punching, kicking
- anger outbursts followed by remorse, repeated cyclically, suggest that the remorse is not leading to lasting changes
- denying anger ("I wasn't really mad") after you have raised your voice, or believing that your major anger episodes are caused by your partner's doing things you don't like ("It's her fault I'm mad"), are particularly noteworthy signs that say *Get Help*

All mates do things from time to time that their partner doesn't like. Those situations indicate it's time for fix-it talk, not for anger outbursts.

A word of warning on getting professional help: Choosing a therapist is not like buying aspirin tablets. All mental health professionals are not equal. Trust your intuition. Even if the person to whom you go is highly recommended and has excellent credentials, if the sessions do not feel helpful to you, speak up. If discussing your concerns does not lead to change, find another therapist.

When two discourse, if the one's anger rise,
The man who lets the contest fall is wise.

—Plutarch

Chapter 6

Receiving Anger Without Fighting

It takes one to express anger, but it takes two to make a fight. Psychologists have noted that in distressed couples one partner's anger typically generates a return of anger. This "negative reciprocity" contrasts with what typically happens in happier marriages (Margolin & Wampold, 1981). In happier marriages, when one spouse expresses anger, the other stays calm.

Whatever your mate does, how you choose to respond affects the outcome—whether the situation becomes better or worse. This is another way of understanding the power of two. Two points determine a line; precipitating words plus a response determine the course of a dialogue.

In what sense then does a spouse on the receiving end of anger have power? Power is options. You can choose to respond to your partner's anger by becoming defensive or launching a counterattack; or you can stay calm, offer soothing, change the topic, or exit.

This idea of options as power is very different from the notion that you bear responsibility for your mate's actions. If your partner is going to continue to be difficult, that's his or her choice. It is not your role to control him or her. You alone, however, have the power and the responsibility at every point in your shared dialogue to determine what your contribution will be.

A cautionary note

We all know "it takes two to tango." Sometimes, however, two angry people are more like a bank robber and a bank teller. That is, responsibility is not always equal, especially when power is unequal.

Research on battering has concluded that once a battering incident begins, nothing the victim does, except leaving the situation, makes much difference. Being nice, being defensive, being apologetic, being angry all tend to get about the same result (Jacobsen et al., 1994).

Even in this kind of situation, however, you have options, particularly between episodes. Leaving, while often difficult, is one option. If you are in this kind of a marriage, seek knowledgeable professional help.

When Your Mate Is Angry

Listen to learn. Listen to determine in as comprehensive a way as possible what the trouble is about. This basic principle offers the key to responding in a way that leads to understanding. Alas, it is a key that can be very difficult to use. If you find that instead of listening to learn you are responding defensively, or becoming angry in return, your best policy probably is to exit as soon as possible.

Listen to learn about your partner

When your mate is angry at you, remember that you are listening to learn about his or her distress, not for what you did wrong. Listening in this way will help you remain calm, keep your perspective, and understand the source of your partner's distress.

Defensive Listening	Listening to Learn
Len (furious): You lied to me when you said you'd meet me at eight o'clock. Everyone at the party was asking where you were, and I looked absolutely foolish when I had to tell them I had no idea!	*Gerald (furious):* You lied to me when you said you'd meet me at eight o'clock. Everyone at the party was asking where you were, and I looked absolutely foolish when I had to tell them I had no idea!
Linda (defending herself): I don't lie. You know that!	*Gina (responding with compassion):* I'm so sorry about miscalculating so badly when I'd be able to get there. I got caught up at work. I would have hated being in your position. I can understand how frustrating and embarrassing my mistake was for you.
Len (continuing to rage): How can you humiliate me like that?!	
Linda (counterattacking): Who's humiliating whom?! You're the one who's yelling and treating me like a disobedient child! Some nerve you have accusing me of lying!	

Linda found that like a wildfire, Len's anger ignited her own. Anger is inherently provocative because it carries a toxic tag of "You did something wrong!" or "You're not a good person!" along with the main message your spouse intends to convey. Linda heard Len's words "You lied to me" and snapped to angry self-defense.

Listening so that you then can express empathy when you feel under attack takes extreme self-confidence and emotional equanimity. How does Gina succeed? The trick is that she listens to learn *about Gerald*. Gerald was upset because he felt embarrassed when he did not know where she was. As Gina listens to learn about her husband's concerns, instead of feeling defensive, she experiences compassion. She can understand his wanting to be able to count on her being where she says she will be. She would have felt similarly embarrassed at not knowing where her husband was.

Once she understands the situation from Gerald's point of view, Gina then can then figure out for herself her own part in the upset. Her conclusion about her need to keep a better eye on the clock at work is motivated by altruism, by wanting to prevent her husband's having to suffer similar distress in the future—not by feeling that she has been a bad person.

When your partner is mad at you, if you, like Linda, are listening for what he or she is saying about you, which given the anger is bound to come out negative, you will both miss the point and set yourself up to become hurt or angry. By contrast, if you, like Gina, listen to hear what your spouse is saying about himself or herself, then you will learn the vital information you need to respond with empathy to the current upset. That empathy in turn will help you prevent a similar upset in the future.

This mode of listening, listening to what your mate is saying about him- or herself rather than about you, is the opposite of "taking it personally." Of course, the more your mate targets you as the source of his or her anger, criticizing or blaming you instead of sticking with when yous, the harder it will be to listen to learn about your partner. At the same time, the more skillful you become at listening to anger to understand what the anger is about, the easier it becomes to listen like Teflon. The toxic words won't stick to you because you will be so focused on trying to understand your partner's distress.

❤ Beware of "What did I do wrong?"

One tip-off that you are listening defensively rather than listening to learn about your partner is if you react like a child to a parent by thinking, "What did I do wrong?" That question focuses you on the wrong person. More helpful questions to guide your listening are:

- What is my mate's concern?
- What is causing the sensitivity?
- What might I do that could help?

After you understand what concerns set off the anger alarm, the question, "What was my part in this problem?" becomes helpful. This sequence can make a significant difference in enabling you to listen helpfully to anger without feeling put down by it.

Change *wrong* to *miss*

Beware of the word *wrong,* which carries heavy, judgmental connotations. If there is a genuine moral issue at stake, then *wrong* would be a suitable word. If, for instance, there has been a theft, or a violation of your monogamy contract, these are clear wrongdoings. Most of the time in marriage, however, anger comes up because you have been tripped up by one of the *mis*-es:

- mistakes
- mishaps
- miscommunications
- misunderstandings
- misinterpretations
- miscalculations
- misconceptions
- misery
- missiles (hurtful words that evoke the impulse to strike back)

As you understand the concerns that gave rise to your mate's anger alarm, you can figure out together which of the *mis*-es may have been involved. Your mutual energies then can focus on the most important post-anger question—how best to rectify the problem situation.

The Triple-A Strategy for Receiving Anger

To receive angry comments safely and have them lead to constructive dialogue about a problem that has set off an anger alarm, try following the three As:

Agree

Listen for what is right, what makes sense, in what your angry mate is trying to tell you. Respond by reiterating all that you can agree with. Listen especially for what your partner wants. Remember that people feel angry when something they value feels threatened or inaccessible. Be specific, detailing what you agree with.

Apologize

"I'm sorry for... I certainly didn't intend for you to feel...when I...And I do feel badly that you felt so..."

Add

After agreeing and apologizing for your part, you may be able to add your perspective. Be sure to add your experience of the incident by using *and,* not *but,* and to use *I* and *when you* statements, not crossovers.

Fighting Back	The triple-A Method
Linda (furious): I'm so mad at you! Before I left to drive Lori to school she was hysterically yelling at me. I was so frazzled by it I was crying as well. When I returned you asked how Lori was, but you never asked about me! I'm furious! Don't my feelings count around here?	*Gina (furious):* I'm so mad at you! Before I left to drive Genny to school she was hysterically yelling at me. I was so frazzled by it I was crying as well. When I returned you asked how Genny was, but you never asked about me! I'm furious! Don't my feelings count around here!
Len (disagreeing): Of course I care about you, Linda. I get sick of constantly being questioned like that. *(defending)* I can't read your mind. Look, instead of being mad at me for not asking you how you felt, you need to tell me if you want me to know.	*Gerald (agreeing):* You're absolutely right, Gina. I never did ask about you, just about Genny. *(apologizing)* I really am sorry about that. I can see that not asking gave a wrong impression. I sure didn't mean to hurt your feelings.
Linda: You have the compassion of a cow!	*Gina:* Thank you. I appreciate that.
Len (defeated, trying to ignore the insult): Besides, I was busy trying to get to work on time.	*Gerald (adding):* My mind was on trying to get out the door and get to work. I did want to be sure you two had calmed down, though. You looked fine, so I asked about Genny. She sure can create a tornado when she's distraught. Were you OK? I definitely do care about you as well.
	Gina (hugging Gerald): I'm fine. Thanks.

When Linda feels hurt and angry, Len misses out on being able to hear her concerns constructively. He misses all three triple-A steps. First, he is listening for what is wrong with what Linda has said instead of for what he can agree with. Having missed the first step makes subsequent recovery all the harder.

After disagreeing, instead of finding something in Linda's angry effusion that makes sense to him, Len proceeds by defending himself. He defends himself by criticizing, by "blaming the messenger," Linda. There is truth in what he says, but blaming when he needed to acknowledge his inadvertent mistake further inflames the situation.

Lastly, alas, because he has not set a foundation by agreeing and apologizing, Len's explanation that he had been trying to get to work on time sounds like an excuse. Instead of soothing, it adds to the animosity.

The sequence of the three parts of a triple-A response is essential. Gerald successfully listens first for what he can agree with. He then acknowledges Gina's anger with an apology. Lastly, the new information he adds helpfully augments Gina's understanding of what happened. Gina is open to hearing Gerald's explanation because his openness to hearing her concerns has reestablished cooperative trust between them. Gerald's explanation for his lack of attention enables her to see the painful situation in a new light, and Gina feels her anger lift.

One note: If the three steps of a triple-A response to anger, or even the first two steps, seem to be generating more anger instead of less, back off. You can return to talk later, letting time offer its calming effects, and then trying the triple-A again.

Top off a triple-A with a new and improved solution

By agreeing, apologizing for your part in the mishap, and adding information about your experience of the problem, you are likely to succeed in regaining a cooperative atmosphere. The threat of a fight will dissipate. Yet, an opportunity remains to convert the upsetting incident into one that leads to a positive outcome.

Kate and Tanner handled one such situation with particular success.

> Tanner stormed into the room. "I called you six times and you never answered! I feel like you're purposely ignoring me!"
>
> As Kate listens she pauses, thinking to herself, "Triple-A." She thinks first what she can agree with, what might be right in Tanner's description of the incident. "You're right," she replies, "I didn't answer. I vaguely heard you, beyond the radio. I hate to admit it but I probably was tuning you out."
>
> She apologized, and then added her perspective. "I'm sorry. I think I'm still simmering over what you said after breakfast, when we were rushing out the door. I am sorry for not answering. That wasn't the most constructive way to deal with my irritation at you. Can we talk over what you said so I can let go of it?"

"I hadn't even realized there was a problem this morning. What are you referring to?" Tanner asked.

"My feelings were hurt when you were so harsh about the red dress I bought for your office party. I don't even want to go now."

Now it's Tanner's turn to use the triple-A system. Angers often come in sequences like this. One anger begets the next.

"I did speak pretty harshly when I said you look like a prostitute in it. I'm sorry. Actually the problem with the red dress is it's too sexy on you. I probably spoke harshly because I felt threatened. I saw it as you trying to look good for other men, to attract other men at the party. I get jealous easily. It doesn't take much for me to be certain you want to dump me for someone else."

Kate smiled ruefully, "I'm actually not a hundred percent comfortable with the dress myself. It's my fantasy of gorgeous, but the reality feels too seductive to me, too. Would you be willing to come shopping with me? I could return that dress and find another. There's one store I haven't gone to yet. I'd love to make a fun evening of supper in the mall and shopping."

"I'd love that. And I really do feel bad that I was so insensitive toward you. I don't want to lose you to some other guy, but acting like a jerk myself is no way to keep you."

"That's for sure. Getting back at you by not answering also was not so cool. What do they call it, 'passive-aggressive'? I was getting back at you by not doing what you wanted, by not answering you. I feel better now though, with the dress problem out in the open so we can solve it."

♥ Detoxify as you listen

Anger can bring toxic comments into a discussion. To protect yourself when you listen to your partner's anger, it helps to be able to detoxify hurtful information that comes your way. Detoxification is a process of translating negative language into more neutral or positive language.

Toxic Comments	Detoxified Versions
You're so selfish!	She doesn't feel that I understand her concerns.
You treat me like a nothing. What I like to eat doesn't seem to matter around here! All you care about is what you like to eat.	He feels uncertain about whether his concerns matter to me. He'd like me to take them more into account, especially when I'm planning meals.

(continued on next page)

Toxic Comments	Detoxified Versions
The table looks so sloppy I can't eat!	When the dinner table is cluttered, she feels uncomfortable. She'd rather we take a few minutes to straighten up and then eat.
If you weren't like a spoiled kid throwing tantrums all the time maybe I'd listen to you more.	He tunes out when I speak negatively and overemotionally. He would be more likely to listen to my concerns if I could speak more calmly.

To detoxify, silently translate the words your spouse has spoken into the language of cooperative dialogue. In your thoughts you can

- change your mate's accusatory *you* to an explanatory *he* and *she*, so you can listen to learn your spouse's concerns
- change complaints to requests
- change toxic words to nontoxic versions of the same idea

The three-part detoxification formula presented in Chapter 2 can help you detoxify aloud. A critical step to remember if you voice your detoxification aloud is that the first word of a detoxification response needs to be *yes*. That powerful word buys time and reestablishes cooperation. Then you can reiterate what makes sense to you in what you have heard, rephrasing toxic phrases more tactfully. This technique may or may not ease your partner's anger, but it can be very effective in keeping your own thoughts busy, blocking impulses you might otherwise have had to snap back in anger.

Safety Rules for Receiving Anger

The following rules can help couples to stay safe near anger. They are rules in the sense that they describe how anger interactions work.

The Ownership Rule

The owner of the anger is the person who feels angry. The owner of anger, like the owner of a pit bull, is responsible for its management and restraint. You may offer to help. But no matter how much an angry person attempts to blame you for his or her anger, or tries to remedy a situation by punishing you with a flood of angry words against you, remember that their anger is not your fault, and not your responsibility to soothe.

This concept can be a difficult one to fully understand, because you may well have done something that triggered an anger response. Your partner's angry response, however, was there to serve as an alert, a stop sign, not as a weapon against you. Therefore, no matter what you did, you do not have to become a victim of your mate's misuses of anger.

Similarly, you are not responsible for deescalating your partner's anger. You and your spouse each own responsibility for soothing your own emotional overheatings. Otherwise you would be setting up a codependent relationship, that is, a relationship in which each of you is responsible for controlling the other. This kind of symbiotic relationship spells disaster, much as if two people riding side by side on motorcycles at high speed were to decide that each of them was responsible for steering the other's bike.

You do, however, own responsibility for how you listen. If your mate is angry at you and you become defensive or start counterattacking, you own these inflammatory responses. Your responsibility, in receiving your partner's anger, is to follow rigorously the guidelines for listening detailed in Chapter 2. Poor listening, like defensiveness or counterattack, is inherently provocative.

Why is poor listening so provocative? As discussed in Chapter 5, when an anger alarm goes off, it announces a message of urgent importance. If this message is pushed aside, or heard but not digested, the original hurt or trespass is compounded. The result is a louder, longer and more livid attempt to get the information through to the intended recipient. The more you appear to be putting up barriers to hearing your mate's anger, the more you are inviting him or her to get out the verbal battering rams.

At certain times you or your partner will be able to help deescalate the other's anger. Soothing ability is a great gift to be able to share as a couple, but bear in mind that helping your mate cool down is a generous, voluntary contribution, not an essential in the marriage contract. Your promise is to be loving, that is, to have understanding and compassion toward your partner's distress; it is not to fix his or her overheating.

When you are the receiver of anger, your job is to hear the message that the anger alarm has said needs to be conveyed, and to learn from it without letting anger's heat lead to your losing your own cool. That is the responsibility—and it can be a challenging one—that as receiver you own.

The Fireman's Rule

If you are close to anger for too long, or close even briefly to anger that is very hot, you too will become angry. While you may be learning skills that can help you hear your mate's anger without becoming angry yourself, and perhaps to help with cooling the anger, putting out fires is dangerous work.

Keep in mind that anger is highly contagious. Be realistic how close to the anger and for how long you can tolerate the heat before you risk exploding. As soon as you begin to feel even a tinge of sparks within yourself, distance yourself immediately from the blaze. There are no prizes, only burns and wounds, for staying and getting burned, or for allowing your own capacity for blazing to ignite.

It takes significant self-confidence to respond with calm listening when someone tells you that he or she is angry at you. If you genuinely believe you are a good person, and that your motives have not been to hurt your partner, then it is easier to hear angry concerns.

On the other hand, if you tend to take others' anger personally; if you are someone who tends to be short-fused; if you are at all tired, hungry, ill, or under stress; or if your spouse is a frequent blamer or highly inflammable, exit the danger zone as quickly as possible.

The Emotional-Matching Rule

When two people are talking, their feelings will gradually ease toward one shared emotional state. How can you be certain that both of you move toward your quiet good humor, not toward matching your partner's agitation? The following guidelines can help:

- *Stay calm.* During the anger incident, keep your own emotional state within the narrow zone within which you can keep thinking. You can become more emotional later.

- *Stay safe.* If your partner is not able to join your calmer state, you are likely to join in on the anger. Therefore if your mate is not being calmed by your presence, disengage.

- *Stay problem focused.* Seek to understand your spouse's concerns and look together for solution options.

The Movie Projector Rule

The more angry your spouse becomes, the more likely that criticism directed at you will be a projection of your spouse's own feelings, thoughts, or tendencies. If the complaints about you feel inaccurate, the likelihood is high that your spouse's view of you is a projection.

When someone projects their difficulties onto you, with you serving as the movie screen, it is helpful to be able *silently* to translate the information. "You have no sense of time!" may indicate that your partner has difficulties monitoring how long things take. "You are full of resentment!" tips you off that your mate may have been harboring longstanding resentments of some kind.

"You just want to spend, spend, spend without worrying about whether we have the money!" may be an indirect confession of his or her own wishes. Again, the further from the mark the criticism of you seems to be, the more useful it may be to think about what those words tell you about the speaker.

Translate first, talk later. This rule of thumb can protect you from unproductive attempts to talk about overly sensitive issues when your mate is already overheated. Translating projections in your own mind can protect you from feeling stung by criticism. Translating can also help you to learn about your spouse as you listen to an angry tirade. By contrast, trying to talk about the projection while your spouse is still angry is likely to fan the flames. Wait. Later, perhaps even the next day, in a calm moment when you can be exceptionally tactful and your spouse is likely to be able to listen, you might cooperatively and carefully discuss the insights that his or her projection seems to have offered you.

The Rule of History

History tends to repeat itself. If the last time your spouse became angry, the ensuing dialogue was draining, upsetting, and essentially unproductive, do not believe that somehow this time will be more positive. Instead, look back. Has allowing the one of you who became angry to engage both of you in a fight ever accomplished anything that a quiet heart-to-heart talk would not have accomplished better? And what were the costs?

If your spouse has any history of violence—verbal or physical—do not stay in a situation where violence could occur again. Either learn to read early warning signals and exit early, or reconsider the merits of staying in this marriage. The Rule of History is especially vital to heed in these circumstances.

The Snapping Turtle Rule

A client of mine has a saying: "When a snapping turtle bites, it won't let go until the thunder claps." Some people have a very hard time letting go of their anger. In these cases, if their mate "escalates over" them, sounding more angry that they themselves feel, the surprise response stuns them back into a normal emotional state.

This strategy can be dangerous. Escalating over can turn out to be escalating with, and the fight is on. By contrast, some angry people do find that their spouse's ability to turn to them and say sharply "That's enough! Stop it!" does enable them to loosen their angry jaws and let go.

Most of the time, however, it is better to let a snapping turtle stay angry and self-soothe. After your partner has calmed down, analyzing what happened may be helpful, but it will not help while he or she is still locked in anger and looking to blame or punish.

Sound and Fury Signify Something

If you are repeatedly receiving anger, blame, and criticism, it is likely that something greater than normal stresses and strains is going on. Your mate may be locked in a distressed emotional state. Anxiety, depression, guilt, shame, or problems at work or with other family members can bring about pervasive negativity. Instead of being able to identify the external problem that is the actual source of these negative feelings, your mate may be displacing generalized negative feelings onto you.

> Lana and Oren both felt angry most of the time. They fought mainly about who was doing how much of the household chores—who made the lunches, who did kitchen cleanup, and who was freed up to sit and play with the children. Underlying these battles, however, stoking the chronic irritability, were unspoken concerns about Oren's pending need to change jobs.
>
> Oren's firm was closing down. He was afraid that he wouldn't be able to find an equivalent or better job in the town where they were living, but knowing his wife's attachment to their home and community, he was afraid to ask her if she would be willing to move to where there might be more work opportunities for him. Instead, he harbored anger at what he believed would be her resistance to moving.
>
> Oren's irritability in turn evoked anger in Lana. "I'm tired of feeling like I'm in the doghouse all the time!" Her angry resentment came out in continual criticisms of Oren, so that he too felt chronically in the doghouse. "Stop fighting Mommy and Daddy!" their two daughters would insist.
>
> Once Oren and Lana began to talk openly about Oren's job dilemma, they realized that they could come to agreement on a plan of action that felt good to both of them. They agreed that Oren would try to find another job in the same city if possible, and they also agreed on a level of increase in income that would make it worthwhile to both of them to move. The chronic anger immediately evaporated. The division-of-labor questions became routine, practical, living-together questions that they could discuss and resolve relatively easily. And the doghouse emptied out.

Oren and Lana stopped their cycle of reciprocating anger by realizing that the anger must be signifying an underlying problem. As they cooperatively sought to understand what the underlying problem was and how to resolve it, the anger ended.

Know where to look

Anger is a stop sign both for the person who feels angry and for the person who is the brunt of it. Anger says *stop* to seek understanding. Once you have stopped, your next dilemma is where to look to understand the difficulty. The essential rule of thumb is to look where the anger is.

If you are the one who feels angry, look inside yourself and ask, "What do I want that I'm feeling frustrated about?" You'll be on the right track if you can phrase your dilemma as "I want..." not "I want you to..." For example, "I want help cooking dinner because I feel overwhelmed," not "I want *you* to cook dinner."

Anger framed well leads to insight and then new solutions. The solution to the dinner anger, for instance, might be that your mate would pitch in, or alternatively you might decide to order pizza, to enjoy cereal and fruit as a simple supper, or to go to the gym and work out together for a while and then decide what to do for dinner.

If your mate is the one who feels angry, look carefully at him or her and ask yourself, "What does my spouse want? What is triggering the frustration?" In other words, if the anger is in you, you look within yourself for a frustrated *want*; if the anger is in your spouse, you need to look there.

In this way you both can stay far from blame or criticism. These toxic expressions of angry feelings mistakenly assume that if anger is in one of you, the other must be to blame. Blame and criticism point you in exactly the wrong direction. Instead, look where the anger is. Likewise, when you are the recipient of your mate's anger, the place to look to find out what the distress is about is at the fire within him or her.

Understanding anger this way provides a foundation for building a relationship of deepest intimacy. If you want to peek ahead at Chapter 12 you will see how. In the meantime, however, the next chapter looks at what you can do if the two of you missed an anger stop sign and crashed.

Give me a fruitful error any time, full of seeds, bursting with its own corrections. You can keep your sterile truth for yourself.

—Vilfredo Pareto, *Comment on Kepler*

"Nothing, so it seems to me," said the stranger, "is more beautiful than the love that has weathered the storms of life..."

—Jerome Klalpka Jerome, *Three Men in a Boat*

Chapter 7
After Upsets, Cleanup Procedures

The skills this book has covered thus far have been preventive—ways to avert irritations that mar day-to-day life. Alas, sometimes prevention doesn't succeed. What can a couple do when their talk has become toxic? How do you clean up after bad feelings have erupted to the point of a major toxic spill?

Ineffective Cleanup Strategies

When things go wrong and tempers erupt, the urge to make things better can easily make things worse. Negative recovery strategies increase the bad feelings on both sides, and do little to prevent similar upsets from occurring again. After an upset do you find yourself using the following strategies?

- *Blame*— looking for whose fault it was
- *Retribution*— looking for ways of getting even
- *Punishment*— finding ways to punish your spouse for having hurt your feelings
- *Humiliation*— making the point about how hurt you feel by trying to evoke shame and guilt

Negative strategies may succeed in giving you a sense of justice fulfilled, but they do not promote healing. Getting even, in fact, turns the tables so that your partner feels injured and wants to retaliate. As a rule, as people feel worse they tend to act worse, not better, and your spouse is probably no exception.

Take Ronald and Pauline, for example. They cared deeply for each other, but their poor skills at recovering from difficulties turned a disappointing setback into a major, marriage-threatening disaster.

> *Ronald had promised his wife that he would stop drinking. He did very well for over a year, and then one night, on a lengthy sales trip, he stepped into a bar. When Pauline found out, she was furious. Ronald, already shameful and distressed at having slipped, felt mortified.*
>
> *For the next several months, Pauline spoke angrily to Ronald almost all the time, greeting Ronald with a scowl when he returned from work, and criticizing him for watching TV, for leaving dishes in the sink, and for not playing enough with the children. From her perspective, Pauline was punishing Ronald so that he would not again slip back into drinking. The actual impact, however, was to demoralize Ronald, further lowering his resistance. Within several months, Ronald had resumed steady drinking. Before long, Ronald's job was in jeopardy as well.*

Ronald made a definite mistake by taking that first drink after his year of sobriety. Pauline's relentless anger then deepened his already self-critical depression. When people are depressed they have a harder time sticking with their intentions to change. By contrast, if Ronald and Pauline had been able to talk over his mistake constructively, they might have been able to work together to help him return to his alcohol-free life.

The following strategies transform upsets into positive growth experiences. All are based on the principle that what comes after the upset determines its lasting impact. In music, a dissonant chord evokes a momentary uneasy feeling. When the odd sound is resolved by a subsequent chord that reestablishes harmony, the sequence evokes a feeling of well-being. So it is with disagreements, misunderstandings, and emotional injuries. Dissonant moments need to be followed by the reestablishment of cooperation and caring.

Healing Strategy 1: *Hearing*

Hearing—genuinely understanding your spouse's concerns—promotes healing. Healing, not more hurting, creates recovery. With hearing, the negative energies generated by upsets can be transformed into powerful opportunities to add to the strength and love in your marriage.

Hearing in the midst of a toxic upset, is a two-step process:

1. First, pause and distract.
2. Then backtrack to hear.

♥ Pause and distract, then backtrack to rehear

In the heat of disagreement, you can easily slip from the ABCDs into defensive irritability. To heal from the minor bruises this slippage causes, it helps to take a break from the sensitive discussion by pausing and changing the subject for a few minutes.

Pause for damage control, to stop the negative words or negative listening that were beginning to contaminate your conversation. This step is a mini version of the disengagement into separate rooms that prevents large fights from escalating. Pausing and changing briefly to another topic of conversation gives you a chance to cool down.

Then, when you both feel cooled down, returning to the difficult topic can give you a second chance to hear each other. In this "second draft" of the discussion, focus on listening well, on being sure that you understand what your partner is trying to tell you. To the extent that you hear each other, you will both feel *healed*.

Newlyweds Ian and Marissa generally got along quite well. Like many couples, however, from time to time they would begin to *yes but* each other. Understanding *yes but* helped them recognize why their conversations sometimes became frustrating. Now they faced the challenging task of converting their new understanding into reliably better listening skills.

> Marissa and Ian, waiting for their dinner in a restaurant, were discussing the role of women in Biblical stories, a sensitive topic for them. "Women don't appear in the Bible as visibly as men," Marissa observed.
> "Yes, but that doesn't mean they are discriminated against," Ian countered.

Ian's *yes but* heralded trouble ahead.

> "I'm just saying that there are not as many stories about women as about men," Marissa reiterated.
> Ian, getting more agitated, repeated his first response, "Yes, but that doesn't mean the Bible puts them in a bad light or makes them second-class citizens."

Feeling unheard, Marissa restated her point, leaving Ian feeling unheard.

> "Ian, please don't keep yes but-ing what I'm trying to tell you," Marissa said, trying to stay calm but feeling a growing impatience.
> "Don't tell me what to do!" Ian snapped.

Marissa's attempt to redirect the dialogue backfired. Her crossover, telling Ian what he should do, fanned the flames of his irritability. He experienced

Marissa's attempt to get the dialogue back on track as an attempt to control him, which sets off a particularly sensitive alarm.

Pause and distract

Ian realized it was time to implement damage control. He initiated a pause in their disagreement by talking about their food, which was just coming out. "What do you think of the salad dressing, Marissa? As good as the vinaigrette I make?" Ian joked.

Backtrack to rehear

Reengagement after a break—whether a brief pause or a disengagement of several hours—needs to start with talking about safe, neutral topics. Ian and Marissa know that they can always return to the inflammatory dialogue at a later time to figure out what went wrong, to do a better second draft.

As they were eating dessert, Marissa asked Ian, "Do you feel ready to return to look at how we became overheated?"

"OK. Good thing our food came," Ian remembered. "With hindsight, hunger probably was a part of it for me. When my blood sugar drops, I get short-fused and negative. Religion is touchy to talk about anyway, and when I'm hungry it's probably highly risky. It sounded to me like you were disparaging the Bible and going into a putdown of religion. Were you?"

"In fact," Marissa replied, "what I was saying was far more benign. My point was just that the Bible is mostly about men, and there aren't all that many females who are very visible. It was just an observation."

"Doesn't sound very controversial now," Ian noted.

"The lesson for me," Marissa continued, "is that when I hear us getting off track, telling you what I think you should be doing differently is guaranteed to make matters worse. Next time maybe I'll ask you what your agitation is about when you get hyper-energized and give yes buts. Or I'll switch topics. Would those be better than asking you to stop yes but-ing me?"

"Any of those would have been vastly better for me. When you tell me not to yes but all my autonomy alarms go off; I get mad almost instantaneously. As for what I've learned, I can see that late dinners may be elegant but they do me in. Next time we're going to eat late, I'll grab something from the refrigerator to keep me going."

Pausing their escalating discussion served as damage control. Then, with their post-upset rehearing, Ian and Marissa converted their unpleasant spat to a satisfying opportunity for mutual growth.

Healing Strategy 2: *Apologizing*

Apologies accelerate recovery from upsets. They alleviate the pain of emotional wounds, disinfect festering bad feelings, and promote rapid healing. How do they work these miracles? Apologies acknowledge what has happened. They offer regrets for any hurt that might have been incurred. They convey that the hurting was not on purpose, but rather an unintended consequence of something that was intended to be positive.

Apologies accomplish a lot. It's no wonder then that while we may think of apologies as a simple matter of saying, "I'm sorry," a fully effective apology generally includes multiple parts. I have found in my work that distressed couples rarely use all steps of apology. Few therefore know the benefits of apologies' full healing power.

In its most basic form, apologizing is a five-step process:

1. Express regret.

2. Accept responsibility.

3. Clarify nonintentionality.

4. Explain the circumstances.

5. Repair the damage.

The apology sequence

Let's look at each of the steps in detail.

1. Express regret

Express regret for any harm you may have caused. If your tone of voice indicates genuine concern, your regrets clarify that you have heard the suffering the other person has experienced.

2. Accept responsibility

Accept responsibility by detailing what you see as having been *your specific part* in the event, for example, "I'm sorry that I forgot to pick up the laundry on my way home from work."

While no one likes to say "I goofed," being able to make that simple statement has enormous power to convert negative moments to positive ones. Apologies do not require groveling. To the contrary, there is great dignity in a straightforward acknowledgment of error.

3. Clarify nonintentionality

Say explicitly that you did not mean to cause hurt or harm. "I certainly didn't mean to leave you without something to wear. I must have driven home in a blur."

Explaining that you did not hurt the other person on purpose has major healing power. If someone hurts us intentionally, we become angry as a defense—to prevent them from injuring us the same way again. By contrast, when we know we were not injured on purpose, we can relax.

4. Explain the circumstances

Describe what you believe happened. "I was preoccupied about my new manager. He's impossible to work with. He takes the fun out of our office."

If the hurt was unintentional, then how did it happen? Your alternative explanation—"a miscommunication", "I was tired and hungry," "It was a casualty of rushing, of overload"—furthers digestion of the incident. These aren't excuses; they are mitigating circumstances.

5. Repair the damage

Fix the problem or offer restitution for damages. "How about if I wash and iron a shirt for you tonight? It won't be quite as spiffy as the cleaners can do, but I'll do my best."

While apologies are complex in that they have several steps, they still can be quite brief. For instance, if you were walking quickly down a street and inadvertently bumped into an elderly gentleman carrying a bag of groceries, how would you apologize when his groceries spilled? In that circumstance you would probably flow quite readily through the five steps:

1. *Express regret:* "I'm so sorry..."
2. *Accept responsibility* by specifying your error: "for bumping into you."
3. *Clarify nonintentionality:* "I sure didn't mean to run into you."
4. *Explain the circumstances:* "I'm afraid that I was rushing to get to a meeting, not looking where I was going."
5. *Repair the damage:* "Are you OK? Here, let me pick up the groceries for you. Let's make sure nothing's broken."

By contrast with this concise apology sequence, in the following situation lengthier apologies lead to interesting discussion. In both cases, apologizing clearly is not the same as saying, "It's all my fault," or "I'm to blame." "I'm sorry" means "I regret what happened and my part in it."

Louis and Julie are athletic, silver-haired retirees. Since retirement they have been spending more time together, and have been exploring new activities. In their child-rearing and career years, when they both worked long hours at separate workplaces, they seldom argued. Perhaps because of many new situations that they face with their increased togetherness, arguments erupt more often than they used to.

Bike-riding on a warm summer day, Louis and Julie came to a main street. They had to cross to get to the low-traffic residential area on the other side. Julie glanced up the street, saw a car coming, and pedaled fast to cross quickly. Louis, riding behind her, also saw the oncoming car and stopped to let it pass.

Seeing Julie racing in front of the car, Louis suddenly felt anxious. "Julie, Look out!" he shouted. Julie braked slightly as she looked about to see what was triggering her husband's alarm. Fortunately, she was still able to make the crossing before the fast-moving car buzzed by.

When she had safely reached the other side of the street, however, Julie felt a wave of fury. "Calling to me like that almost made me get hit!" She spoke sharply to Louis, "I could see the car. I'm not a child."

Julie's anger triggered a quick retort from Louis, who felt unfairly accused. "Why did you race the car? That was foolish!"

Now, both angry, they pedaled for a few minutes in silence. The pause gave them time to calm down. They each began to be able to think about what had happened without blaming. They both had felt wronged, so thinking about the incident without blaming took careful self-direction. Louis realized that he needed to focus on his own role in the upset instead of ruminating on what Julie had done. Doing so, he was pleasantly surprised that he soon felt calmer and began to have insights into his part in the upset. After a few more minutes he was able to speak with Julie.

1. Express regret

"I'm sorry," Louis said, "that I shouted to you to look out when you were crossing the street." Regret arose spontaneously as Louis realized that he had made a mistake and that had caused his wife potential harm.

2. Accept responsibility

"I misjudged the distance of that oncoming car," Louis continued. "It looked unsafe to me, but I see now that you did see the car coming and made a reasonable decision. My panic call to you probably did put you in more danger, not less."

Louis's statement of what specifically he was apologizing for assures Louis and Julie that they are talking about the same problem. At the same time, his noninflammatory description of what he did detoxifies his error.

*"I misjudged the distance" offers a neutral alternative to Julie's interpreta-
tion that he had treated her like a child.*

*Louis's ability to admit his error rests on his understanding that humans
are not designed to be error-proof. The ability to make mistakes distin-
guishes us from angels and keeps us humble.*

*Julie appreciated Louis's apology: "Thanks Louis. I appreciate that. I was
scared when you called out. I almost stopped in the middle of the road to
see what you were shouting about. Stopping would have been a disaster."*

*By verbalizing her acceptance of Louis's apology, Julie kept the apology
sequence moving forward.*

3. Clarify nonintentionality

Louis continued, "I didn't mean to scare you."

*"I see that now," Julie concluded. Knowing that Louis's mistake was inad-
vertent left her feeling considerably better about the incident.*

4. Explain the circumstances

*"I think I get anxious and am more likely to misjudge danger when I'm so
hot. The sun is really intense," Louis continued. Understanding the situational factors allows Louis to save face. It also puts his error into an appropriate perspective. Most upsets occur because of difficult circumstances.*

5. Repair the damages

*"Are you feeling OK now?" Louis asked, checking for any remaining damage.
"Definitely. Thanks. Except that I've had too much sun, too," Julie added.
"Let's stop somewhere soon for shade and rest."*

By checking to be sure no remaining damages need fixing, Louis has completed his end of the apology process. Julie feels better. The bike trip and life
go on.

This apology, which took several minutes, made all the difference between
a fun day and an unpleasant one. Apologies are worth learning to do well.

Look at all three sides

Interestingly, couples can recover from an upset as long as at least one
of them is able to complete a full apology sequence. When both partners are able to whiz through an apology, this two-sided process brings calm
and harmony faster and more fully. Best of all, when both partners apologize
and are also able to add an explanation about the part played by external circumstances, this "three-sided" apology will resolve the mishap with a maximum of goodwill.

Good enough: The one-sided apology

Louis's initial apology to Julie could suffice in this instance. He apologized to her, and their calm was restored.

Better: The two-sided, symmetrical apology

Louis did succeed in reestablishing goodwill with his apology. Still, Julie could have picked up the ball and run with it from there by adding, "Actually, Louis, your misreading of danger from that car was not so far off. Darting across the street in front of it was a bit risky. I'm sorry for having taken a risk that panicked you."

She could also have added, "And I'm sorry to have barked at you. I knew that you were just concerned for my safety. I was shaken from the incident, and when I feel scared, I have a bad habit of acting mad."

Best: The three-sided apology

The apologies of both parties plus an understanding of the context the upset occurred in yields the most satisfactory conclusion: "So we both goofed," Louis summed up. "And is it ever hot today! It's easy to get irritable in this heat. Next time we ride, let's go earlier in the morning or late in the afternoon, when the sun is less intense."

Now no one is to blame. Both spouses have acknowledged their mistakes. Both have gained some understandings about themselves, each other, and the external circumstance—heat—that can help to prevent similar upsets in the future.

Strive for symmetry

If either you or your partner seems to be doing most of the apologizing, be wary. The difference could be a simple matter of skills. Alternatively, sometimes family-of-origin experiences have given one partner a tendency to believe that if something is wrong it must be his or her fault. Gender differences also may play a role. In traditional families, women generally have been regarded as responsible for the emotional well-being of a family, and consequently have often assumed the main responsibility for upsets.

A lopsided relationship, in which one person does considerably more apologizing than the other, can also indicate that one partner has a serious problem that he or she is apologizing for but not fixing. If you have a serious anger problem, for instance, a cycle of anger, apology, calm, and more anger, you are not succeeding in making adequate changes. Procrastination, lateness, disorganization, and messiness can get caught in similar cycles, in which regret does not result in genuine change.

Another possible reason one person may be doing more apologizing than the other is that one partner may be in the habit of blaming. If you are not accustomed to using insight to look at your part in what happened, you may be at risk for routinely blaming when things go wrong.

If you tend to assume responsibility for problems and your partner is blame-oriented, or vice versa, both of you are likely to end up unhappy. The partner who takes excessive blame will tend toward depression, and the blaming spouse will be at risk for polluting the household with chronic anger, as in the following example.

> Marina and Leo looked like a perfectly matched couple, both tall and blond, and in their late thirties. Their asymmetrical apologizing, however, proved disastrous to their marriage.
>
> Marina, generally a self-confident mother and schoolteacher, was considering leaving her marriage. Her husband, Leo, appeared mellow and charming to everyone else, but in the privacy of their home was frequently angry. Marina was tired of feeling defensive, especially about enjoying anything, which seemed to be a particular trigger for accusations.
>
> Marina felt, as she had seen her mother feel toward her father, that their problems were her fault. Her usual playfulness had gradually given way to persistent self-criticism, a hallmark of depression.
>
> Finally Marina told Leo that she had become too demoralized. The only way she could feel better was to leave the marriage. Leo was stunned, then furious, accusing Marina of abandoning him and their daughters.
>
> Marina and Leo had been living separately for almost a year and were about to finalize their divorce when Leo suddenly woke up—literally woke up in the middle of the night—to what he had been doing. He realized that he was deeply, unconsciously ashamed about what felt to him like a large and terrifying secret. From time to time Leo had been using cocaine. He had not admitted even to himself that he was addicted, but he suddenly understood that his anger at his wife had been a way of covering up his drug habit.
>
> Rather than show his weakness to his wife, Leo had masked his habit and the anxiety it caused him with anger. He had been criticizing his wife as if tearing her down would somehow lift him up. Subconsciously, he had been escaping his guilt and shame by transferring them onto Marina.
>
> As Leo understood his part in the asymmetrical apologizing in their relationship, he and Marina were able to talk openly for the first time about his drug use. To his surprise, rather than adding to his despair, admitting his difficulty to his wife actually brought Leo relief. Hearing that their problem had been drugs, not anything she had been doing, Marina felt the dark cloud around her lifting and her self-confidence returning.

Unfortunately, by this time Marina had accepted the end of her mar-
riage. She had begun dating other men and was not willing to risk a return
to Leo. While Leo's awakening had been in time to make their subsequent
years as coparents that much more cooperative, it came too late to save
the marriage.

Healing Strategy 3: *Piecing Together the Puzzle*

Sometimes when arguments erupt neither of you may understand how the situation became so inflamed. Again, the seemingly easy solution is for each mate to blame the other. The minor solace of believing the upset to be the other person's fault exacts high costs in ill will and negative views of each other. Alternatively, you can learn to approach a confusing upset as a jigsaw puzzle to be pieced together. The pictures that emerge provide understandings for preventing similar upsets in the future.

This strategy sandwiches an apology between puzzle-making and learning.

1. Piece together the puzzle of what happened.

2. Apologize.

3. Learn to convert the upset into an opportunity for shared growth.

Starting with assembling the puzzle makes cleaning up intriguing instead of painful. The learning orientation at the end offers the reward of increased understanding of yourself, your partner, and the situations you share.

1. Piece together the puzzle of what happened

To succeed in piecing together an understanding of what happened, it is essential to follow the rule about crossovers. You get to talk about what you experienced; your partner tells what he or she experienced; neither talks about the other. Any mention of what the other person did needs to be included within the safe framework of the "When you... I..." formula.

Emma and Daniel, a dignified couple in their late forties, generally
treated each other with respect. A major argument erupted, however, when
they tried to talk after an unpleasant incident at the airport. They and
their son Pete had been rushing to catch a plane, and Daniel had spoken
uncharacteristically angrily to the airline ticket agent. Several minutes after-
ward Emma expressed her chagrin. The two of them then began attacking
each other. They did succeed in disengaging to stop their rapid escalation,
but not until both of them felt wrongly accused and emotionally injured.
Daniel and Emma waited several days—until they had cooled down

enough to have had some normal interactions—before they tried to piece together the puzzle. They chose a safe, quiet, and unhurried time and place to talk.

Emma said to Daniel, "When you chewed out the airline ticket agent, I felt mortified. It's one thing when you get mad occasionally at home, but I've never seen you speak so harshly to anyone in public. Like I said then, I felt embarrassed for you; it seemed so out of character."

Emma's *when you* launched the puzzle-solving. Daniel was able to follow suit, sticking with *I* and *when you* statements.

Daniel thought for a bit. "I was reacting to your comment about my anger being out of character. When you had said that I went ballistic, I thought you were saying that my real character is to be mean and intimi-dating. Was that what you meant?"

Questions are particularly helpful in piecing together the puzzle.

"Not at all," Emma reassured him. "I was shocked to see you because your usual character is so gentlemanly."

Already the first two puzzle pieces had clarified as a misunderstanding.

Daniel continued, "When the airline clerk told us there was no reserva-tion for Pete on our flight, she wanted us leave him to travel alone on a later flight. How stupid! I had to intimidate her in order to get her to do what she should have done in the first place, which was to put him at the top of the list for standby seats. So I did chew her out. I thought you would be proud of how strongly I dealt with the situation. I was crushed when you criticized me; I thought I'd been a hero."

Gradually the full picture of what happened became clear, with Daniel's pieces of what he felt, thought, said, and did interfacing with what Emma felt, thought, said, and did. By the time the puzzle was complete, both of them were able to see the same full picture.

2. Apologize

When both partners each take full responsibility for their part in an upset, the symmetrical apologies result in rapid healing.

With the puzzle clear, Emma and Daniel were ready to move on to the middle part of the cleanup, apologies. They took turns, each acknowledging and regretting their mate's frustrations in the incident.

"I'm sorry my comment sounded like I was saying you were a bad person. I don't like that kind of angry scene, but I still think you are dear, kindly, and genteel," Emma said.

"And I'm sorry that once I got defensive I stopped listening to you. I was supercharged from fighting with the agent. In fact, I agree that it was an ugly scene. I probably could have asked right away to talk with her supervisor. I got carried away. I went into my prosecuting attorney mode and treated her like an opposing witness in the courtroom. It's not pretty to treat people like that. I was like a boxer beating up on people outside of the ring. I see now why you were embarrassed for me."

Daniel had experienced what psychologists call "flooding," the sudden rush of explosive anger described in Chapter 5.

3. Learn, to convert the upset into shared growth

The final phase of cleaning up after a toxic spill involves learning something positive from it, both to deepen your understanding of yourself and your partner, and to prevent similar difficulties from occurring in the future.

Emma concluded, "As much as I didn't like being seen next to a man who would get so mad at a poor airline clerk, I do appreciate that I have a husband who I am sure would come to our family's defense in any dangerous circumstance. I've learned that you have a side that I hadn't seen before. I just hope we won't need to let it loose again."

"Good thing you don't see me in the courtroom!" Daniel chuckled. "And I've learned that I have to keep that kind of behavior where it belongs. Cross-examining witnesses is one thing. Out in the world I can hold the line at being firm without getting nasty. What is it they say? 'Attack the problem; not the person.'"

Reality is messy

Shakespeare tells us "the course of true love never did run smooth"; the same is true of the course of the three steps described above. The flow is likely to begin with a couple of puzzle pieces, add an apology or two, return for more puzzle pieces, advance for some learning, and then maybe even return for another apology.

Also, the three pieces are seldom of equal sizes. Often the bulk of the talking needs to be in puzzle-solving. Once the details of what each of you experienced have been fully elaborated, the apology and learning phases may take only a few brief interchanges.

Cleaning Up Old Negative Feelings

Old upsets have remarkable power to leave lingering resentments. Fortunately, though, older upsets often prove relatively easy to clean up, because emotions become less sensitive with time. The steps for cleaning these up are the same as above.

> *Merry and Gil both have earned national prominence in their respective careers and have enjoyed an excellent marriage. As the last of their three children left for college, they were surprised when Merry suddenly experienced a surge of angry resentment toward her husband. The ending of her parenting years had rekindled a long-smoldering anger.*

By utilizing the steps of cleaning up after toxic spills, Merry and Gil came to a new understanding of an earlier era in their life.

1. Piece together the puzzle of what happened

> *Merry shared with Gil the nagging doubts she had long harbored when their children were growing up. "I enjoyed my work, but I felt forced into it. If I had been able to choose, I would have been home when the kids got out of school."*
>
> *Gil was surprised. He explained why he had insisted on her working. "I was concerned about the deep depression you seemed to be sinking into. I felt like I had to do something, not just to help you, but because we were all sinking along with you. When our neighbor suddenly needed someone to rescue his family business, it seemed like a gift from heaven. I thought if you had to go off to work every day maybe you would go back to feeling normal. I knew you'd do a great job, because organizing and marketing have always been your strengths. I thought maybe staying home all day was getting you down. I hoped the business would help you to feel good again. And it looked to me like it worked."*
>
> *Merry thought a moment and then replied, "I never knew that's why you wanted me to work! I always assumed that it was because you wanted us to have more money. I felt used, like you wanted me to be the family slave, earning money and handling the kids and the house, too."*

Sharing the puzzle pieces of their thoughts and feelings began to clear up a misunderstanding that had troubled Merry for years.

> *Gil had become curious. "I thought you loved your work. Did you?"*
> *"Yes and no," Merry answered. "You were right that the job was a*

*good match for my skills and interests. And it probably did pull me
out of the awful dark hole I had sunk into. The problem was the hours.
Too many!"*

2. Apologize

*Gil and Merry were able to offer symmetrical apologies, each taking
responsibility for their own part of the misunderstanding. "I'm really sorry,
Merry," Gil said with sincerity, "for my part in your having worked more
than you wanted to. I'm relieved that my interpretation of what you needed
wasn't completely wrong. But I can see now that it would have been better
to ask you what you wanted, instead of assuming I knew best and making
decisions for you."*

*"Thank you, Gil. I really appreciate your willingness to admit your part
in the mess up. I wish I'd told you that the hours were too long. I assumed
you knew that the job kept me at work too late. I complained. I hinted. But
I never looked you, or myself, square in the eye and said that what I wanted
was to work fewer hours and have more time to be a mother."*

3. Learn, to convert the upset into shared growth

*Merry continued, "When I hear that people need me—you, the kids, my
boss—I become deaf to what I want. I guess I make myself into a slave."*

Merry had a strong case of excessive altruism. Like many women, she had
trouble hearing her own needs when others needed her. While altruism is
essential for mothering an infant, whose needs do really need to come before
your own, for most other relationships altruism needs to be tempered with
information about your own desires.

*Merry continued, "I see now that when I want you to hear me, I need to
start by hearing myself. Instead of just feeling angry at you I need to ask
myself 'What do I want?' and to start asking you what you want instead of
reading your mind— as if you're my master."*

*"Slave driver wouldn't be my first choice of occupation," Gil laughed. "I
see things differently now, too. I'm opting out of my job as decision maker
for everyone. As our boys need to make job decisions, or choose wives, same
thing. I'll talk it over with them, but I won't take over. It's hard enough making my own decisions."*

*"Thanks for talking, Gil." Merry smiled. "And the truth is that our kids
seemed to do fine in spite of my working. I lost out. I lost the chance to be
at home when the kids got home from school. I lost the chance to bake
them cookies. But with luck I'll get a second chance. If the boys marry and*

have kids, I'm going to be the world's most available grandmom.

"Actually, all those years of working so hard are why I have work that I love today at an income that I never dreamed of. We're both at the peak of our careers. Your pushing me to work was probably how we made it... Just don't try it again," Merry joked.

"Not a chance," Gil laughed.

The Power of Healing

Upsets with your partner can alter your sense of personal
power and decrease your sense of well-being.

If you react to an upset with anger, blaming your mate for the difficulty, you may actually feel more powerful, puffed up with righteous indignation. This feeling of larger-than-normal size brings a spurious sense of power, a power to control or hurt your mate, but does not necessarily give you the power to feel good yourself. In contrast with this negative energy of angry power, true empowerment is not at your partner's expense. True empowerment does not depend on hurting your mate for you to feel good.

After an upset, if you do not have a process for healing, you may experience what I call a depressive collapse. If so, like a balloon losing its air, you will feel your sense of personal power diminishing. If you close your eyes then and visualize yourself and your partner interacting, your mate is likely to look large and you quite small. Depression is a disorder of power with feelings of helplessness, hopelessness, and smallness.

One sign of depressive collapse is the presence of self-critical or self-demeaning thoughts. Another can be the sense that your world is covered by a dark cloud. After upsetting interactions, these depressed thoughts and feelings can last for quite some time, especially if you continue to feel like your mate is large and powerful and you are smaller and helpless.

Fortunately, on a happier note, your positive sense of power, of yourself as a mature, competent, and resilient person, is likely to return immediately if you and your partner can successfully negotiate any of the three healing strategies in this chapter. As both of you resume feeling a full personal sense of self-worth and appreciation of each other, your sense of the power of the two of you will again feel strong. The good-to-be-alive, great-to-be-together feelings will return.

Notes

Notes

Ah! When shall all men's good
Be each man's rule, and universal peace
Lie like a shaft of light across the land?

—Alfred, Lord Tennyson, "The Golden Year"

Chapter 8

Shared Decision Making

In traditional ballroom dancing the man led and the woman followed. So it has been in traditional marriages. Hierarchical decision making worked fine, provided the husband made good decisions, the wife trusted the man's decisions, and the man's decisions routinely incorporated input from his wife. In today's world, however, wives expect to be co-choreographers in the dance of their married life. To make decisions together with the grace of traditional ballroom dancers, couples need skills for collaborative decision making.

What kinds of questions can be resolved with shared decision making? Decisions that affect both of you—and that at least one of you doesn't want delegated to just one person—need to be made jointly. Issues that many couples decide together include how to spend money, how orderly and how clean to keep the house, where to live, how many children to have and how to raise them, as well as day-to-day decisions of what time to go to bed, when to leave a party, and what TV programs to watch.

Decisions that involve personal self-care need to remain the responsibility of each individual. How much you eat, what you wear, whether you put on a coat when you go outside, what you do with your leisure time—these kinds of personal questions need to be left up to each of you as individuals. Otherwise you will find yourselves irritating each other by crossing over the boundaries of who is who. What I do, feel, and say needs to be up to me. By contrast, which house we buy or apartment *we* rent generally is a shared decision.

In between the clearly *we* and the purely *I* decisions lies a third category of decisions, the "designated driver" decisions. Designating spheres of responsibility simplifies running a household. Who is in charge of what can be jointly decided. Subsequent decisions for the most part can be handled by the person in charge. You might jointly decide to eat more fruits and vegetables; the designated shopper then would implement that shared decision.

This chapter focuses on various ways to make decisions collaboratively.

- Both of you offer input about your concerns, about what is important to you in the decision.
- Both of you feel you have equal say, equal power, in deciding the outcome.
- Both of you feel good about the decisions you make.
- The decisions are win-win, responsive to what both of you want.

By cooperating in this way, you as a couple can make far better decisions than either of you alone could have made. Shared decision making, however, can be challenging. There is no place for selfishness—"my concerns are the only ones that count"—in this process. Nor is there a place for competition, one-upmanship, or for that matter, excessive altruism.

When Decisions Are Not Made Cooperatively

Without collaborative problem solving, decisions that affect both of you can easily trigger negative reactions from minor irritation to large upheavals:

- *Anger*— Decision-making by who argues more strongly or can outlast the other evokes anger. Force-it decision making (see Chapter 4) invites unpleasant bickering and will often result in decisions that please neither of you.
- *Depression*— If one of you makes a decision that does not take into account the other's concerns, and the other goes along with it, depression is the by-product. As explained at the end of the last chapter, depression is a disorder of power.
- *Anxiety*— Unresolved decisions evoke anxiety. If you leave a significant decision unmade for fear that discussion will provoke undesirable conflict, tensions will hover over your household. Meanwhile, postponing decisions can exacerbate problem situations.
- *Obsessive-compulsive disorders and addictions*— To escape from potential conflict, one (or both) of you may resort to distractions such as drinking, drugs, eating disorders, or hypochondriacal preoccupations. Distraction leaves decisions unresolved. Self-destructive distractions also create additional problems.

If you were animals, say two dogs fighting over a bone, you would have only the four above options: *fight,* the anger route; *submit,* the depressive route; *freeze,* the anxiety route; or *flee,* the addictions route. Fortunately, people can use words. With words to express ideas and share information, collaborative decision making becomes a fifth, very gratifying option. People can squander their gift of language by using it on lower-level animal strategies, or they can learn to use language to discover mutually satisfying, win-win solutions. These five options are summarized in Table 7 (Heitler 1993).

Adversarial versus collaborative decision making

Collaborative problem solving depends upon both parties maintaining the cooperative stance of allies who are facing a problem together. Both of you need to regard the problem as the problem, not each other. In adversarial conflict, by contrast, you feel like opposing sides in battle rather than like life partners facing choices together. As you read the following lists, you might keep in mind a decision you and your partner recently may have faced. Were you primarily adversarial, cooperative, or some of each?

Adversarial Dialogue	Collaborative Dialogue
Either-or thinking	Yes and thinking
Description of the problem in extremist, inflammatory language	Attention to realities, with neutral language
Accusatory, critical and/or blaming stance	Focuses on the problems, not the people
Focuses on past mistakes	Focuses on the present dilemma and on solutions for the future
Listening for what's wrong with or missing in what the other says	Listening for what's right and useful in what the other says
Disparaging the other's input	Respecting the other's input
Generates negative energy and impulse to harm the other side	Creates positive energy, compassion for the other
Creates an atmosphere of hopelessness	Creates an atmosphere of enthusiasm
Invites personal attacks on the other to invalidate his or her position	Invites consideration for the other's concerns
Yields win-lose outcome	Yields mutually beneficial solutions

TABLE 7   The Five Basic Conflict Strategies

Strategy	Canine Behavior	Human Equivalent	Emotional Results
Fight	Growling or biting each other for possession of the bone.	Insisting on your preferred solution, without regard for your spouse's preference • Demanding, raising your voice or speaking in an irritated tone • Blaming, accusing, criticizing • Shouting or using force • Belittling your mate's opinions to minimize their influence • Passive-aggression, such as agreeing but not following through, sulking, and manipulating by guilt	*Anger*
Submit	Allowing the other dog to take the bone, sitting or lying in a submissive posture, tail between legs.	Yielding, lowering your aspirations, settling for less than you want in order to keep the relationship • Giving in or giving up • Agreeing so as to end the conflict and keep the peace • Surrendering to what your partner wants at the expense of your own preferences	*Depression,* feelings of hopelessness and helplessness; excessive altruism
Freeze	Hovering around the bone without definitive action.	Becoming immobilized • Taking no action, using a wait-and-see approach • Staying aware of a problem without gathering information or choosing a course of action	*Anxiety,* passivity, feelings of panic
Flee	Going on to something else rather than risking a fight.	Escaping, withdrawing • Leaving the scene of the conflict physically or changing the topic • Ceasing to talk or escaping into drugs or other distractions	*Obsessional thinking, compulsive behaviors,* such as drinking or eating disorders; denial
Problem Solve	Dogs can't talk.	Seeking options that satisfy both of you • Talking, listening, gathering information • Generating options for mutually satisfying solutions	*Healthy feelings of well-being, a strong and loving marriage*

Pseudo-consensus—the several flavors of domination

Couples sometimes confuse agreement by domination with genuine consensus building. What is the difference, especially when there has been no overt fighting? When decisions are made by domination, by one person either issuing directives or wearing the other down with persistence, the outcomes do not reflect the concerns of both. When the preferences of only one mate hold sway, decisions are not collaborative, even if there is apparent mutual consent. In the following two examples, for instance, there was no overt fighting, but the processes were dominant-submissive, not cooperative.

> "Will you please tell those kids to hold off on their showers until I finish mine?!" Gerson shouted angrily down the stairs. "She knows there's not enough water pressure for two showers at once," he muttered angrily as he returned to the bathroom. "Doesn't she give a darn what I want?"
>
> "Oh dear," thought Holly as she turned to the children's bathroom. "That means they'll miss the schoolbus again. Which means I'll have to drive them, and that means I'll be late for work. If I lose my job, none of us will be very happy. But if he doesn't get hot water, he gets hot tempered, and I don't want another big fight. I don't have the energy to deal with that today. And the kids get too upset when we fight."
>
> ....
>
> "I really would love it if you would play tennis with me on Sunday morning," Penny told her husband Oscar.
>
> "No, Penny," Oscar answered. "We played golf this morning, and tennis tomorrow feels like too much,"
>
> "The golf was fun, and the tennis will be, too. Can't you please?"
>
> "No. Too much sun for me, and besides I have work around the house I want to get done."
>
> "Oh please. Can't you possibly join me? Just for an hour? It's been so long since we've played together, and I've already reserved a court."
>
> "I really don't want to."
>
> "Oh please, just this one Sunday, let's play."
>
> "Well, all right," he reluctantly agreed.

What is missing? What makes these two stories examples of pseudo- rather than real cooperative decision making? Gerson in the first example and Penny in the second lack *bilateral listening*. They each hear their own desires much louder than those of their mate. Consequently, they feel like the decision has been mutual, when in fact their partner has given in. Decisions made by submission do not pass muster as shared decisions. Both parties are involved, but the concerns of only one have been taken into account.

In fact, as often happens with couples who use these dominant-submissive decision-making patterns, the partners took turns being winner and loser. Gerson won the shower, and Holly withheld affection in return. Penny got her tennis game, and Oscar spent a lot of money on a car that his wife didn't feel they could afford. All four people became increasingly angry and depressed.

By contrast, once you have genuinely mastered the art of shared decision making, all your decisions will feel positive to both of you. Neither mate will feel the frustration of giving up on concerns of either minor or major importance. Both of you will consistently feel that what you want matters.

Good intentions are not enough

Before we look at how sharing decisions can be accomplished, let's take a close-up look at how attempts at shared decision making can go awry.

Our old friends Len and Linda, who we know have problems with basic communication skills, also lack a process other than tug of war for making shared decisions. In this section, we'll see how they go about trying to make a decision together; then in the next section we'll look at how Gina and Gerald handle the same dilemma.

> Linda and Len, expecting another child in several months, came home tired from work to find a note from the handyman saying that their old washing machine cannot be repaired. "We'd better bring the kids and go out tonight to get a new washer," they agreed.

Making decisions when you are tired, hungry, or overloaded stacks the odds against cooperative dialogue.

> At the appliance store, feeling rushed, tired, and stressed by having their bored children along while they were shopping, Linda said, "I like this one with all the different settings. Let's just buy this one."
> "This one is much cheaper, and the manufacturer has a better repair record," countered Len.

Instead of validating her concerns about the features and then offering his concerns in addition, weaving their dialogue together, Len speaks as if his wife had not said anything.

> "But I don't want a washer that limits me to just a couple of options," reiterated Linda.

Linda's reply, starting with a *but*, continues the pattern of each spouse arguing for their own preference and against the other's. Linda *buts* away Len's concerns for money and repair record in order to try a second time to make her concern known.

"That's foolish if it's going to cost us more money," insisted Len.

Feeling also that his concerns are being ignored, Len belittles Linda's concerns. Again he is negating her concern instead of entering it into a shared information pool.

"You never listen to what matters to me!" pouted Linda, resenting Len's comment.

When dialogue slips off track, the first priority needs to be getting it back on track. Instead, Linda responds to Len's criticism with a counter-complaint. Since a complaint says what she doesn't want, not what she does want, the negativity of the dialogue escalates.

"Let's be sensible about this!" urged Len, trying to contain his anger. "We have big expenses with the kids."

While Len does sense that something needs to be done to improve the tone of the dialogue, his response disparages his wife's concerns in hopes of strengthening his position.

Linda could feel herself heating up. "I know we have kids at least as much as you do. You're just being selfish about the machine. You always want things your way."

The pattern of attack and counterattack has by now been established and is becoming increasingly personalized, leaving the problem of washing machines and focusing instead on the people.

"What do you want me to do? Buy foolishly and then have no money for other things we need?" Len hissed. "You're the one who's selfish. How will we pay for all the things the kids need, never mind save for their college!"

Additional weaponry, manipulation by guilt, is being brought to the scene of battle. While his money concerns are legitimate, by using them against his wife, Len makes it impossible for her to agree with him. Agreeing with his concerns would mean accepting the toxic message that her concerns are selfish.

Linda was glad they were in the store; if they'd been at home, both of them would be shouting by now. Still, the tension embarrassed her. She wanted to calm things down. "Oh well. We have to get something to wash clothes. I hate the limitations of that poorly designed machine you want to buy, but we've got to get the laundry done somehow."

Every couple has a typical escalation ceiling. Linda and Len usually bicker, insult each other hurtfully, and then retreat.

*"Well, if you're going to make such a big deal of it, let's waste our money
and buy the one with the gimmicks that you want," Len conceded angrily.*

The outcome is a decision that neither of them can enjoy. The solution has
been besmirched by an unpleasant decision-making process, and it does not
meet the full range of either of their concerns. Len and Linda both end up feeling frustrated and hurt, and they have a washer that will long remind them of
the unpleasant evening when they bought it.

The Win-Win Waltz

How would Gina and Gerald face the same dilemma? They would stick with
the communication fundamentals, and they would follow the three steps of the
Win-Win Waltz:

1. Express your initial positions.
2. Explore your underlying concerns.
3. Choose a mutually satisfying solution.

> *Gerald and Gina have also just returned from work. They discover a simi-
> lar note regarding their unfixable washing machine.*
> *"I'm so tired," Gerald moans. "I can't deal with this tonight."*
> *"Me, too," Gina adds, "And waiting to do something about it sounds
> even worse. We're way behind on laundry. We do need to get a new machine,
> and the next several days look even worse in terms of overly full schedules."*
> *"How about if we eat some supper, rest a bit, ask one of the high school
> kids next door to come baby-sit, and try going to the appliance store about
> eight-thirty?" Gerald asks.*

Gerald and Gina are aware of the impact that being tired, hungry, or overloaded can have on their ability to dialogue cooperatively. They show an ability to listen to themselves, to their physical cues about fatigue and hunger, as
well as to listen to each other.

> *"That plan would help me," Gina answers. "We'll both be less brittle
> that way. Let's try it."*

Gina and Gerald are so good at the Win-Win Waltz that they whiz through
the three steps right away to decide on a plan of action. Gerald's initial position is to wait until another day to get a new washer; Gina's is to go out and
get one that night. Their underlying concerns include: being too tired right
after work, being hungry, and feeling like bringing the children will overload

them. Their solution—to eat dinner and rest, get a baby-sitter for the children, and then go out later in the evening—puts them in a good mood by the time they actually do go out.

After eating and then relaxing as a family as they clean the kitchen, Gina and Gerald do in fact feel up to a visit to the appliance store. They head out in good humor discussing washing machines as they drive.

1. Express initial positions

Neither Gina nor Gerald have a specific washing machine in mind to buy, so they can pass over this first step. When, like Gina and Gerald in this instance, you do not have a solution in mind at the outset, you are free to explore options in more relaxed way. Because neither of you is attached to a particular solution, you can build consensus as you gather information.

2. Explore underlying concerns

"What kind of machine do you want? Any ideas about what's important to you?" Gerald asks Gina.

"Well, I don't know for sure," Gina muses. "I think though that the main considerations for me are the practical pieces. I want dials that are easy to read, a lid that stays open when you raise it and lots of different settings for different size loads and kinds of fabrics—the kind of things that I would notice every time I use it if they're not right. And capacity. I don't want to have to do laundry more than once a week, so I'd like a huge one."

The dialogue follows the ABCDs. Gina and Gerald each express their own concerns and ask about the other's, never talking for or about each other. Gerald's question indicates receptiveness to his wife's input, and Gina's comments indicate that she has the skill of insight, that is, of being able to focus inward to figure out and put into words her concerns and preferences.

Gerald chuckles, "You can see who does the laundry in this household. I never would have thought of dials and lids as something to pay attention to. I just think dollar signs and repair records. Repairs are the hidden part of the appliance's cost. A cheaper machine that keeps breaking would be a mistake. My salary sure is better than it used to be, but with the kids and all of those college educations down the pike, I'm concerned about watching our pennies."

Gerald listens to add Gina's concerns to their shared information pool. Digesting aloud the information he has taken in lets Gina know her concerns are being heard. He then adds the dimensions of import to him in the decision, braiding their dialogue.

As Gerald and Gina continue to talk, they utilize the Four Ss. The both speak in *short segments,* not long speeches. They maintain *symmetry,* speaking with more or less equal airtime and considering both their concerns with equal regard. They speak in *specifics* not just saying "I want the machine to work well," but noting the precise aspects of "working well" of import to each of them. And they *summarize* frequently the data they have accumulated. By using these basics, Gerald and Gina build consensus as they talk, setting themselves up for an easy decision by the end.

As Gerald and Gina browse the selection of washing machines, they begin by vetoing the machines with poorly designed dials or doors. They also note cost, and Gerald checks a consumer guidebook for information on frequency of repairs. As they look at the various options, they add to their criteria. Gerald realizes that color is important to him. He'd like a white washer, to match the rest of the kitchen. Gina realizes that buying a large-capacity machine is not worth the extra money because, with their modest-sized dryer, the extra size in the washer would not speed up completion of the task.

3. Choose a mutually satisfying solution

Gina and Gerald easily agree which machine most fully meets their shared criteria. In a very short time, they decide on a machine from a reliable manufacturer, in white, with visible dials and a door that can be locked open. They leave feeling contented, having enjoyed the evening together and with their mission accomplished.

Gerald and Gina both speak up comfortably for what they want, in part because each knows that the other will listen readily, and in part became they know that exploring underlying concerns will lead them to a win-win decision. Instead of a tug of war, their process feels like the fun of dancing together.

Solutions versus concerns

When an issue comes up that needs a joint decision, it may be a quick mini-issue, or a larger, major issue. Which video to rent would be a mini-issue; which church to join might be a major issue. Both, however, can be decided upon by following the same three-step sequence.

To succeed in this dance, you need to be able to distinguish between *solutions* and *concerns.* Solutions are plans of action. Concerns are the underlying preferences, values, and fears that your solutions are meant to address.

Two proposed solutions can be in direct opposition. Either we will buy a new car, or we will not, but we cannot buy and not buy simultaneously. On the other hand, a set of concerns has many possible solutions. Being able to switch from espousing solutions to exploring underlying concerns is therefore essential to finding solutions that please you both.

The solution you eventually choose need not be—often will not be—one either of you suggested initially. It just needs to be responsive to both of your concerns to be win-win.

Let's reexamine the three steps in the light of these definitions.

1. *Express initial positions.* Positions, the starting preferences in a conflict, can be expressed either as concerns or as preferred solutions.

   "I'd like us to go visit my sister this weekend. What are your plans?"

   "I was counting on going clothes shopping."

2. *Explore underlying concerns.* Concerns are the desires, fears, preferences, and values to which a given plan of action is a solution.

   "We haven't been out to see my sister in almost a month. With her illness, I'd really like to keep in closer contact."

   "Winter's almost here, and with the weight I've put on I have to buy new business clothes or go to work in my jogging pants."

3. *Design a solution set.* A solution set is a multifaceted plan of action. It is multifaceted in order to meet all the relevant concerns.

   "Would you like me to handle the kids on my own one night this week so you could go shopping after work? I'd be glad to feed them dinner myself and take them out to the park until you get home if you want to go to the mall after work."

   "Alternatively, we could go visit your sister for the weekend, and I could shop out there one afternoon. The discount shopping malls near them would be great."

Sensitive and complex decisions

The same three steps can guide you through more complex decisions. When a topic is sensitive or complex, however, deciding together where and when to talk starts you off with good climate control.

   When Aaron and Donna, whom we meet first in Chapter 4, were first married they kept separate bank accounts. Now, married for some time, they want to reevaluate their money arrangement.

   "I'd like to talk about money. Is now a good time, or would you rather wait until after dinner?" he asked.

   "Now's fine. What's on your mind?"

1. Express initial positions

> *Aaron began by suggesting, "I'd like to see us pool our finances. If we're going to be a couple I'd like to make all our finances joint. Instead of my money and your money I'd prefer if we had our money."*
>
> *"I'm worried about that," Donna responded. "I feel out of control at the thought of all our money being together. We've always had separate checking accounts, yours for what you earn and mine for mine, plus the small shared savings account that we each contribute to each month. I like the way we have it now."*

Aaron and Donna had different initial positions, but they succeeded in putting these out on the table in a quiet noninflammatory way.

2. Explore underlying concerns

> *"What worries you about combining our finances?" Aaron asked.*

Concerns are expressed in thoughts and images. These need to be spoken aloud in order for both of you to fully understand the preferences, facts, and fears relevant to the decision.

> *"I'm worried," Donna answered, "because I like to be sure that there's always at least some cushion in my account. When you panic at the end of the month that you've overspent your individual account, I panic along with you. I don't like getting anxious like that. That's why I'm such a careful planner and record keeper. I hate surprises."*
>
> *Aaron thought about Donna's concerns. "I think I overspend because I don't tally my book as I go. I always have a ballpark idea of how much I've spent. Then at the end of the month I panic because I think I've spent too much. Once I actually do go through my account though, I almost always discover that I'm fine. I don't know why I put myself through this emotional roller coaster every month."*

Donna and Aaron each take seriously the information the other offers and braid in their own perspectives, building on what the other just has said. In this way both of them can express their concerns and know that their partner will take these into account.

> *Donna continued, "Yes, and that emotional roller coaster is exactly what I don't want to join you on. I feel fine about your actual spending, although some months you do overdraw by thirty or forty dollars or so. It's the not knowing and then the panic that I don't like."*
>
> *"I agree with you," Aaron nodded. "I'm not a big spender, just casual about record keeping and then prone to panic."*

> *"Why is combining our earnings important to you?" Donna asked, to try to understand her husband's underlying concerns in proposing that they share bank accounts.*
>
> *"For me," Aaron answered, "it's a symbolic thing. If we're going to be a married partnership, it seems we should blend our money."*

Each concern that has been mentioned by either partner merits exploration.

> *"I like the idea of more sense of a union," Donna agreed. "At the same time my independence radar is going off. Does it have to be an either-or thing? I'd feel best if we can find some way to give you, and me, the sense that we're one couple financially, and yet still set aside some money that's mine to do whatever I want to with. In addition to not wanting to join your emotional roller coaster, I don't want to feel like I have to ask your permission every time I buy something."*
>
> *"For me, too," Aaron agreed, "the worst would be to get into a mother-may-I relationship with you. I'm looking for a way to have our earnings all go into one pot. I want a sense that what I earn or you earn is for our joint benefit. And at the same time I agree with you that when it comes to everyday spending decisions, I want to feel a sense of freedom of action, like no one's looking over my shoulder, at least for all but the big-bucks decisions. Maybe our earnings could all go into one savings account, but our spending could come out of several different accounts."*

By reiterating and expanding on the concern that Donna has expressed, Aaron makes it clear to both of them that her concern has been entered into their shared information pool.

As they understand the specifics of each other's concerns, solution possibilities begin to emerge.

> *"I think if we each had a couple of hundred dollars a month for personal discretionary spending I'd feel like I still have individual freedom. How much do you think you've been spending?" Aaron asked.*
>
> *"That feels like the right ballpark, or maybe somewhat more, but I want to go back and look at my actual bank records over the past six months," Donna said.*
>
> *"So it sounds like we both want more sense of being one financial team. We both want to retain a sense that we can make at least some independent financial decisions. And neither of us wants to continue my panic attacks at the end of each month," Aaron summarized.*

A summary provides a formal bridge from Step 2 to Step 3 of the Win-Win Waltz. Note that in the summary, both participants' concerns are combined onto one list of *our* concerns.

3. Choose a mutually satisfying solution

Aaron continued, "I see now that riding my emotional roller coaster stresses me unnecessarily, and it's no fun for you either. That would be easy enough to change, though. Instead of going into panic mode and then looking at the facts of what's in my account at the end of each month, I'll tally my checkbook before I start emoting about what I've spent. What I've been doing reminds me of how when my brother and I used to fight my mother used to punish us first, then ask what happened. It was like we were assumed guilty and punished before anyone looked at the facts, even if we were innocent."

"That would sure help me," Donna agreed. "And how do you feel about the idea of keeping a cushion?"

"I can see that it works for you. For me, I'd rather know exactly how much money I have to spend, and then work within that. If there's cushion in the account, I'll be too tempted to spend it. If our discretionary spending is from small separate checking accounts though, you could keep a cushion in yours, and I'd keep mine in my style. Would that work for you?"

"Probably. I'm still afraid though that if you panic, I will too."

"I have an additional idea on the panics. I think I want to sit down and analyze just what our money goes to. If I break the overall budget down into specific expenses, then I'll feel less in the dark. And I can set aside the cash for discretionary spending. Then I'll know exactly how much I have."

To be certain that the solution includes responses to all the concerns raised by both parties, the solution generally needs multiple components. In this regard it is helpful to think in terms of building a *solution set* rather than simply of finding *a* or *the* solution.

In addition, each spouse needs to focus on what he or she can do in the way of solutions. Beware of focusing instead on what your partner could do. No crossovers!

"I can do something about my part of the panics as well," Donna continued. "Now that I understand better why you go into panic mode, I can let you decide how you handle your individual checking account. I panic along with you if I feel like I have to fix your problems for you, like I used to fix everyone's problems in my family growing up. If you make messes I need to let you clean them up yourself. In our old system, when you overspent we took it out of our joint savings.

If you overspend could you deduct that from your next month's discretionary spending? Then I would no longer end up paying for your mistakes."

Sometimes discussing solutions clarifies additional underlying concerns. Note also that as Donna sees something that Aaron could do that would help her, she asks, rather than telling him what to do, avoiding a crossover.

"So how's this for the plan then?" Aaron reviewed. "One combined sav-ings account for everything either of us earns, and a combined checking account for our standard monthly bills, for the us factor. Separate checking accounts for discretionary spending. We'll figure out a set monthly amount to put in each of our individual accounts. You can keep a cushion in yours. I'll look first and panic after with mine. And I'll take any overspending from my next month's discretionary money, not the joint money."

A summary is essential, to conclude with certainty that your understanding of the plan of action is shared.

"Are there any pieces of this that still feel unfinished?" Aaron asked.

This vital last question can make the difference between a plan of action that works and one that doesn't quite take care of the problem.

"When to start it." Donna said. "How about by the beginning of next month?"
"Settled."
"And credit cards? How about if we have one for standard expenses like food and gas, and then each have our own for discretionary spending?"
"That's fine. Also, let's make a list of everything either of us pays for to be sure we agree on what's a couple expense and what needs to come from our discretionary accounts."
"I think that takes care of all the last details for me."
"Me too. We did it!"

First moves set the style

If you pay particular attention to first moves—that is, the way one of you initiates decision making—you are likely to discover that these starters may set the course for whether your decision making will be coopera-tive or antagonistic, unilateral or bilateral.

Unilateral Starters	Cooperative Starters
I'm taking the car tonight.	I'd like to take the car tonight. Will that work for you?
It's my basketball night. You'll have to handle the kids on your own.	It's my basketball night tonight. Will you be OK with the kids on your own? Is there anything you'd like me to do to help out before I leave?
(continued on next page)	

Unilateral Starters	Cooperative Starters
I want you to start coming home from work earlier and at a predictable time. That's it on drifting in whenever you please.	I'd feel better if you could come home at a regular time after work, and preferably earlier. That way I'd have more incentive to make nice meals, and we'd have nicer evenings together. What are your thoughts on that?

Expressing your desires as if they are all that count in making plans will almost certainly generate opposition. By contrast, "I would like... Would that work for you?" launches a cooperative process by inviting bilateral listening.

Make one list of *our* concerns

In a loving couple, any concern of one mate's is by definition a concern of the other. Helping you get your concerns met is a priority of mine, and getting my needs met is a priority for you. Therefore we don't need yours and mine lists of concerns, just an *ours* list.

Similarly, when you make personal decisions that have pros and cons, instead of listing pros on one side and cons on another, list all of your concerns, pro and con, on one list. The decision will depend on finding an option that is responsive to all these concerns, or at least to all of the more significant ones. Two lists imply two sides, that is, adversaries. One combined list launches consensus building.

Donna and Aaron faced a decision reminiscent of discussions about dogs in Part I. After Aaron's dogs broke a vase that had belonged to Donna's grandmother, Donna wanted to get rid of them. Aaron was horrified.

His (or Pro)	Hers (or Con)
I've had them for years. They've been my closest friends.	They get wild in the house, and their big tails swish things off tables.
They bring joy to me.	I'm afraid of them.
They love me. They're especially fun on mountain hikes	They need a bigger yard than we have. They jump on me and want to lick me, which I don't like.

This two-sided list feels discouraging. Donna and Aaron might have fought over this decision. Fortunately, they rearranged their concerns to read as one list. Notice as you read this reformatted list how your mind begins thinking of win-win solution sets instead of either-or solutions.

They get wild in the house, and their big tails swish things off tables.
I've had them for years. They've been my closest friends.
They bring joy to me.
They love me.
They're especially fun on mountain hikes.
I'm afraid of them.
They need a bigger yard than we have.
They jump on me and want to lick me, which I don't like.

In response to the list above, Donna and Aaron arranged for a neighbor with a large yard to keep the dogs during the day. Donna "dog-proofed" the house so that the dogs' swishy tails would no longer knock over breakable treasures. She read books on dogs, especially on golden retrievers, like Aaron's, and spent more time with them to get over her fears. Aaron trained the dogs so that they would no longer jump up on people or lick them. Donna learned to tolerate the dogs, and Aaron was able to keep his longtime friends and hiking companions.

Other Joint Decision-Making Strategies

Not every we decision needs the full Win-Win Waltz. Simpler strategies also can work, particularly for lesser decisions.

One long-standing method by which couples have always avoided battles over decisions has been by agreeing ahead of time on who makes decisions in each sphere of activity. If he, for instance, is in charge of everything inside the home and she is responsible for decisions outside the home, each adult has clearly defined realms of decision making. She hires the new baby-sitter, and he invests their savings. She handles cooking, and he makes sure the lawn gets cut. While for many families these traditional gender roles no longer fit, the idea of dividing up the realms is very useful. If both work outside the home, for instance, within the home she may cook and he may keep the kitchen clean, and she may bathe the children while he's in charge of storytelling.

The One-Step

Once a couple has decided whose decision-making realm a particular decision falls into, a single step suffices. If the decision falls in your territory, you make it. You always have the option of consulting your spouse for input, but the buck starts and stops with you.

Decisions	Decider
Who shall we invite for dinner this Friday night?	The social secretary
How can I fix the broken toilet?	The repair person
What breakfast cereals shall we buy?	The shopper
Which baby-sitters shall we entrust with our children with when we go out for an evening?	The baby-sitter finder

> *Gina and Gerald were planning a camping trip for their daughter's birth-*
> *day. "I'll go buy the flashlights and pocket knives we agreed on as gifts for*
> *each of her friends, and take care of renting the tents," Gerald offered.*
> *Gina replied, "That's fine. I'll handle food planning. She's making her*
> *own invitations, but then I'll take care of phoning each of the parents to*
> *answer their questions."*

"You should have..." is out of bounds

Gina and Gerald understand that once one of them is in charge of a decision, the costs of commenting negatively on each other's decisions can be high. That is, if Gerald comes home with the flashlights and pocket knives, and Gina then says, "You paid too much for them," this kind of crossover could undermine Gerald's desire to take responsibility in the household. Instead Gina and Gerald offer appreciation for the decisions their partner makes.

Sometimes you may have a concern you think is important for your partner to bear in mind in making a decision. Offer that information before the decision rather than after, if at all possible. Input is easier to hear than criticism. Second-guessing your spouse with "Don't you think you should have...?" just demoralizes both of you.

Note that the one-step mode of decision making depends on the two of you having similar values, making reasonably good decisions, and appreciating each other's solutions. When input from both of you is not essential, one step gets the job done most efficiently.

The Two-Step

The input-first version

This strategy prevents frustrations down the line in cases where an issue that falls into one partner's decision making affects the other partner.

1. *Consult*— The decision maker first requests input about the other's concerns and preferences.

2. *Decide*— The decision maker then takes this information into account in making the decision.

> Gerald tells Gina, "I want to take our savings and invest as much as we can in a good mutual fund while the stock market is down. What are your feelings about that?"
>
> "Will it be liquid?" Gina asks. "With the house looking so shabby I want to be sure we have access to enough funds to pay to get it painted, and I think the roof probably will need repairs also."
>
> "I forgot about that. I think I will make a mutual fund purchase, but I'll hold out enough to be sure we can handle painting and reroofing, plus a slush fund for unexpected expenses. That will cut down by quite a bit what I thought I'd invest, but we'll be better off."
>
> ....
>
> Gerald has agreed to take on responsibility for planning a family trip to visit national parks. Before making the reservations, however, he checks first with Gina to find out the exact dates she and the children have for vacations, and how much driving she will be comfortable with. He wants to know what factors will make it a good vacation for her, asks himself the same questions, and then moves forward on making reservations.

The veto-after version

This strategy depends on prior agreement that before decisions are put into action you will find a solution that both of you feel good about.

1. *Preliminary decision*— The main decision maker makes a decision.

2. *Veto option*— The second party has veto power or can add input afterward so that the decision can be improved.

> "What do you think of this new bedspread? I picked it out to match the curtains in our bedroom."
>
> "I wish I liked it, because I know you've put time into finding it. But that pattern feels busy. I'd prefer something calmer, simpler, since we do spend a lot of time in our bedroom now that we have comfortable chairs in it."
>
> "I'll go later this week to pick out another option or two that I'd be happy with and then run them by you."
>
> ....
>
> "I've grounded Genny for the next two weeks."
>
> "That sounds awfully harsh. Besides, we'll be fighting with her for two weeks about it. Is there some way she could earn back her privileges sooner?"

"Since she's being punished for swearing in the house, what if we tell her that every day she doesn't swear takes two days off her punishment?"

"That sounds much better to me. It gives several days of concentrated learning to get the no-swearing point across without antagonizing her with punishment overkill."

Dancing Cheek-to-Cheek

When you make decisions as a couple, you will almost always find that each of you attends to a different facet of the problem. Decisions become fun as you become accustomed to contributing your own underlying concerns, sharing them, and then brainstorming to find solutions that incorporate these concerns. Instead of feeling like tests of who has how much power, decisions become opportunities for shared creativity.

Without skills of shared decision making, issues that you need to resolve together can become rife with tension. Once you master the Win-Win Waltz, however, decisions are a dance. Best of all, when two perspectives are brought to bear cooperatively on a problem, the collaborative solution generally proves better than either party would have been able to create individually. In sum, with these skills, differences that might otherwise have been divisive become opportunities to enjoy your collaborative power of two.

Notes

The test of a man or woman's breeding is how they behave in a quarrel.

—George Bernard Shaw, *The Philanderer*

Chapter 9

Conflict Resolution

Inevitably in marriage there are times when one of you wants to turn somewhat to the left and the other a bit to the right. Sometimes you may seem to pull in exactly opposite directions. Sometimes you may collide head on. These tugs, pulls, and pushes in response to apparent differences indicate conflict. A conflict is a situation in which your priorities or preferences appear to be incompatible and exert force in opposing directions.

Conflict can also be defined as a situation in which one or both of you experiences anger. When one of you feels injured in any way, or if you want one thing, your partner wants another, and the stakes feel high, before long one or both of you are likely to feel anger rising. As explained in Chapter 5, anger has its risks. While angry feelings warn that there's a fire burning somewhere, a dispute that needs to be addressed, acting in anger typically leads you away from, not toward, equitable resolution of disputes.

The earlier chapters of this book have covered many of the secrets to averting angry conflicts. The basic skills of cooperative dialogue minimize conflicts from provocative crossovers, toxicity, or poor listening. Fix-it talk can enable you to resolve minor differences without argument. Anger regarded as a stop sign can lead to thinking, information gathering, and constructive problem solving. Cooperative decision-making skills build consensus in the face of choices that might otherwise breed disagreement.

In fact, if you have read Chapter 8 you have already learned the essentials of conflict resolution, because arguments are resolved with the same three steps as cooperative decision making.

1. Express initial positions.

2. Explore underlying concerns.

3. Choose a mutually satisfying solution.

The differences between shared decision making and conflict resolution lie in the tone of the initial discussion—comfortable or contentious—and in whether the dialogue keeps moving forward or becomes stuck at one of these three steps.

For example, imagine that you and your partner need to decide which television program to watch together. If you maintain a tone of cooperation and comfortably follow the three steps, arriving at a choice of program that fits the criteria important to both of you, you have accomplished a shared decision. If by contrast, one of you insists on a choice that the other finds objectionable, or your tone becomes antagonistic, then you have arrived at a conflict.

This chapter shows how to return from conflicts to the cooperative decision pathway and how to devise mutually acceptable options.

Why Do Conflicts Occur?

Most marriage fights do not result from incompatible differences of opinion. Rather, they arise out of insufficient dialogue skills, hot tempers, hot topics, or frozen thinking.

The first of these sources probably triggers the most difficulty. Most conflicts arise out of straying from the communication basics:

- *Misunderstandings*— when one partner didn't say explicitly, with adequate specificity, what he or she thought or felt, and the other made assumptions rather than asking questions.
- *Defending turf*— because of crossovers in the form of you messages.
- *Hurt feelings*— from toxic comments that convey insult, criticism, blame, or fault finding.
- *Not feeling heard*— because the listener is pressing the mute button or responding with negative *yes but* listening.
- *Escalations*— from insufficient climate control.

Dry tinder flares quickly

If one of you is emotionally fragile, minor communications violations can be enough to trigger upset. Similarly, a single you message or subtle toxic comment can strike a blaze if one of you is exhausted or stressed about other issues.

A family history of depression or chronic anger or traumas in younger years can cause a person's neurological system to develop extra sensitivity. If one of you tends to be particularly fragile emotionally or quick to flare up, medication and/or counseling can make an enormous difference. Selective serotonin-reuptake inhibitors (SSRIs), for instance, which reduce depression, also reduce quickness to anger. Depression and anger are two sides of the same coin. Enough of either can signal a problem that could benefit from professional help.

Arguments also erupt when a topic is inherently sensitive. One word with a slightly negative connotation can trigger a full-scale battle. Most couples can readily identify the sensitive issues in their relationship. I have seen in my clinical experience that the following issues tend to be particularly volatile.

- *In-laws,* especially if:
  - one partner is closely connected to parents in a way that blocks sufficient objectivity.
  - one partner speaks uncharitably, critically rather than compassionately, about the other's parents.
- *Division of labor,* especially if:
  - problems are raised as complaints or demands rather than as requests.
  - decisions are made by assignment rather than by volunteering.
  - the system feels unfair.
- *Money and time,* especially if:
  - one or both are in short supply.
  - the partner who earns more money feels justified in spending more or in having more say in how time and/or money is spent.
  - the partners have different values on spending versus saving, investment risk, and how to spend their time.
  - both partners' preferences are not taken into account.
  - decisions made by one partner result in major financial losses.
- *Cultural and religious differences,* especially if:
  - either partner is disrespectful of the other's beliefs or traditions.
  - one partner is unable to accommodate the other's deeply held traditions or beliefs.
- *Parenting,* especially if:
  - the partners have significantly different ideas on discipline.

+ the partners are unable to share what they each know, to learn from each other.
+ one or both partners are unwilling to read books, attend parenting classes, or consult a counselor to develop shared views.
+ the partners blame each other when their children have difficulties.

- *Sex,* especially if:
  + the partners have radically different ideas of appropriate frequency or sexual behavior, and one insists on his or her own way rather than both attempting to accommodate.
  + only one partner wants a monogamous relationship.

- *Drugs or alcohol,* especially if:
  + partners' views differ on what and how much are acceptable.
  + one partner denies the detrimental effects drugs or alcohol is having on him- or herself or the marriage.
  + one partner is more attached to the drug than to the marriage, choosing to continue the habit rather than heed the marital impacts.
  + one partner takes on responsibility for controlling the other's intoxicants.
  + the "more is less" rule of intoxicants is being ignored. More substance use yields less marital harmony, stability, and love.

- *Weight and appearance,* especially if:
  + one partner is unable to accept the other as is, and tries to change him or her.
  + one partner neglects his or her hygiene, and in consequence is becoming less attractive.
  + the partners have radically different ideas of adequate self care.
  + one partner is unable to accept changes in the other's appearance caused by age, injury, or illness.
  + one partner takes responsibility for controlling the diet or exercise of the other.

Frozen thinking

I have virtually never seen a couple whose fighting was about differences for which there was no solution, provided both partners wanted to find a solution and were willing to use a cooperative process to get there.

However, if one side locks into a fixed perspective and ceases listening to the other, constructive conflict resolution grinds to a halt. Any *yes but* indicates at least a temporary blockage in listening. A lack of affirmative responses to indicate that you have been digesting what your partner has said also can suggest that listening is breaking down. When the ability to take in new information ceases altogether, however, this "frozen thinking" poses the biggest obstacle to negotiations.

How can you tell if your thinking, or your partner's, has become rigid? If you have ceased taking in additional information to broaden your understanding of the dilemma at hand, your thinking may have frozen in this way.

Rigid, Frozen Thinking	Flexible Thinking
Your ideas are fixed. Your mind is closed to new information that does not confirm what you already believe.	Your mind is open to new ideas. You curiously take in new information, even when it seems to challenge what you have believed to be true.
You see yourself as right and different opinions as wrong. You disparage other points of view and think in terms of either/or. Either I am right or you are right.	You look for how you can be right and others with different opinions can be right as well. You like the words and and both.
You use inflammatory language to highlight your rightness and your partner's wrongness.	You keep your language neutral, describing what you see without describing your partner in words with negative connotations.
If you are not getting what you want, you resort to criticism and blame. You lack insight with respect to your part in difficulties.	If difficulties arise, you are willing to look at what you yourself might do differently to improve the dialogue or the problem situation.

Frozen thinking spells major problems:

- It means you are stuck. Information gathering is essential for progress in resolving conflicts.
- Frozen thinking provokes irritation. The nonfrozen partner is likely to become frustrated by the futility of trying to convey information about his or her concerns.
- Frozen thinking, with its deafness to the other's perspective, is the opposite of bilateral listening. It makes healthy dialogue impossible.

Strategies for When You Get Stuck

Sometimes differences feel impossible to negotiate. Rather than continue with increasing strife, however, you can convert your clashing stances to cooperation. The following pages suggest strategies for effecting this transformation.

Of course, the further you have gone in battle—the more fire or ice—the more difficult converting antagonism to cooperation becomes. All the options on the following pages can be implemented more easily if you launch them sooner rather than later.

Once cooperation returns, if you think of your conflict as an opportunity to use your shared problem-solving skills, you are likely to find that you gradually begin to see encouraging new options. Table 8 offers a quick review of the three steps in conflict resolution, which are the same as the three steps of the Win-Win Waltz.

Start by doing less of the same

The first secret to making headway when you feel like you're up against intransigent differences is to pass beyond the "more of the same" myth. As a wise person once said, more of the same will get you more of the same. Nate and Nicole provide a case in point.

> *Different views proved a daily challenge for Nicole and Nate. The more frustrated they felt, the more they intensified explaining, insisting, wishing, and resenting. Explaining became persuading, insisting became shouting, wishing became denial of the facts, and resentment mushroomed into fury. With three children who fought incessantly with each other, however, Nicole and Nate needed to learn to resolve differences between themselves if only to become better models for their children.*
>
> *When Nate and Nicole agreed that they wanted to join a church, which church to join became a major controversy. Nate wanted to join a nearby Protestant church. Nicole felt more attracted to a Catholic church like the one she had grown up in. Nate held firm, increasingly certain that his solution was the correct one. Nicole resented that Nate didn't seem to be listening to her.*

As Nate and Nicole discovered, intensifying an ineffective strategy just evokes more intense versions of the same responses. At some point, a proverbial straw may break the camel's back, and one partner either gives up or explodes—yielding depression or toxic emissions. In a branch of mathematics called catastrophe theory, an early form of chaos theory, the point at which a system suddenly shifts from smooth to turbulent flow is called the critical point. In marriage, it usually is called a fight.

TABLE 8 Conflict Resolution Sequence

Steps	Secrets to Success
Express your initial positions	Say it, don't hint. Symmetry: Did both of you express initial positions? Summarize by defining the problem in a no-fault, umbrella way that includes both and blames neither.
Explore the underlying concerns listing all the concerns of each of you on one joint list	Use the Four Ss. If you are getting stuck, ask: • Are we maintaining *symmetry*, exploring equally both of our concerns? • Are we giving long speeches or talking in *short segments?* • Are we talking in generalities or in *specifics?* • Have we put together a *summary*, listing all the concerns each of us has, as a bridge to the third step, finding solutions?
Determine mutually acceptable solutions responsive to all the concerns	Create solution options by adding modifications to your original positions and by devising completely new options. Think in terms of solution sets, taking into account all of the concerns. Summarize the plan, to be certain you both leave with the same understanding. Ask the final essential question: Are there any pieces of this that still feel unfinished?

Stop, look, listen

As suggested in Chapter 5, *stop*, to step out of the current debate, cool down, and gain a broader perspective. Then *look* and *listen* to understand more fully your partner's perspective.

> Nicole said to Nate, "Wait a minute. We're getting nowhere here. I'm going to get a big pad of paper and write down all the reasons you've given for why the Protestant church down the block appeals to you. I want to be sure I fully understand what you would like about joining that church."
>
> Nicole listened closely to Nate, listing his concerns as they talked. Within a few minutes the tone of their talking switched from debate to affectionate banter.
>
> Nate enumerated what he liked about the Protestant church. He felt drawn to its smallness and to the friendliness of the people who gathered there. There seemed to be many children in the Sunday school; finding a church where the children would feel a sense of belonging and receive a strong religious education were essential objectives for him.
>
> Feeling finished, Nate reached for Nicole's pad of paper. "Your turn," he grinned. "I'm listening."

Gather more information

Where there is disagreement on factual matters, the best antidote to argument is information. For instance, Nate and Nicole had argued about whether to tell their eldest daughter they would pay for her to go to an out-of-state college. Getting the actual costs of in-state and out-of-state tuition quickly yielded a consensus.

An objective, outside opinion also can make a difference. Nate and Nicole, for instance, had battled about how often the lawn needed to be mowed until they learned from their neighbors that almost everyone on their block mowed their lawn once a week.

Books and experts can contribute vital information. In the following instance, Nicole and Nate had been fighting about how to respond to their daughter's avoidance of reading.

> Nicole was worried because their nine-year-old daughter, Deirdre, appeared so resistant to reading. Nate insisted that most children in these times are more drawn to the hot media of TV and computers than to reading. "Let's not start thinking that she's some kind of oddball," he insisted.
>
> Rather than continue to argue, Nicole and Nate decided to gather more information. They each took time in the evenings to sit with Deirdre and have her read aloud to them. Deirdre surprised them both by how haltingly

she read, and how often she lost her place. They also consulted her teacher. The teacher said that Deirdre was a bright girl—her input in class discussions was creative—but she did poorly on tests because she ran out of time before she could finish. She read so slowly that she often had to stay at her desk to finish her work while the other children played at recess.

At this point, Nate agreed that Nicole seemed to be right about their daughter's resistance to reading having a basis in some kind of problem. At the same time, he was inclined to think that it was the kind of problem that children grow out of with time, and he continued to be more concerned that Deirdre not think of herself as a kid with problems. Nicole, by contrast, feared that the problem might grow worse with time. They bickered again about what to do.

To resolve this round of conflict, Nicole and Nate decided to consult someone with expertise in the area of reading. The reading therapist who tested Deirdre diagnosed significant eye-coordination difficulties. Because Deirdre's eyes were not working together, reading for her was arduous, and she was significantly below her grade level. In addition, the reading specialist pointed out that Deirdre was getting headaches if she read for more than a few minutes at a sitting.

With this information, Nicole and Nate easily agreed on a strategy. Their consensus included enrolling Deirdre in an eye-coordination treatment program and signing her up for a soccer team to highlight her athletic abilities and keep her feeling like "a normal kid."

Sometimes arguments occur because partners have different information about a situation. While Nate's concerns that Deirdre feel normal, not "different" from other kids, were valid, he was genuinely misinformed about the seriousness of her reading problem. Gathering additional information eliminated the controversy. At the same time, Nicole validated Nate's concerns that their daughter have a "normal" childhood and feel good about herself. With additional information, their conflict gave way to cooperative planning.

Change the game from tug-of-war to exploration

Sometimes conflicts feel like a tug-of-war, with each of you pulling toward a different point of view. A tug-of-war indicates that you have slipped into either-or thinking. How can you return to a mutual-satisfaction consensus-building mode? It can be challenging to implement bilateral listening when it feels like you and your spouse have opposing desires.

Roger Fisher and William Ury, authors of the book, *Getting to Yes* (1981), that first popularized win-win decision making, contrast what they call *positional bargaining* with what they call *interest-based bargaining*. In formal dispute resolution, solutions proposed at the outset of the negotiation are called positions. Positional bargaining is a tug-of-war. Each side pulls for an opposing plan of action. Interest-based bargaining, by contrast, explores the interests—what I refer to as underlying concerns—of the participants, and then comes up with a new strategy responsive to the dimensions of importance to both participants.

Switching from debating plans of action (positional bargaining) to exploring underlying concerns (interest-based bargaining) transforms conflict resolution from a frustrating power struggle to a cooperative effort. Exploring concerns puts you on the path to eventually being able to find a plan of action you will both like.

As the Christmas holidays were approaching, Nate and Nicole hit another brick wall—whose family to visit for Christmas.

Tug-of-War	Exploring Underlying Concerns
Nate insisted that the family go to his parents' house for Christmas. Nicole was determined that they have Christmas at home. They couldn't be both places at once. The conflict felt impossible to resolve.	Nate had to stop and think. He turned his attention inward to explore his inner landscape of concerns. He wanted to go to his parents' home for Christmas because his siblings, both his brother and his sister, were going to be traveling there from the Northwest this year. He hadn't seen them for a long time, and he treasured the opportunity for his family to reconnect with theirs.
To avoid a fight, Nicole and Nate stopped discussing vacation plans, but the tensions kept rising.	Nicole also explored her underlying concerns. Hers were religious—to go to midnight mass and for her children to share the meaningful dinner rituals her family had enjoyed.

Nate and Nicole hardened into tug-of-war positional bargaining when they first began to talk about Christmas plans and discovered that each had envisioned something different. On their second try at the discussion, however, Nate and Nicole both succeeded in loosening their attachments to their initial preferred solutions long enough to explore the underlying concerns that made these solutions appear attractive. To convert to exploration, Nate asked Nicole a key question, "What are the concerns that your proposal answers?"

> Nate asked Nicole what religious ceremonies in particular she was picturing when she thought about Christmas in their home this year, or in her home as a child.

*In addition to midnight mass, Nicole pictured family prayers as they
sat down to a big dinner. Their family custom was for each person around
the large family dinner table, old and young, to offer thanks for the gifts
from Above they had received and for the help they had given each other
in difficult times.*

*Listening to Nicole, Nate at first was tempted to say "Yes, but," to argue
for going to join his family in Florida. He consciously focused instead on listening to learn, to understand in the best possible light his wife's concerns.
"Yes," he acknowledged. "That kind of religious experience changes holidays
back into holy days. I never experienced anything like that growing up. I'd
love it for our kids—and for me, too."*

Nate's determination to switch from tug-of-war to cooperative decision making enabled Nicole to feel heard. Then she was able to invite Nate to explore his underlying concerns as well. They took turns talking, describing their concerns, and asking questions for specifics about their spouse's concerns. The more precise the description of underlying concerns, the more easily mutually agreeable solutions begin to emerge.

*Nate elaborated on his concerns. He said that his siblings and their
families were going to be staying together in a motel near his parents' home
on the Florida coast. They planned a week of golf, tennis, swimming, and
boating together. "Santa will probably arrive by surfboard," Nate mused.*

As conflict resolution switches from tug-of-war to exploration, the tone changes. Antagonism and tension give way to cooperative curiosity. This change in tone enables both parties to think more flexibly.

Nicole and Nate also did well with the Four Ss: *symmetry* of speaking time, speaking in *short segments*, getting out the *specifics* of their concerns, and from time to time *summarizing* what had been said. As a result, they arrived relatively quickly at the third stage of conflict resolution, finding a mutually comfortable plan of action.

*Multiple plans of action now emerged as options. Nicole suggested going
to Florida with Nate's family, finding a church there with a midnight mass,
and introducing Nate's family to dinner-table rituals.*

*Nate suggested that since his family was going to be together for a full
week, he and Nicole might celebrate Christmas as a nuclear family with
their children, and then join his family in Florida the following morning.*

Both of these suggestions take one of the initial solution ideas and modify it so that it meets both partner's concerns. Both Nate and Nicole tried to be as flexible as possible, finding ways to augment their mate's preferred plan so they could feel comfortable with it.

> *"Well," Nate said, "we have two options now, either of which would be fine with me. Do any other concerns come to mind for you?"*
> *Nicole thought some, and then added, "What about money? We'll be stretching to pay for the plane fares plus the motel costs. Can we make it?"*

Beginning to look at solutions often raises additional concerns.

> *"From my perspective that's another reason to spend Christmas day here with our family and then go to Florida. My family goes overboard on the gift-giving. They buy more expensive gifts than we usually do. In our own family we've been able to play down the commercial aspects of Christmas in favor of the spirit. Especially if we're going to pay for airfare and the motel, it would help a lot if we could keep our gift-giving to homemade items. Frosted cookies or jam or fudge won't look so low-budget if they're not handed out next to bicycles and portable TVs on Christmas morning."*
> *"Looks like we've flip-flopped on who wants to go where," Nicole chuckled. "The more I think about it, the happier I am with the idea of connecting with your family, and a week in the sun sounds like paradise. Let's agree that we'll do Christmas Eve here at home, just our family, and get reservations for the first flight out the next morning to Florida."*
> *"Sounds perfect."*

Nicole had offered a summary of their consensus plan. Now she asked the critical last question.

> *"Are there any little pieces of this that still feel unfinished?"*
> *"Actually, I do feel nervous about one thing. How do you feel about my playing golf? We've had arguments about that in past when we've visited my family," Nate asked warily.*
> *"I know you like playing with your family. When the children were small I used to feel overwhelmed when you'd be off on the golf course for six hours at a time. Now that they're older they'll be busy with their cousins. I can take your golf time as alone time or spend it with my sisters-in-law, either of which sounds appealing."*
> *"Settled. Merry Christmas!"*

Nate and Nicole succeeded in using the exploration strategy to successfully resolve their Christmas conflict. They were able to succeed in part because they could recognize and name the problem they were having i.e., tug-of-war, also known as positional bargaining.

Establish ground rules

Children often have standard formulas for situations that would otherwise regularly trigger fights. If they are going to split a piece of cake, for
instance, they can rely on the "one person cuts, the other chooses" rule.
Similarly, "taking turns" prevents fights when there is one tricycle for two children. Adult couples can benefit from many similar simple agreements:

- *Whoever cooks, the other cleans up* can give a sense of fairness over
  dinner routines.

- *A place for everything, and everything in its place* can resolve the
  "where did you put the scissors?" frustrations.

- *One week on, one week off* for who gets up in the middle of the
  night for crying children.

- *Consult with each other on any purchase over $100* or whatever
  dollar amount makes sense for your financial state. This kind of
  agreement settles which purchases can be made by individual
  decision making and which need OKs from both of you.

- *No talking about tough topics after ten at night* maintains climate
  controls when fatigue could invite fighting.

- An agreement like *Mondays for men's night out, Thursdays for
  Mom's night off, and Saturday nights we go out together* gives him
  one night a week for basketball with friends, her one night off-duty,
  and time for the two of you to spend together as a couple.

Depth dive to understand concerns more fully

If you find yourself frozen in a polarized position from your mate, a
"depth dive" may help uncover what is locking you into that viewpoint.
Your underlying concerns may not be readily apparent, and could go back to
childhood or another, earlier relationship.

To dive into earlier sources of your reaction, ask yourself when you have
had a similar feeling or have seen others reacting similarly to this kind of situation. Chapter 12, on intimate talk, elaborates this depth dive technique
more fully, but this simple version often can yield surprisingly helpful insights.

> Nate became agitated when they were packing to go on a trip and he
> was ready to depart far sooner than Nicole. The intensity of his frustration
> surprised Nicole, who didn't understand why he was so distressed. To her it
> seemed obvious that more needed to be done before they could depart. If
> Nate could pitch in and help they soon would be able to leave. Nate saw
> the logic in her response, but still felt strongly annoyed at having to wait.

A depth dive provided a quick answer. Nate recalled how irritated his
father used to become, almost as a matter of routine, waiting for their large
family to get ready to go somewhere. His father typically was ready first,
while Nate's mother ran hither and thither organizing the children, the lunch,
and herself. Nate had internalized a miniversion of his dad's impatience.

Having discovered the source of his pattern of departure irritability, Nate
then could make a decision to rechoreograph their departure routines, dividing the work of leaving more evenly and eliminating the conflicts.

Use structured listening to get unstuck

Sometimes you may feel that dialogue is not moving forward, that one
or both of you keep repeating the same concerns. Repetitive dialogue
indicates either a problem in bilateral listening, or that the point you want to
make isn't quite clear to you yet—you're still figuring out your concerns.
Strategic reiteration (Chapter 2) can help.

Alternatively, the technique of structured listening can help you move forward again.

- Mutually agree on an amount of time, say five minutes. Setting a
  timer helps.
- During that time only one partner talks and the other only listens.
- The listening partner then reiterates what he or she has taken in and
  asks questions to get further information or to clarify a point.
- Then switch roles. The partner who listened in Step 2 now has five
  minutes to lay out his or her concerns, and the other partner listens.
  After the five minutes, digests aloud what he or she has heard.

Note that this technique contrasts with the recommendations for short segments and braided dialogue. Sometimes when one approach isn't working its
opposite will. Both short segments and structured listening are strategies for
enhancing hearing. Short segments let you digest bite by bite. Structured listening's longer monologues separate talking and listening. This separation
helps you focus solely on understanding your mate's point of view while you
are listening. It also lets you, when you are the speaker, talk long enough at
one time to discover the missing piece of what you were trying to say.

The hardest part of structured listening is getting yourselves to do it. If one
conflict keeps resurfacing or you feel that you are stuck, spinning your wheels,
it can help to formally schedule a meeting at a time and place conducive to
uninterrupted, thoughtful talking.

♥ Good moods yield better resolutions

Research in various areas of conflict resolution—politics, business, and home—has found that when people are in a positive mood they are able to discover more flexible solutions to their conflicts. The opposite is also true. The more contentious bargainers are, the less effective they are in finding win-win solutions (Pruitt, 1981).

In one study, subjects (college students) were divided into two groups and then into pairs. The pairs in Group A were given a difficult business negotiation to attempt as representatives of two simulated companies. The pairs in Group B were given the same instructions, but first they spent five minutes sorting through funny cartoons. Those who began in good humor negotiated substantially more effective solutions. (Carnevale & Isen, 1986).

When you and your mate are grumpy, rushed, tired, hungry, or irritable, you are most likely to find yourselves in conflicts. Trying to talk them through at these times, however, is likely to lead to relatively poor solutions, that is, to solutions that do not maximize your joint benefit. Take a break, and plan to talk again when you both have regained better humor. Schedule a relaxed time when you can be most resilient.

If you cannot identify a time when you will both be in good humor because irritability is constant, set aside a special quiet time when you can use the techniques in Chapter 11 for helping each other with distress. Chronic grouchiness means that something is amiss.

♥ When tensions run high, take a hike

Researchers Lewis and Fry (1977) found that placing a physical barrier between high-conflict bargainers reduced their tendencies to use hostile tactics and increased the likelihood that they would find mutually agreeable solutions. Other researchers since have confirmed that eye contact increases preexisting hostilities. Not being able to see each other, by contrast, enables bargainers to relax and to find more creative solutions (Carnevale & Isen, 1986). Eye contact in competitive situations feels threatening. It seems to invite angry people to attack.

Marriage partners talking about issues that bring up negative feelings can benefit from this finding. Going on a walk together is a good way to approach a conflictual subject, especially if you walk in a lovely and quiet place. The loveliness improves your mood, the quiet will decrease your sensory overload, and talking side by side as you walk decreases the eye contact that can increase competitiveness.

Discussing sensitive personal issues is inherently difficult. Choosing a soothing setting and side by side positioning increases your odds of success.

For mental rigidity, take a break

When dialogue slips into conflict, one or both of you may become locked—overly attached to your specific position, solution, or plan of action. Locking on brings mental rigidity. Your ideas and information become frozen, fixed rather than flexible. The main sign of frozen thinking is that when you hear new information that does not conform with what you already believe, you brush it aside or argue against it instead of adding it to your thinking about the problem. Inability to take in new information signals that your cognitive system is stuck, much like a computer that has frozen.

When a personal computer freezes, pressing the Control, Alt, and Delete keys simultaneously breaks up the jam by shutting down the programs and restarting the computer, hopefully returning it to normal, i.e., able to access and enter information. The equivalent strategy for loosening rigid ideas in an argument is to take a break from the discussion and then start up again later.

This strategy works if the computer of your thinking has frozen temporarily. At times the problem is more serious. Paranoid disorders, for instance, can bring about a mental state in which people develop fixed delusional systems that are beyond what a simple pause can release. The delusion needn't be overtly "crazy" or bizarre, just fixed and out of accord with reality. Occasionally a person develops a fixed but erroneous negative set of beliefs about a partner. These frozen thinking states are frustrating to understand, because the person suffering with one will appear totally normal in other aspects of his or her life. Usually, the frozen idea system is confined to one area or one person. If your spouse has developed a fixed negative ideational system about you, you have a serious problem.

Chronic frozen thinking may be treatable; it merits professional consultation. Talking as a couple with a psychologist or other mental health professional can offer significant help. If your spouse shows signs of frozen thinking and is not willing to seek help with you, consider getting help for yourself.

Eight Styles of Solutions

So far in this chapter we have been focusing on strategies for bridging the transition from oppositionally expressing initial positions (Step 1), to cooperatively exploring underlying concerns (Step 2). While this transition can take the conflict out of differences, it is not necessarily enough to bring the differences to resolution. Choosing a mutually agreeable plan of action (Step 3) still needs to be accomplished. One secret to creative solutions is to know a number of standard win-win solution structures, such as those described below.

A basic rule of thumb applies to all of these solutions. Each of you needs to focus on what *you* can do, rather than spend your energies on what you want you partner to do differently. This theme should sound familiar by now. A crossover, suggesting what your mate should do, seldom proves as helpful as insight, seeking what you can do differently.

Compromise

Compromise, while sometimes handy for bringing differences to closure, often leaves both spouses feeling compromised. Splitting the difference means both of you have lost some. Nonetheless, compromise is suitable for quickly ending conflicts in which a problem is quantifiable, that is, can be reduced to numbers. Compromise solutions are generally preferable to a tug-of-war. Usually, however, by switching to exploring underlying concerns, you can create far better solutions than a simple split-down-the-middle compromise.

> Nate and Nicole again found themselves locked in controversy over vacation planning. Nicole wanted to take their two-week vacation on her parents' farm. Nate only wanted to go for one week. They considered a compromise, a ten-day stay.

Notice the other solution options that open up, however, as Nicole and Nate switch from arguing over their initial positions to exploring their underlying concerns, and *then* reconsidering solution possibilities.

> Talking again the next day about their spring vacation, Nicole and Nate began to explore each of their underlying concerns.
>
> Nicole's main concern was that because her parents were aging, she wanted as much time with them as possible. She also wanted to see her old friends in her hometown, as she feared losing touch with them.
>
> Nate's main concern was wanting to plant their garden, which otherwise tended not to get planted until well into summer. Also, the sports Nate enjoyed, like mountain biking and vigorous hiking, were more enjoyable to do at their home than at Nicole's parents'.

Logrolling

Logrolling means an exchange of favors or trade-offs. Each party gets his or her main concerns met and lets go of others.

> Nate suggested, "You want to see your parents as long as possible, and I want to have one of our two weeks at home so I can plant my garden. How about if you take the children and spend two weeks with your parents on their farm, and I'll take a week first at home to plant my garden and then

join you. That means we'll have just one week together, but that seems to be
less important for both of us.

Club sandwich

When the underling concerns are complementary rather than oppositional, an additive solution or layered approach may be quite feasible.

If Nicole wanted to see her parents, but didn't feel that it needed to be
the full two weeks of their vacation because of her parents' questionable
health, they could spend one week with her parents and one week doing
sports and gardening at home.

Sequencing

A sequencing solution—let's do one of ours now and the other's preferences later—works for some kinds of conflicts.

"How about if we take our spring vacation here at home, and then spend
our end-of-summer two weeks visiting your parents?" Nate suggested.

In this case, Nicole's concerns for her parents' health made her reluctant to agree to this plan.

Expanding the pie

By expanding the resources of time, money, space, personnel, and so forth, often new solutions can emerge.

"I could take more of my vacation time at once," Nate suggested. "I
could spend a week at home first, then during the two weeks you have off I
can go with you and the kids to Kansas."

Incorporating

Sometimes one solution can be included as part of the other.

"I know," Nicole brightened. "Let's buy plane tickets for my parents to
come for two weeks to visit us here. It would be good for them to have a
vacation from the farm, and they would love helping you and the kids with
planting the garden."

Integrative synergies

Integrating or weaving together into one solution all the concerns raised by both partners sometimes brings an entirely new picture into focus. Such a synergy can be responsive to the full range of your concerns—the whole is greater than the sum of its parts. These positive breakthroughs provide the ultimate reward for collaborative thinking.

> *"You know," Nate mused, "we seem to get into this same argument every vacation. I have an idea that would end the problem forever. Your parents are getting too old to manage the farm. Maybe now is the time to look at either us moving and taking over the farm for them or encouraging them to sell the farm and move out near us. What do you think?"*
>
> *"Wow. That's radical. But feasible. Let's think about that. That's a whole new perspective. A real breakthrough."*

A solution set

If you have kept a list, mentally or written, on which you have included all the concerns of each of you, you can aim for a solution set rather than just a simple solution. The idea is to keep adding pieces to the solution until all the concerns are accounted for in your final plan of action. The examples below describe two situations that start out seeming to be intractable conflicts and end up with excellent win-win solutions sets.

> *Ken and Jane faced a serious conflict. Ken wanted more children: Jane did not. Jane simply didn't like babies. She felt awkward with them and experienced their total helplessness as burdensome. In addition, nighttime awakenings to tend to an infant's needs triggered depression in her sensitive neurochemical system. She loved being a mom with their six-year-old, Netta, and felt that Netta fully satisfied her urges to nurture a next generation.*
>
> *Ken, by contrast, regretted deeply that he and Jane did not have a larger family, and especially regretted that their daughter had no siblings. With this latter concern, Jane agreed.*
>
> *Their solution: to adopt a child, but one who was a toddler or older. Ken and Jane are currently in China, and they will be returning shortly with Netta's new sibling.*

> . . . .

> *When Lana and Ron moved to a new city where Ron had been offered an excellent job, Lana wanted to pick a home in town, rather than in the suburbs, and in a neighborhood with lots of children. Ron wanted a house with plenty of space so he could have a home office. He also wanted the house to be bright and sunny with lots of windows. Both were concerned that the house be reasonably priced. Lana and Ron began to squabble, as houses in the affordable, in-town, family-oriented neighborhoods were all too small and too dark to meet Ron's preferences.*

> *Rather than have one of them giving up on a major concern, they decided to buy a small, inexpensive house that they both liked, in town, in a child-oriented neighborhood. They then would renovate the detached garage into a large study for Ron, and would add skylights and extra lighting to make the relatively dark house considerably brighter.*

Concluding Conflict Resolution Dialogue

As with shared decision making, two final ministeps can determine whether a resolution to a conflict will be successful or will turn out to be yet another skirmish in an ongoing war:

- *Summarize together*
  Reiterate out loud the plan you have agreed upon.
- *Ask the essential last question*
  "Are there any little pieces of this that still feel unfinished?"

> *Nicole and Nate, after lengthy discussion, decided that they would buy Nicole's parents tickets to spend several weeks with them this spring. Nicole concluded, "So the plan is that we'll buy them tickets for the first two weeks of May?"*
>
> *"Does we mean you or me?" Nate asked to clarify the plan.*
>
> *"I'll call the travel agent." Nicole said. "Are there any other pieces that still feel unfinished?"*
>
> *"The only other piece for me is whether you and I can spend some time alone during our vacation," Nate said.*
>
> *"My parents could baby-sit if we took a three-day trip in the mountains," Nicole smiled, "I just read about an inexpensive YMCA camp with facilities for biking and hiking. How about if I make reservations?"*

Without this kind of closure, a few weeks down the line Nate and Nicole could have found themselves arguing about who was to have bought the plane tickets or about the extra money that tickets bought at the last minute would have cost. They would also have missed out on the chance to spend part of their vacation alone together.

Allies, Not Adversaries

Conflicts put couples at a choice point. Each can try to overpower the other, as a conflict is essentially a battle that determines who has more power. No matter which defeats the other, however, as soon as you turn against each other, you are taking away from your mutual power. You are injuring each other rather than enhancing each other's lives, and while one of you may temporarily feel more strong from the confrontation, the sum power of the two of you as individuals, as well as the strength and love within your marriage, will have been diminished.

Alternatively, you can beat your swords into plowshares. As soon as you begin to battle, pause, and choose instead to implement the secrets to conflict resolution set forth in this chapter.

Chapter 10
Out-of-Bounds and Fouls

In sports, rules and boundaries clearly delineate when the ball is inbounds, and when it has gone out-of-bounds. In dialogue, the equivalent of the ball is words and the boundaries of the playing field are the ABCDs.

The difference between out-of-bounds play and true foul play is measured by the impact on the receiving partner. Fouls are words and actions that can hurt someone. Foul play is unsafe. Fouls in a marriage result in hurt feelings, wounded pride, damaged trust, loss of self-esteem, shattering of faith in the marriage contract and questioning of the marriage commitment. Fouls can include hurling angry insults, cursing your partner, physical abuse, dishonesty, financial irresponsibility such as spending beyond what you can afford, flirting, emotional intimacy or physical involvement in an extra-marital affair, and similar potential marriage deal breakers.

Chapter 7, on cleanup strategies, described ways to restore well-being after arguments. The initial techniques in this current chapter are for using before arguments have erupted. The chapter then explores two other marriage challenges—what to do if only one person plays by the ABCD rules, and what to do if one person has committed an action that is a major foul.

Getting the Ball Back on the Field

Out-of-bounds communications—hinting, blaming, listening with *but,* or getting overly heated up—indicate that your dialogue is heading away from your goal or off the field of play. When your conversation has strayed, how do you get the ball back into play within the boundaries of the ABCDs?

Call a time-out to retrieve the ball

In sports, after the ball goes out-of-bounds play stops momentarily. Once the ball has been brought back and placed more or less where it was before it went out, play resumes. As we have seen in prior chapters, the same principle can apply to out-of-bounds communications. You can pause the dialogue momentarily, figure out where the dialogue went out-of-bounds, and then resume the dialogue at that point.

Talking about the other person instead of about oneself, for instance, is out-of-bounds.

> *Gerald and Gina have been shopping at the mall. Gerald has become irritable; he is tired and impatient to leave. "You should know that I like to leave by eight o'clock!" he snaps.*

A pause here gives Gerald a moment to think, to realize what he has just done, and to figure out what to do about it. To resume the dialogue, Gerald has two positive options. He can talk about himself:

> *"I'm tired. I'm shopped out, and impatient to get home. I want to be sure I'm not exhausted tomorrow at work."*

Or he can ask about Gina:

> *"How much longer do you want to shop? Would you be willing to go now?"*

Fouls need apologies

Suppose Gerald made a worse error, talking about his wife in a nasty toxic way, which would have been both out-of-bounds and a foul, that is, hurtful.

> *"You act so selfish, ignoring me when I want to leave!"*

Given his fatigue and frustration Gerald might have spoken like this, blaming and name-calling instead of saying what he felt and wanted. In that case, in addition to pausing and resuming the dialogue within bounds he would have needed to offer a cleanup apology.

> *"I'm sorry. I got carried away. I lose it when I'm this tired. I get frantic. I really would like to go home."*

In marriage, as in informally organized sports, no referees stand by to blow a whistle for fouls or to halt play when the conversational ball has slipped out-of-bounds. Players need to know the boundaries and judge for themselves.

Restart play inbounds

Sometimes, especially in a sport like tennis, the receiving player may be able to see where the ball has landed better than the person who hit it. The receiver then needs to make the out-of-bounds call. That is, if your mate goes out of bounds but doesn't call it, you can be the one who pauses, backs up the conversation to where it went out of bounds, and runs it again more constructively from that point.

> When Gerald said, "You should know that I like to leave by eight o'clock!" Gina initially felt hurt and defensive. No one likes to be talked to in an irritated manner. She felt tempted to reply in kind. "Oh yes, if we're shopping for me you want to leave by eight. But if we're shopping for you it's a whole nother story."
>
> Fortunately, Gina knows better. She thought to herself, "Pause. That's always a good first move when I'm getting heated up. Now, it takes two to make a fight. Think, then resume. Use your power to get back on track. What was Gerald trying to tell me?"

Now Gina can turn to Gerald and reiterate, in a nontoxic tone, what she has heard him say. She pictures herself on a soccer field, bringing the ball back to where it crossed the line.

> "So you said you're tired and want to leave, and your irritated voice sounded like you've had it."
>
> "Exactly," Gerald said, sounding a bit calmer.

Now that they are back on track, Gina can keep the dialogue moving forward. She is tempted just to cave in, having heard the urgency in Gerald's voice. At the same time, she too has a pressing agenda. Giving it up without even verbalizing it would be a setup for her to feel resentful, bullied, or depressed. She decides to take a chance, hoping they have successfully returned to the ABCDs, and state her concern.

> "My situation is that I have about twenty minutes more shopping to do, and then I will have bought what I came here to get. Is there a way you could handle twenty minutes more? The sale ends tonight, so it's now or never for me."

Gina is doing a good job of getting the dialogue back on track without criticizing Gerald. After her initial calming pause, she had several options for restarting the dialogue back in bounds.

Ask a question

A question that invites your spouse to describe his or her concerns in I statements prompts an inbounds answer.

- "Why do you want to leave?"
- "What happened that you became suddenly agitated just now?"
- "Would it help, Gerald, if you sat and had an ice cream while I finish up a last twenty minutes of shopping? Or if you waited in the sporting goods store where they have a TV for customers to sit and watch sports videos?"

Remember, if you are going to focus on your mate's thoughts or feelings, do it with questions, not crossovers.

Defuse, then proceed

A change of venue can help bring the conversational ball back inbounds. If you step out of the fray, bring down the tension level, and then resume, your dialogue is likely to proceed more amicably.

> *"Let's step into the coffee shop, where it's quieter, for a few minutes to confer. Then I can explain why I want to stay, I can hear why you want to leave, and we can come up with a plan that works for both of us."*

Explain your concerns

Adding information about your priorities can help your partner gain a broader understanding instead of seeing only his or her concerns.

> *"I do want to be able to get both of us home as soon as we can," Gina began. "And at the same time I would feel terribly frustrated to come all the way to the mall, see exactly what I want at a bargain price, and have to leave before I can get it. I really need another outfit for work. With these sales we can save fifty percent."*
>
> *Gerald thought for a moment. "I guess I could go to the music store while you finish. They have earphones for listening to new CDs.*

Correct listening errors

If you suddenly realize that you've had the mute button on or you have been listening for what's wrong with what your mate said rather than listening to learn, getting back on track is simple. "Can you repeat what you said and let me try listening better?" is pretty much guaranteed to win your mate's heart again.

The harder part of the equation is when your partner is not listening well, and you are looking for a way to get your message through. A *you* statement can wrench you further off course; your mate is likely to become defensive as well as deaf. Fortunately, an *I* statement can work magic.

You Statements	*I* Statements
Len: You're not listening to me! *Linda (defensively):* I am too listening. I just think you're being selfish not letting me finish my shopping.	*Gerald:* I'm having trouble conveying what I want to tell you. Let me try again. I'm feeling frantic. I'd rather we pay more for your clothes than stay another minute. I've past my limit. *Gina:* I'm sorry. I hear you now. At the same time I do feel caught in a bind. That one red suit...

Gerald keeps in mind that his goal is not to correct Gina or to show her that she is doing a poor job on the listening end. His goal is to get his message through, to keep the information flowing and the dialogue going. He remembers that Gina is on his team, that they are together against the problem, not playing against each other.

Ask "What can we do?"

When you or your mate has slipped out-of-bounds, in the heat of the moment focusing on what you can do individually to remedy the situation is probably the most you can hope for. On the other hand, after the heat of the incident has cooled, if you and your mate can step back and discuss together what happened, you may find more possibilities for growth than you would have thought.

The secret to a *we* approach to change is to emphasize to your mate that, rather than looking at what he or she did wrong, you are willing to look at the situation as a problem to which each of you contributed. Your focus will be on what *you* might do differently in the future; your partner's focus will be on understanding his or her options.

Several days after the shopping mall incident, Gina and Gerald sat over coffee discussing what each of them might do differently the next time they want to shop together. Gerald realized that in the future if he was going to accompany his wife on shopping trips he could bring a book. Or they could plan at the outset to spend some time at the mall together and some separately on their own pursuits. Following his wife to serve as her consultant was a role that he had only limited tolerance for, though for a brief time he did enjoy it.

Gerald also realized that he had barked at Gina as a result of "nice-guy-itis." He had subdued his early warning signs that his tolerance for shopping was wearing thin. As a result, by the time he did say something, he had passed the point of being able to say quietly, "I'm running out of steam." Instead his words had burst out in an angry eruption. Next time he would voice his budding impatience at its first indications.

Gina similarly realized that shopping for clothes probably was not an activity best enjoyed with her husband. Because she liked having a companion and second opinion for shopping, she concluded that next time she might bring a woman friend instead of Gerald. She also realized that she had spent the first hour or so looking at minor purchases. Next time she did bring Gerald, she would take care of her most important purchase at the outset, while Gerald was still enthusiastic, and look at scarves and belts and the like after he had lost interest in the shopping expedition.

When Your Mate Won't Play

You may sometimes feel that while you are playing the game of cooperative dialogue, your mate is competing to find out who's right and who's wrong or is playing a round of force-it talk. If you had hoped your partner would play catch with you, but he or she was playing keep-away instead, you would probably feel similarly frustrated.

It is likely that one of you will learn the ABCDs faster than the other, or that one may choose not to learn at all. One of you may persist in a habit that is provocative for the other and show no ability to change. Fix-it talk is a good place to start in such a situation, but if that doesn't work, what then?

You can lead a horse to water...

The bad news is, you can lead a horse to water but you can't make it drink. The bottom line is that you cannot control your partner. As much as you may want to see some changes, only your mate can control whether or not these changes will happen.

Leading a horse to water is helpful. "Water" in this situation is information about the changes you would like to see. By contrast, attempts to control your mate's behavior, to insist, or demand that he or she make the changes you want, generally does not work, and is in itself out-of-bounds communicating.

Several "leading" strategies can succeed. You can bring this book to your mate's attention. Alternatively, you can:

- Give your partner feedback. You can explain the consequences to you of your spouse's words or actions. Using a *when you* ensures that the subject of the feedback is *I*, what *I* feel, think, and would like. A quiet tone of voice may help to avert a defensive response.

- Describe the specific behavior that is troubling for you, again using a *when you,* rather than giving a general label.

- Talk about what you *would like* rather than negatives—what you *don't want*—in hopes that this information will motivate your partner to want to make changes.

The good news is that if you are now able to lead the horse to water, you must be learning the ABCDs. If the secrets, skills, and strategies in this book are helping you feel more personally empowered, then you can feel thankful that the ability to learn is one of your gifts. Perhaps you can let yourself feel compassion instead of irritation toward your partner who has not yet received this gift, at least with regard to the specific growth you would like to see. At the same time, as your spouse secs and appreciates your changes, they may well prove contagious over time.

Fortunately, if your partner just doesn't get it, you are not responsible for forcing him or her to change. You needn't waste your energies on that frustrating project. You can be happy even without the change. You can use your energies for projects you enjoy, for living your life, rather than wasting them on the fruitless project of remodeling an unwilling mate.

The strategies and secrets you have learned from this book will continue to be available to your partner in the future, should he or she become open to them. While few people want to be taught to drive by their mate, and probably even fewer are willing to learn new dialogue patterns from a mate, many eventually are willing to learn from a neutral third source like a book, audiotapes, classes, or a counselor.

Ask yourself "What can I do?"

"What can *I* do?" is exactly the question to ask. "What can *I* do differently so that *I* will be more comfortable?"

Fortunately you always have an almost infinite number of options, including humor and compassion. The following lists just a few. Remember, though, that the goals of these responses are to enable you to feel better and to get the dialogue back on track, not to change your spouse.

- If your mate blames you when things go wrong:

  + you can observe, "I'm not a fan of blame these days. I see what happened differently."

+ you can reassure yourself and your spouse, "It is upsetting when things go wrong."

- If your mate criticizes or gives *don't-wants:*

  + you can ask, "What are you telling me you would you like?"
  + you can offer a *when you:* "When I hear you criticizing me, I lose my desire to please you."

- If your mate hints instead of speaking outright:

  + you can invite more information—"I really would like to know exactly what you think."
  + you can clarify, "Even if I don't like what you tell me, I'll appreciate the information."

- If your mate bullies, using an insulting, angry, or domineering voice:

  + you can leave the situation, explaining, "I'm not for bullying. Let's talk again later." Then later, when your spouse is calmer, you can explain, "I expect my opinion to count, and I don't want to fight. So if my opinion isn't welcome, I leave the conversation. Also, when there's an unpleasant tone of voice, I choose to stay away."

- If your mate listens with *but:*

  + you can respond with *yes and:* "Yes, I agree with you that ... And, as I said before ..."

Assume your partner won't change

If you assume that what you see is what you will continue to get, that the person you see now is the person you will see tomorrow, the realization can be liberating. You only need to figure out how to work with the facts as they are. Changing what you do is not only easier than trying to change anyone else, it often results in turning around the overall situation.

For example, Suzanna, on vacation with her husband, David, and their teenage children, Colin and Shana, focused on the question "What can *I* do?" when David had developed a temporary case of "deafness."

> *Suzanna felt left out. David and their children were leaping in the surf and laughing together in the swimming pool, ignoring her. Initially, Suzanna told David she felt left out and asked him to include her. She suggested that if he could look at her some of the time when he talks, direct at least some of his comments to her when the family was together at meals, and find activities that she could participate in, she would feel much better. Instead of responding helpfully though, David brushed off her concerns.*

Suzanna tried again to convey her feelings. David reacted defensively, denying that he was doing anything problematic and attacking the messenger by accusing his wife of being controlling. When Suzanna had said she felt left out, David had felt criticized. Though Suzanna's requests for his help were well intended, David heard them as attempts to control him. She felt increasingly alone, excluded, and desperate.

At this point Suzanna had several choices. She could rant in anger, withdraw into depressed isolation, or she could start thinking.

Trying to get David to include her was not succeeding. Suzanna focused her thoughts by saying to herself, "He doesn't get it, and he's not going to change. What can I do to get what I want, which is a fun vacation and good connections with my husband and children?"

As she stopped to think, Suzanna remembered to regard anger as a stop sign. She realized that although she was tempted to shout at David to berate him for his selfishness and insensitivity, she would do better by continuing to pause and to think. She considered the questions "What do *I* want?" and "What can *I* do differently to get this concern met more effectively?"

"What do I want?" she asked herself. "I want to enjoy this vacation, and to connect in fun ways here with David and the kids." Beginning now to seek new solutions, she thought, "I'll stop putting my husband in the role of gatekeeper. Instead I'll make arrangements myself with each of them for activities that we can enjoy in pairs. Individual time with each of them will bypass the problem of my feeling excluded when the four of us are together. And when the three of them are together, I can take photographs or read, activities I enjoy doing alone. When David and the kids come back from fishing, I'll suggest this plan."

When David and the children returned, Suzanna invited her husband to sit on the deck with her for coffee. Now feeling upbeat instead of beat-up, Suzanna could enjoy the sunshine and her husband's companionship. After considerable pleasant time together, Suzanna suggested her plan. By saying what she would be doing instead of what she wanted David to do, she avoided triggering David's defensiveness and engaged his listening. The rest of the vacation went delightfully.

Use compassion

When you see your mate doing something you don't like, and he or she is unwilling or unable to change, how you think of your partner will determine whether you feel small and depressed, resentful, outright angry, or at peace with the reality in front of you. Compassion is the key. Compassion gives you the ability to accept that your mate has a problem and to see his or her limitations in an understanding rather than a condemning way. You don't have to like your mate's limitations; you just need to accept them as a fact of life—the way you accept fatigue, occasional illness, and losses by your favorite football team.

Compassion can take a number of forms:

Regard faults as handicaps

What do you see as your partner's biggest "fault?" Now notice what happens if instead of defining your mate's unfortunate tendency as a fault, you regard it as a handicap. Handicaps—such as blindness and deafness—invite a paradoxical blend of acceptance and practical thinking.

For example, does your partner tend to be self-centered? Selfishness is a handicap in the development of bilateral listening. Can you learn, together, to work with and around this handicap? That's love.

Look at the flip side of negative traits

A second way of viewing your partner's provocative habits in a more positive light is to flip over the coin. The reverse side of a negative habit is often a positive trait. For instance, does your mate sometimes become too domineering? Perhaps you chose your mate in part for his or her personal strength.

The admirable strength and the tendency to become overpowering may be inextricably linked. Is he or she too rigid? Perhaps you have a partner who can be counted on for consistency. Is he or she fragile? Perhaps one of your mate's strengths is this sensitive, if painful, radar for when things are not quite right.

Regard annoying habits as nascent positives

Try reading your spouse's negative habits as fledgling strengths. Is he or she bossy? Maybe this suggests not yet fully developed leadership skills. Is he or she disorganized? Maybe the chaos comes from a high-energy willingness to tackle multiple projects that has yet to be tempered with understanding of how much is enough.

Allow time to work its magic

If your attitude toward your mate's faults is compassionate, this understanding can give you patience to let time be your ally. Time is in fact a notoriously unreliable magician; as often as not, it brings no change. However, giving your mate the opportunity to absorb new perspectives at least takes the pressure off you. And you never know. Like the miraculous green fuzz of new growth on brown earth in springtime, changes may eventually emerge.

After a Major Foul

Fouls can injure players, make play unfair, or destroy the pleasure of the game. Fouls therefore require more than just a pause before play is resumed. They need an apology—at least "I'm sorry" and better yet a full run-through of the five-step apology sequence described in Chapter 7.

Apologies are in order after any toxicity: hurtful sarcasm, insulting comments, or a bullying tone of voice. After major fouls (see list at the end of this chapter), your apology needs to be much more comprehensive. It is also likely to be asymmetrical. If you have fouled, you need to take responsibility for your error and acknowledge your significant responsibility for the upset. If you have developed a serious problem, such as gambling, drugs, infidelity, anger outbursts, or violence, no matter what irritations from your mate may have been involved, the responsibility for your actions lies squarely on your shoulders.

Look in the mirror

When you have done something that you know was wrong, if you can rectify it, apologize thoroughly, verify that your spouse has healed, and learn from the situation so that you are certain that you will not repeat your mistake, your error becomes a part of your having lived and learned.

Look clearly in the mirror of your mind's eye in order to understand as fully as possible what you did and why. The point is not to criticize yourself, which helps no one. Rather, look to understand, to see as clearly as possible:

- what you did
- how you came to do it—the time, place, or events that triggered it
- toward what purposes you did it—what you were intending to accomplish
- what was mistaken in what you did
- what the costs were to you, to your spouse, and to others
- what you would differently next time

Looking back in your life can help you to understand both childhood sources of current problems and more recent contributing factors. Understanding the intentions behind the mistaken episodes might help you understand the current difficulty.

Some people do this kind of self-exploration best aloud, with a mate, a relative, a friend, a religious counselor, or a therapist. Others succeed on their own by writing in a journal, by taking long walks, by lying in bed and thinking, or by sitting in a favorite place in meditative self-analysis. The important thing is that you do some kind of serious introspection, and then that you share the results of your understanding with your partner. Your mate needs to understand what you now understand in order to feel confident that history will not repeat itself.

Unfortunately, self-awareness itself is not necessarily enough to prevent recurrences of most fouls. Once you understand the *hows* and *whys* behind your problem, you will need to devise a strategy to ensure that the same situations in the future do not bring the same behaviors.

With major or repeated mistaken behaviors, self-correcting on your own probably is not a realistic goal. Consult a mental health professional or seek a self-help group. For addictive problems such as alcohol, drugs, and gambling, these groups are often free of charge and can be very helpful.

Recover together

Insight is only half of the recovery process. The other half is the talking you must do with your mate. For a full recovery, each of you needs to do your part of the cleanup if the outcome is to be a stronger and more loving marriage. Psychologist Jean Marie Hamel (1995) studied highly positive marriages, or as she calls them "transformational marriages." She found that when these couples go out-of-bounds or foul, they don't feel embarrassed to talk about their mistakes. Like good athletes, after a difficult game they analyze their errors and devise corrections.

The steps that will help you learn, grow, and leave behind an upsetting period in your life are the strategies for cleaning up after any toxic spill: full hearing of each other to put together the puzzle pieces of what happened, apologies, and listening to learn so as to prevent recurrences. You need to be able to discuss the upsetting event as a couple, with both of you following the principles of braided dialogue—open talking, honest verbalizing of feelings, and careful listening to learn each other's experience of the incident.

> *Suzanna was furious. She had just discovered that David had forgotten to pay his self-employment tax, had forgotten to file a crucial deed, and had forgotten to pick up dinner on his way home from work as he had promised. A mistake or forgetfulness is human up to a point, but Suzanna had begun feeling that she couldn't rely on David to follow through on anything he promised. She questioned, "Is it because he doesn't love me? Doesn't he care enough to do the things for the family that he has promised? Is he hopelessly like a child, doing just what he feels like doing?"*
>
> *David apologized sincerely. He, too, was baffled. His apology included an attempt to piece together how each of these lapses had happened.*

Suzanna and David, by talking at length through the full series of steps for cleaning up after upsets, explore the problem to the point that they discover a surprising explanation for why David had repeatedly disappointed Suzanna and himself, an explanation with clear-cut remedies.

> *Suddenly the picture came clear in a new way. Suzanna had just read an article about attention deficit disorder. Maybe David had a classic case of ADD. Throughout his childhood, although he had been a highly intelligent student, he was always getting in trouble for being out of his seat, not finishing his work, and bothering other children. At home as a child he had been in trouble equally continuously, and had never understood why.*
>
> *Suzanna and David pursued their new hypothesis. David spoke with his physician, who prescribed medication for this disorder. To his amazement, on the medication David found that he could concentrate on his work with unprecedented ease, stay focused on one project at a time, and remember side projects such as his taxes, filing the document, and picking up dinner. Their full apology sequence, including piecing together the puzzle of what had happened and learning from it, had been radically successful.*

Be wary of tactics that make matters worse
If you have committed a foul

After you have made a serious mistake in your marriage, if you deny that you have done anything wrong and refuse to participate in the cleanup process, you can make matters much worse. In most instances, resistance to acknowledging your mistakes will exacerbate your situation.

This kind of self-defeating resistance typically takes one of four forms:

- Denial
- Minimizing
- Blaming the messenger
- Blaming someone else

> *Mickey was a quiet but very responsible post office clerk. For a while, however, he was working with colleagues whose chronic teasing left him feeling fragile. To cope, he began drinking when he came home. As he drank, he would become verbally aggressive toward his children, taunting them.*
>
> *Mickey at first responded to his wife Lana's concerns about his drinking with denial: "I didn't have anything to drink! And I'm not being mean to the children!" In response to Mickey's denial Lana felt her anger rising. She told him sharply and clearly that she didn't buy a word he was saying.*

When denial was obviously not succeeding in convincing his wife, Mickey turned to minimizing. "It's really no big deal," he insisted. "I only had a beer or two!"

Mickey's minimizing further infuriated Lana. She feared that her husband was endangering his physical health as well as the emotional health of their marriage and their children, and she was appalled at what seemed to her to be a lack of appropriate remorse.

Mickey's third strategy, blaming the messenger, continued to make the situation worse. "You shouldn't nag me! You're too controlling!" he insisted.

"Fine," Lana snapped, "I won't control you; I'll leave you."

Mickey's final attempt at denial of responsibility, blaming someone else, also backfired. "It's because of those guys at work. You need to pick on them, not me!"

To which Lana immediately responded by packing up herself and the children and going to live with her parents until she could sort out her options.

This case actually had a happy ending. Lana's clear message that Mickey's drinking and mistreatment of their children constituted unacceptable fouls paid off. Mickey realized that he did have a problem. He obtained help. The entire family thus became happier and emotionally healthier.

If you've been on the receiving end of a foul

Sports generally specify penalties for foul play. In a good marriage, the penalties, or negative consequences, occur naturally. That is, if your mate does something that is out-of-bounds, you will feel angry, may lose confidence in your mate as a partner, feel disgusted at his or her behavior, and see him or her in a lesser light. Ultimately you may decide to separate or divorce. These natural consequences need to be verbalized to your mate, as this feedback helps your partner to understand the impacts of his or her mistakes. Everything we do has consequences. When people engage in wrongdoings, they generally have been at least temporarily unaware of the consequences.

Punishing your partner with extended criticism, lectures, or withholding affection tends to breed resentment more than it motivates growth. However, you need to be willing, like Lana, to implement natural consequences. Consequences are different from threats or punishments. They are the simple realities. If your mate has acted in ways that potentially endanger you, for instance, you must, for your personal survival, take whatever measures are necessary to protect yourself. Similarly, you may find you have emotionally and physically withdrawn from the relationship. Using *I* statements and *when yous,* these new facts on the ground need to be communicated for you to begin to heal.

Each partner bears responsibility for managing his or her own recovery from the upset. It is not your responsibility to impose further penalties and punishment. You need to take care of yourself; you are not responsible for fixing your mate.

Help yourself when you've been hurt

The person who has been the receiver or victim of a foul also needs to employ recovery strategies. Recovery from major fouls is not automatic, even when the mate who committed the foul has been able to acknowledge and apologize profoundly for an error. In some cases, in fact, recovery never quite happens. Like a glass that has been broken, trust, once shattered, sometimes cannot be pieced back together.

To take care of yourself, you will need skills of three types:

- Self-soothing
- Insight
- Reality testing

Self-soothing

Ruminating on how badly your mate acted will reinforce how distraught you feel afterwards. The sooner you can soothe yourself by refocusing on your own merits and by indulging in your enjoyments in life, the less harm you will have allowed your mate's mistakes to have caused you.

This is a tough one, because after someone has hurt you, you may feel an urge to prove how terrible the error was by showing how long and painfully you suffered in response. While such a strategy may increase your mate's guilt, it leaves you paying further for his or her error.

By contrast, healing yourself will enable you to feel better as soon as possible. In addition, your spouse, seeing you at your attractive best, is more likely to feel motivated to try to deserve being married to you.

Insight

In every upset lies a nugget of wisdom. It may take considerable searching to discover that golden reward, but as you find it you will discover also that your self-soothing will accelerate. The nugget of wisdom may be about human nature or an insight directly about yourself.

Learning about how to handle life's challenges more effectively is a lifetime project. We learn especially in high-intensity moments. Your job is to turn the intensity triggered by your partner's upsetting behavior into an opportunity for your own personal growth.

Reality testing

Self-soothing and insight by themselves can get you into trouble. Once you feel better and have some understanding about your role, small or large, in what happened, remind yourself that focusing in on yourself does not give you the whole story. The inward focus reempowers you and helps you feel better, but it can be dangerous to stop there. The essential third stage is a reality check. What does the fact that my partner did this say about him or her, and about our potential for having a safe, strong, and loving marriage?

If the offending mate does not understand the gravity of the foul, for instance, then your problem is bigger than just the foul alone. You may be looking at someone who lacks the requisite moral development, empathy, personal sense of responsibility, capacity for insight, or desire for growth to handle the role of partner. Marriage is for grown-ups. Some people have adult bodies but not the emotional maturity to handle the power of two.

If that is the case, wishful thinking that your mate will change can be a dangerous strategy. On the other hand, you may have reasons to believe that however disappointing your partner's behavior has been, the benefits he or she brings to your life merit tolerating the bad times. You may also see signs of serious commitment to growth and change. These are serious decisions. Hopefully you and your partner will never have to confront them.

Get professional help

Cleaning up after toxic spills is like first aid after cuts and bruises.

Cleaning up after major fouls is more like setting a broken limb or doing surgery.

To recover from the inevitable natural consequences of pain, anger, shame, and regret that occur in response to these major fouls, a thorough cleanup is important. Genuine healing and reconciliation occur only after the full process of turning the curse into a blessing has been completed. To get there, professional consultation can be a big help. The following case exemplifies the therapeutic process.

> Joyce was a warm, gracious, hardworking young mother. Her husband, Roger was more reserved and stern. For some time their marriage had been punctuated by emotional storms. Joyce would suddenly erupt in furious anger, ranting and shouting and sometimes throwing things.
>
> Joyce and Roger initially tried to handle Joyce's rages on their own. They understood that the point in talking after an upsetting incident is not punishment or blame. Rather, they tried to piece together an understanding what happened, apologize, and learn to ensure that the foul would not occur again.

Eventually, however, realizing that they had been through the cycle of upset-apology-calm multiple times, they decided they needed to seek professional consultation.

Therapy began with exploration into the background causes of the anger explosions. These understandings led to additional insights about what Joyce and Roger each could do to prevent recurrences.

I asked Joyce what thoughts and feelings immediately preceded her rages. She identified three factors that had preceded her most recent explosion and that seemed also to have been present in others. She was exhausted from the stress of having been working two jobs for several weeks. She felt frustrated when her husband was not listening to her side of what they had been talking about, and instead was blaming her for the problem. She felt further frustrated when, feeling her fuse get shorter, she had tried to go into another room and her husband had blocked her way.

I also suggested that Joyce explore what in her background taught her that anger explosions were a viable option.

Joyce thought at length about this question. "In my large family, the best way I had to get heard when I really wanted something was to make a dramatic scene. Otherwise no one seemed to care what I wanted. What my brothers wanted mattered, but girls' and women's desires didn't count unless we made a big fuss."

We then worked on strategies for preventing further explosions.

Their first strategy for preventing more anger outbursts was stress reduction. Joyce and Roger agreed to reevaluate the hours Joyce was working and to look for ways her responsibilities either at work or at home might be lightened somewhat.

A second prevention strategy was to practice their disengagement routines, so that Joyce would be able to nip growing tensions before she erupted into full-scale anger. Roger needed to learn to give Joyce time alone to cool off rather than insisting that she talk when he wanted to talk irrespective of her anger levels.

A third strategy was to work on the ABCDs so that Joyce and Roger's attempts to talk over problems—especially child-rearing questions—would be more effective.

Fourth, we agreed that Joyce would begin taking antidepressant medication, which reduces the tendency toward angry outbursts. Joyce had experienced the kind of intense upsets in her childhood that can alter people's biochemistry, making them more emotionally volatile as adults. Antidepressant medication eased this biological vulnerability.

❤ It often takes two to tango

Sometimes, as you look in detail at what actually happened in an upsetting incident surprising realizations come to the fore.

Joyce and Roger were relieved to find Joyce's emotional explosions decreasing. When she felt herself beginning to anger, Joyce was able to extricate herself quickly, before she began to rage out of control. Some months later, however, Joyce and Roger returned to treatment because the night before she had erupted again with all the furor of her former episodes.

This time Roger insisted that it was all Joyce's fault. On one level this reasoning made sense. Angry behavior is ultimately the responsibility of the angry person. On the other hand, as we looked more closely at the actual incident, a surprising pattern emerged. Joyce had seen a potential rage attack coming. Roger had been criticizing her parenting skills, a subject that both of them knew was sensitive, and one that he generally discussed in a much more tactful manner. Feeling herself getting defensive, Joyce had excused herself, appropriately removing herself from a situation she feared she might not be able to handle.

Joyce went to her space, the kitchen, but contrary to their disengagement agreement, Roger came in soon after to continue their dialogue, insisting that she agree with his criticisms. "He's not listening to me!" had been Joyce's desperate last thought before her rage exploded.

Remembering this sequence of events, Joyce and Roger suddenly saw the pattern in a new light. Since he had returned from a recent business trip, Roger had been hostile. They realized that Roger's anxieties about something work-related had often been a precursor to Joyce's upsets. Roger worked for a television station and was worrying about losing his job. In fact, he had a significant history of job losses, more even than the frequent job changes typical to his industry. When he was feeling insecure about his work, his pattern was to come home and goad Joyce until she would finally explode. Then they would talk about how she was the problem.

As they continued to explore Joyce's rages, and now also Roger's role in them, Joyce realized that at some level of consciousness she had known all along that her explosions had an element of cover-up for her husband's job difficulties. As long as they both agreed to make her the one with problems, neither of them had to address the underlying difficulty, namely that Roger's "I'm right/you're wrong" attitude at work provoked bosses to fire him.

Joyce had learned from her mother not to expect that men would be able to speak about their difficulties. Roger had learned growing up to blame rather than to accept responsibilities for mistakes. Now was a learning time for both of them.

Joyce and Roger's case proved complex and multifaceted. In general, it's a good idea to seek professional consultation after a major foul.

Reevaluate: Terminate the game or renew the contract

Psychologist Lois Davitz (1988) found in her research that healthy marriage teammates take the continuation of their relationship as a given. They figure out how to get the ball back in play instead of threatening to leave the field when difficulties come up. Problem solving focuses on the problem at hand; it doesn't expand to question the whole relationship.

At the same time, if one partner engages in behavior that violates the marriage contract by seriously harming rather than cherishing the other, at some point the contract itself must be reevaluated (Medved, 1990). The following major marital fouls say get professional help and reevaluate the marriage.

- Persistent lying
- Infidelity
- Verbal abuse (rageful name-calling, threats, foul language, etc.)
- Physical threats or abuse (pushing, hitting, choking, etc.)
- Threats of punishment for telling friends, other family members, or authorities about abusive behavior
- Alcohol or drug abuse
- Gambling in an amount that causes financial or family problems
- Serious inadequacy in marital responsibilities (abuse or neglect of children, financial irresponsibility, etc.)
- Psychotic or other irrational behavior (hearing voices or paranoid beliefs)
- Extreme jealousy, control, or possessiveness (following or checking up on the other, restricting who he or she can talk with, accusations of unfaithfulness)

After major marital fouls, the cleanup can seem hopelessly open-ended. It can be helpful eventually to determine a date at which time you will both reexamine and either end or renew your marital vows.

If you decide to recommit to one another, a renewal ceremony can help you to delineate clearly the pre-foul, contaminated, and post-cleanup eras of your marriage. The ceremony might include just yourselves or invite others who are close to you. It may include a symbolic act, a joyful gathering, or quiet thoughtful words of rededication to each other and to a clear set of marriage understandings. Ceremonies and rituals help to clarify transitions between what was then and what is now.

Keep the Team Strong

Allowing out-of-bounds communications and fouls to disrupt your lives seriously undermines a marriage. The last several chapters have clarified how to handle anger and prevent fighting, how to resolve conflicts that seem intractable, and how to heal when prevention and resolution have not succeeded. These skills, plus the communication basics of Part I, are secrets to keeping a marriage strong. The chapters ahead focus on the remaining agenda of this book, keeping your marriage loving.

Part III

MAKING A GOOD RELATIONSHIP GREAT

In retail sales it is said that while it is always important to satisfy your customers, the ideal is to *delight* them. The same is true of marriage. This final set of chapters offers dialogue strategies for maximizing the upsides of marriage.

- *Support*— helping when the other hurts, so you can help each other through life's inevitable emotional ups and downs
- *Intimacy*— developing deeper emotional and more satisfying physical understandings of yourself and your partner
- *Joy and love*— maintaining a joyful home, with emotional health, an optimal balance of sharing and separation, comfortable division of labor, and ample affection

Being there for each other in difficult times, talking openly with each other, sharing affection, laughter, activities you both value, and joy—in these ways couples interweave and enhance their lives. If you not only live and work amicably together, but also fully delight in your partnership, you have created a most special union.

Why is connection vital?

While these bonus dimensions of marriage would have their appeal in any era, they satisfy a particular thirst in the fragmented social structures of contemporary America. In the introduction I mentioned that while a marriage can be considered successful if the couple lives amicably side by side, many people now crave more interconnection.

In previous eras, couples were more likely to live in large extended families and to belong to a community where neighbors interacted frequently for fun, support, and camaraderie. Embedded in a close-knit network of family and friends, a husband and wife could spend most of their time in separate spheres, living out their lives in parallel tracks, without loneliness. This parallel marriage structure may have been less inherently strong than one with more interconnections, but if a couple had only minimal contact in their day-to-day lives, the marriage still felt good enough. Other social needs could be met elsewhere. Caring people were always close by for sharing good times and for commiserating over troubles.

By contrast, in today's world the parallel-lives arrangement no longer suffices. Most people's extended families now are smaller and widely scattered. They can gather together physically only on holidays or vacations. Although the telephone and, increasingly, electronic mail keep a fragile connection alive, face-to-face contact is minimal. Friends also tend to live apart from each other, both geographically distant and pulled in multiple directions by divergent interests and commitments. Moreover, for many people long work hours and commutes devour time that formerly would have been available for social and community activities. Thanks to the mixed blessing of cars, people's lives are dispersed over large geographic areas, rather than concentrated in a single town or neighborhood.

With so little social support, marriage partners often have to turn to each other. An enriched relationship with a mate becomes all the more a treasure.

Notes

What wisdom can you find that is greater than kindness?
—Jean-Jacques Rousseau, *Emile, ou De l'Education*

Chapter 11

Supporting Each Other

Life is a bumpy road. As you travel along it, looking ahead you may feel anxious. As you look behind, you may feel regrets. As you proceed, you may feel weary, overwhelmed by the challenges, frustrated by the steep inclines, discouraged when the way seems too difficult, or injured as the bumps jar you.

The good news is that you have a companion on the journey—a partner with whom anxiety, fatigue, and frustration can be shared. You have a friend who can lend you energy, help you up when you stumble, tend your cuts and bruises, and help you find your way. One of the many benefits of marriage is that it brings each of you your very own personal talk therapist, with no additional fee, and with lifelong availability.

Some people are natural helpers, just as some people are natural athletes. Some are not. If you feel uncertain what to do when your partner appears distressed, however, there is no need to panic. This chapter gives step-by-step guidelines.

The basic strategy is fairly simple: When the going gets tough, the tough play baseball. More on that in a bit. First, let's look at some basic principles.

How Talking Helps

One person listening empathically to another can have remarkable healing power. Why should this be? The healing power of two talking together comes from multiple dimensions.

Listening is a necessary comfort

Feelings often need soothing, and listening provides it. Our bodies go on hyperalert when we are stressed. Sympathetic listening and kindly words offer verbal stroking to a troubled mind.

Psychologist Harry Harlow (1958) studied baby monkeys. He found that when the monkeys felt upset or alarmed, hugging a parent monkey, or even a terry cloth on wire surrogate, provided essential calming. Without the soothing option of a parent or parent substitute to hug, young monkeys developed "neurotic" signs of chronic tension. Feeling heard is like hugging and being held. Especially if your listener remains calm when you feel troubled, you will find that his or her quiet listening soothes your tensions.

If you can invite your troubled partner to put words to troubling feelings, and you are able to give evidence that you hear and empathize with these feelings, you will be providing invaluable emotional support.

Where *id* was let *ego* be

Freud explained the process of emotional healing with his famous phrase "Where id was let ego be." *Id* refers to fears and desires; often these impulses lie just below consciousness. *Ego* refers to conscious thinking. Freud's great realization was really a remarkably simple one. He said that situations and feelings that bother us can hover in our subconscious, nagging at us and dragging us down. When you are unable to see clearly enough what a feeling is actually about, emotions feel burdensome instead of helpful. The essence of Freud's talk-therapy idea was that talking gives you a chance to bring troubling feelings and the situations they stem from out into the light of ego, of conscious awareness, so you can *think* about them. If you talk aloud about your feelings, your feelings lead you to understanding of the problem.

Talking is therapeutic because it enables you to take a troubling situation, place it out in the open where you can look at it clearly, and describe all facets of it, and gradually see the problem from refreshing new perspectives. A listener's questions can help you access the data about the problem that exists subconsciously. Sometimes a listener can also add information that expands your understanding of the difficulty.

Talking brings conflict resolution

Bad feelings are a bright sign that flashes PROBLEM. We feel emotionally distressed when we feel stuck in or struck by a life problem, a conflict that we cannot solve.

Talking is therapeutic when it helps you to use your feelings to identify the troubling conflict, explore the elements of that conflict, and conclude with a plan of action for handling the conflict in a more effective way. Interestingly, the conflict doesn't necessarily have to be resolved for you to feel better. Gaining a new view of what you can do often suffices.

Conflicts that create emotional distress can develop within one person, between two people, or between a person and a situation. Internally, for instance, you might feel pulled between wanting to watch a football game and feeling you should visit a sick uncle. You might feel conflicted between changing jobs to something more interesting and staying where you have been working because the pay is good. These conflicts are *intrapsychic*.

Conflicts can be *interpersonal;* that is, they may occur between two people. Depressed, anxious, or angry feelings may indicate a conflict between you and your mate, or between you and a colleague, a friend, or a family member.

Conflicts also can arise between a person and a situation, such as if you want to be healthy yet have an illness. You may want children and can't get pregnant. Or you may need employment but can't find a job.

When the Going Gets Tough, Play Ball

In baseball, in order to score you need to make it to first base, go on to second, touch third, and continue on to home plate. To feel better when you are troubled by a problem you need to travel three bases before you can return to the home base of feeling comfortably normal. This kind of baseball obviously needs no bats or balls or even a sunny day, but the metaphor can help you to remember a process that can bring comfort when one of you is distressed.

Uncomfortable feelings are the sign that you need to "go to bat" on a problem in your life. If your mate has uncomfortable feelings, you serve as coach. Let's look at what the coach does in this form of baseball.

- First, the coach does not solve the problem. The coach is there to help the player work his or her way around the bases, not to do the batting or running for the player. Generally the most helpful role for you as a supportive mate is not to solve your partner's problem but to support your partner in the problem-solving process.

- Second, a good coach listens and looks very intently at what is going on. Your closely attuned attention assures your troubled mate that he or she is not alone in grappling with the challenge. It also offers a second set of eyes and ears for understanding the problem.

- Finally, a good coach helps player morale. "You can do it!" can provide an invaluable boost when your partner faces tough challenges.

The remainder of this chapter focuses on these coaching skills, since this chapter is about how to be a great partner, not on how to heal your personal emotional woes. Nonetheless, if you prefer to handle problems in a more solitary fashion, you can guide your self-soothing the same way. The three bases correspond to the three ways that talking helps.

The three bases

Your job as supportive listener is to help your partner to get around the diamond. If you can just help your mate get to first base, that is already a boon. If you help him or her make it around all three bases, both of you can enjoy scoring a return to full well-being.

- *First base*— Identify the conflict or problem that has been generating the negative emotion. The coach helps the player to focus on feelings in order to uncover the source.

- *Second base*— Gather data, through questions and answers, about the various concerns and facts of situation. The coach asks questions about the player's concerns, the facts of the situation, and other participants' concerns.

- *Third base*— Find solutions. The coach asks questions that lead to a plan of action to alleviate the negative feeling.

These three bases should be familiar from earlier chapters in this book. They correspond to the three steps of shared decision making and the three steps of conflict resolution. These similarities make sense when you think about it. If feelings signal conflicts, and the process of feeling better is a process of conflict resolution, then therapeutic talk should have much in common with both making joint decisions and resolving conflicts.

First Base: Expressing feelings

Any evidence of emotion—an emerging tear, a furrowed brow, an anxious voice—merits attention. The only way you can get your player to first base, to express feelings and the thoughts that go with them, is by encouraging him or her to focus on feelings. Your interest as a listener makes it safe for your partner to put his or her feelings into words, to explore the thoughts that go with the feelings, and thereby to start the movement toward feeling better.

In a research study on emotional support, bereaved parents and spouses were asked what gestures others had made to them were helpful and what had been unhelpful (Lehman et al. 1986). They listed the following:

Unhelpful Responses	Helpful Responses
Encouraging recovery	Expressions of concern
Giving advice	Simply being there and listening
Minimizing the loss	Providing opportunity to ventilate and validating the feelings
Forced cheerfulness	Sharing similar experiences

If you see or hear a sign of feelings, you may be tempted to offer a quick distraction to keep your partner from feeling bad. In baseball terms, this is like coaching your player to strike out. Feelings are your best clues to finding out what the problem is. Feelings are like Geiger counters. They tick faster and louder as they near a place where essential information is buried.

Unhelpful: Tuning Out	Helpful: Focusing on Feelings
Len (noticing that Linda is frowning): Hey, Linda, come see what a gorgeous morning it is!	*Gerald (noticing that Gina is frowning):* What's that frown about, Gina?

Len means well, but his attempt to fix Linda's feelings by distracting her is likely to be the opposite of helpful. Gerald, by focusing on the clue, will find that it leads them to important understandings.

Responses that show respectful understanding of your mate's feelings complete the trip to first base.

Invalidating Response	Respectful Response
Linda: I'm so mad at myself. I can't find my new leather jacket. I've looked everywhere. Maybe it was stolen out of the car; I don't know. It was by far the nicest jacket I've ever owned. I loved it.	*Gina:* I'm so mad at myself. I can't find my new leather jacket. I've looked everywhere. Maybe it was stolen out of the car; I don't know. It was by far the nicest jacket I've ever owned. I loved it.
Len: It's only a jacket. It's not like someone died or something. Gone is gone. Let's go out for a walk.	*Gerald:* Oh! What a disappointment! It looked great on you, too!
Linda: I don't feel like you understand. I loved that jacket.	*Gina:* Yes. It meant a lot to me, to be able to wear something that special. Oh well. I guess gone is gone. Let's go for a walk. I'll wear my old coat.
Len: It's not like it was a person or something.	

Again Len means to be reassuring, but he is actually invalidating Linda's feelings by saying, "It's only a jacket." Instead of soothing Linda, he is adding frustration to her already negative emotional state.

Remember, communication requires a speaker and a listener. To be fully comforted by expressing a feeling, your partner needs to receive a genuinely interested reply. Listening to feelings means that you not only hear what your mate has said about the emotion and the thoughts that go with it, but that you then think about what you have heard, and answer in a way that indicates that you have understood.

Amplify to empathize

Empathy is the ability to hear the feelings of others and to respond in a way that shows that you have understood the feeling. When your partner expresses an emotion, your ability to respond empathically to that feeling will determine the course of the ensuing dialogue.

To convey empathy, one reliable formula is *amplify to empathize.* Amplification is part of what makes some people seem warm and others cold. Amplification is the process of taking seriously what you have heard and expanding on it. In the following example, while Linda does empathize—she gives evidence that she hears her husband's feelings—Gina empathizes in a way that feels considerably warmer.

Minimal Response	Empathic Response
Len: I'm anxious about how much work I have to get done this week before we go on vacation.	*Gerald:* I'm anxious about how much work I have to get done this week before we go on vacation.
Linda: I can see that.	*Gina:* It does sound like you're juggling a lot of projects at once. I don't know how you manage so much at one time, and with the vacation week coming up, I can see why you would feel stressed about finishing it all.

Conveying that you have heard what has been expressed, has an intriguing impact on the upset person. When joyful emotions feel heard and amplified, the joy is augmented. When sad, frustrated, or angry emotions are shared and amplified in response, the empathic response tends to decrease the feeling. In this regard amplifying to empathize is a particularly useful all-purpose formula for listening to feelings.

Listening feels good

How is trying to listen to your spouse's feelings likely to affect you? Are you at risk for seesaw syndrome, that is, for feeling increasingly down as your spouse begins to feel more up?

Psychologists Clifford Notarius and Lisa Herrick (1988) asked their subjects, female college students, to talk with a depressed student who was actually a drama student role-playing someone who was depressed. After they had talked for 15 minutes, the subjects filled out questionnaires about how they felt after the conversation. Subjects who had relied on giving advice, chitchat, or joking to try to distract or lighten up the depressed person's mood afterward felt somewhat depressed themselves. They also were not interested in talking again to the depressed person. By contrast, those who used supportive listening techniques such as the ones suggested above felt quite positive after the conversation and tended to want to talk again. The specific listening responses that felt good to both the talker and the listener included:

- Emotional echoing such as, "Boy, that must have been rough."

- Commiserating by mentioning similar problems. "My boyfriend dumped me recently, too, and I've been feeling down just like you."

- Offering encouragement that focused on the emotions "Everyone feels badly like that when they break up. Fortunately it's a phase, and then you'll probably feel better." Note that encouragement is different from minimizing: "Oh it's not a big deal. Everyone feels that way." Encouragement agrees that the feeling is hard now and then adds information about what will happen later.

Second Base: Exploring

Second base is where you gather information. As coach, you need to ask questions. Learn all you can about the difficult situation. Explore your mate's underlying concerns; find out the facts of the dilemma; find out about the other people involved and what their concerns might be. Your questions help your partner to gather the data he or she will need eventually for devising solutions.

Common second-base errors include:

- focusing on the person, on what he or she did wrong, instead of on the problem

- assigning blame instead of analyzing the dilemma

- gathering information about the problem, without placing blame or finding fault, leads to helpful new solutions.

♡ Let your curiosity be your guide

If you're not sure what questions to ask when your loved one is distressed, let your natural curiosity guide you. Think of yourself and your partner as confronting a mystery. You are the assistant detective. What information will help you get to the bottom of the mystery of your mate's problem? What would either of you need to know to understand what is causing it and what kinds of solutions might alleviate it? Remember, that specific details about concerns generally hold the key to finding new solutions.

For this second-base task of gathering information, the coach sometimes has additional information that can be helpful. As a general rule, ask questions first, then add your own input.

Interestingly, being able to talk about emotionally distressing situations is in itself therapeutic, even if the problem itself does not get solved. In addition, the feeling of camaraderie, of knowing that there is someone who cares enough about you to want to help, adds a significant emotional boost that can help a difficult situation feel lighter.

Third Base: Solution possibilities

Third base involves devising possible solutions. Solutions often take the form of variations on a few broad themes:

- do something different
- bring in additional resources
- think about the situation in a new and less distressing way
- leave the situation for a better one

Common errors at this stage include the following:

- *Short-circuiting the explorations*— Did you give your mate enough time at second base? Are you beginning to propose solutions before your partner has had time to explore all the dimensions of the problem?

- *Offering your own solutions*— A listener can be tempted to take over responsibility for fixing the problem. Enthusiasm and knowledge can pump your eagerness to offer solutions.

Instead of too quickly offering solutions, move together gradually toward a more detailed understanding of the problem. Solutions will then emerge.

Facilitating your spouse's problem solving, rather than taking over the problem and solving it yourself, is generally the most helpful. In desperate circumstances, your immediate suggestions may be appreciated. Or, if your partner has run out of ideas, at that point your suggestions may be welcome. In most circumstances, however, first encourage your spouse to generate his or her own possible solutions. Then, if you ask before offering ideas—"Would you like me to offer some solution suggestions?"—you are likely to be greeted with less resistance.

♡ Remember whose problem it is

The biggest difference between shared decision making and therapeutic talk lies in who recommends and selects solutions to the problem. In shared decision making, both spouses are involved in the problem, so each of them needs to offer ideas for what they themselves can do. In therapeutic talk, by contrast, the solution is most likely to fit just right if it is proposed and selected by the player, not by the coach.

If you do offer solution suggestions, the hard part is to do so in a way that makes clear that your ideas can be accepted or rejected. Your suggestion is not you, so a rejection of your suggestion is not a rejection of you.

Remember also that persuading, insisting, or pushing your particular solutions will just interfere with your mate's problem-solving process. If your idea sounds perfectly reasonable to you, and yet your partner resists it, instead of lobbying for your solution you can ask what is wrong with it. That way, both of you can delineate a clearer understanding of your partner's underlying concerns, which in turn will move you closer to effective solutions.

> Donna realized that she felt lonely and vulnerable in their new home in the mountains. Aaron felt badly for her, and somewhat guilty because they had moved there so that he could live in beautiful natural surroundings.
>
> "You have to go out and meet the neighbors," he told her. "You just are going to have to pick one neighbor each weekend and walk up and say hello. I'll go with you if you want. That's what you have to do."

In many ways Aaron's solution was a good one. Donna, however, felt uncomfortable with it. She was shy. Going to a stranger's door and introducing herself felt overwhelming. The more Aaron insisted on his solution, the more what had started as loving support was becoming an argument. Aaron genuinely wanted to be helpful. But creating solution ideas for his wife, and then feeling insulted when she didn't pick up on what for him felt like the right solution, created divisiveness between them.

Suggestions from the listener can be a big help. The person with the problem may run into a block on solutions. At other times, the listening partner has additional knowledge that yields a particularly helpful idea. The key is for the therapeutic listener to offer, but not to insist on, solutions. The person with the problem generally knows best what solutions he or she can utilize.

Donna thought for a bit and suggested, "I think I need to start attending neighborhood activities. I could join one of the book groups that the town library runs. That way I'd be most likely to meet other book-lovers like myself. Then, once I've met some people, I'll invite them over, just one at a time, for coffee on Sunday afternoons."

Additional Coaching for the Coach

Like all skills, learning to facilitate your spouse's problem solving takes practice. Practice means you will make mistakes. That's OK. There will always be another inning.

Fortunately, your willingness to roll up your sleeves and focus your attention on your distressed partner is likely to be appreciated. Whether you barely make it together to first, head for second, take third, or see your mate arrive at home plate with the problem solved, you will have contributed positively.

♡ Respect gender differences

When it comes to support talk, generally men and women feel comfortable in different arenas. Women tend to make it easily to first or second base. They are often sympathetic listeners and are very good at asking questions to gather data about the problem. They tend, however to stay on second base rather than asking, "So what can you do about the situation?"

By contrast, men tend to err on the side of skipping second base in a fast dash to third. They cut short the gradual process of information gathering that enables the person with the problem to generate his or her own new ideas. At third, they also err, this time in being too quick to give advice. Good therapeutic talk requires plenty of time asking the questions that help the person with the problem discover new solutions.

Conventional wisdom has it that men and women also differ in when and if they want their partner's help. As John Gray (1992), popularizer of gender differences, has pointed out, when men feel distressed, they tend to want to be alone, to go off on their own to work out their own problems. Women, on the other hand, tend to want to talk when a problem is troubling them. Both genders' modes of self-soothing can work. You are best off if you can use both systems—if you are able to benefit from helping and being helped by each other and from turning inward and relying on your own coping capabilities.

In my experience men seldom seek therapy on their own, but once they discover its benefits, perhaps because their wife has insisted they come for couple counseling, they find that being able to talk over difficulties with someone can in fact be extremely helpful. What begins as couple therapy continues with the man utilizing additional therapy to explore further issues of his own. Similarly, women often find it liberating to discover that they can think through emotional upsets very well on their own. They feel empowered, for instance, seeing that they can figure out whom they are mad at when they feel depressed, or how to handle upsets with less distress.

If you bark when you need to hug

Some people find that when someone expresses to them a feeling of emotional distress, their first impulse is to become angry. They may realize that sympathy would be more appropriate, but what comes from their mouth is blame or criticism. Why does this happen, and what can you do about it?

> Aaron intensely disliked expressions of feelings from his wife. When Donna would cry, he'd feel the impulse to shout at her to shut up. When she expressed other vulnerable feelings, he would feel guilt and then rage welling up within him.
>
> The breakthrough came when Aaron realized that he believed that if Donna had a negative feeling, it must be his fault, and it was up to him to fix it. Feeling guilty and inadequate, he reacted defensively when his wife needed his solace.
>
> The notion of empathy as an alternative to self-blame, guilt, and the impossible task of fixing his wife's negative feelings gave Aaron major relief. He learned to say simply, "That's a shame," when Donna said she felt overwhelmed. This phrase felt easy compared with feeling responsible for the cause and for the cures of her feeling. And "That's a shame" enabled Donna to feel heard and understood, feelings that she had longed for all her life.

Advanced helping strategies

Once you're sure you have the baseball techniques down solidly, you can help to ease the pain of specific negative emotions with the following additional strategies.

- Sadness
  - Inquire about the loss: "Tell me about him. What was he like?"
  - Express understanding, amplifying the significance of the losses: "I can understand missing him, such a kind person."
  - Eventually, ease the person back into the stream of life: "Let's take the children for a picnic."

- Anger
  - ✦ Agree, listening for what's right or makes sense about the anger: "I can see that the mess in this house is distressing to you."
  - ✦ Validate the concern: "I have a kind of deafness to mess, but I can understand your feeling frantic when the house looks frantic."
  - ✦ Find ways to improve the situation: "How about if we routinely walk through the house for a quick pickup every night before bed? And let's both work with the kids on picking up after they play."

- Depression
  - ✦ Identify who or what your spouse is angry at: "If you close your eyes and picture at whom or what—not yourself—you feel angry, what do you see?"
  - ✦ Explore more empowered options for dealing with the situation: "Picture yourself as suddenly huge in that situation. Then what would you see and do differently?"

- Anxiety
  - ✦ Identify the problem: "What brings that anxious feeling?"
  - ✦ Specify the fears: "What about your chest pain scares you?"
  - ✦ Gather information with respect to each fear: "Does your chest pain hurt only when you exercise, or at other times, too?
  - ✦ For each fear, devise a plan of action: "Who could evaluate it so we'll know for sure what it means?"

- Physical pain
  - ✦ Validate the pain report: "Those migraines do seem debilitating."
  - ✦ Problem solve about possible solutions: "What helps you deal with them? Can I do something to help?"

- Frustration
  - ✦ Ask for additional information: "What parts of the problem are especially frustrating?"
  - ✦ Join in problem solving: "Let's look again at your options."

Notes

Chapter 12
Emotional and Sexual Intimacy

The innermost layer of the walls of arteries and veins is called the *intima*. In Latin, *intus* means *within*. The superlative of *intus* is *intimus,* or inmost. When two people share the inmost parts of themselves, they enter the mysterious world of intimacy.

Intimacy generally involves a gradual process of getting to know each other, a process that begins at the first encounter and continues throughout a couple's lifetime. Not all marriages become intimate, and as long as you are compatible teammates, you can enjoy an excellent partnership. Intimacy simply enriches marriage.

To whom, if anyone, do you open the deepest inmost secrets of your soul? To have an intimate relationship takes great trust, trust that your partner will take care to cherish your private thoughts, to hear with compassion your desires, to lovingly caress your most vulnerable aspects of soul and body.

Why be intimate?

Being able to talk openly and to hear your partner's inmost thoughts seems to satisfy a profound human urge to move beyond the oneness of self to a joining, becoming part of and partner with another.

When we talk intimately with someone, the desire for physical intimacy tends to arise as well. For women particularly, verbal and sexual connection are closely coupled.

Intimacy enhances bonding. The more sharing, the more bonding, just as the more fibers that are intertwined in a rope, the more weight it can hold. The more you and your spouse share yourselves with each other, the stronger your connection becomes.

Intimacy has a practical side as well. The more openly you share your thoughts and feelings, the more your partner will understand what you like and want, and therefore the more responsive he or she can be to your needs. To make effective shared decisions or to resolve conflicts, for instance, verbalizing your concerns is essential. The more deeply and broadly the two of you understand each other, the more easily upsetting moments can be remedied.

Lastly, intimacy offers opportunity for spiritual growth. The more intimately you know yourself and your partner, the more accepting you can be of both yourself and each other. Learning about yourselves is like taking a journey inward. Just as travel abroad is enlightening, travel within can provide unending discoveries.

Intimacy as talking openly

The key ingredients of intimacy, of a willingness to openly express your feelings and thoughts, are trust and trustworthiness. When you share the *intima* of your life, you are exposed and thus vulnerable. The intimate details of our lives are those that involve the most tender, humble, sometimes shameful, sometimes sad, sometimes joyous and proud emotions. To share these memories, wishes, and fears, it is important that you feel safe.

Safety means that your listener will treasure the information you share, handling your confidences with tender care. Safety involves confidentiality, keeping private thoughts within the bounds of your relationship rather than telling them to others. Safety also involves hearing with empathy, with caring understanding. To allow deep intimacy, you must feel certain that no criticism, blame, or negative judgments of any kind will enter into your conversation— no *shoulds,* no crossovers. Only insight, acceptance, and compassion belong in the delicate realm of intimate dialogue.

It can be interesting to observe what kinds of information you offer about yourself to different people in your life. The information you share offers a kind of litmus test on the nature of each relationship. If you feel grouchy because your car is in the shop and you have to take the bus to work, sharing this information with a total stranger sitting next to you is likely to seem odd or inappropriate. On the other hand, it would probably seem fine to tell a friend or colleague, "I've had a frustrating morning. My car wouldn't start. I had to have it towed to the mechanic and take the bus to work."

Other concerns, however, are more private. If you are having difficulties at work, for instance, you would probably share this distressing information only with a small group of friends. A problem with a parent or child might be reserved for an even more select group.

In contemporary marriage, couples often choose their partner to be the one person with whom they are most open about virtually all their concerns. If your relationship is not toxic or adversarial, virtually all your emotional reactions can be potential entry points for exploring your experiences. Your deepest fears, dreams, wishes, and values, as well as all you have experienced in your personal history, color the many facets of who you are. In an intimate relationship, these many dimensions all can be shared.

What Are Deep Concerns?

Sometimes when you feel an emotion, you are responding to the immediate situation. When your mate seems to be brushing aside what you say, for instance, you may feel frustration. This emotion probably indicates a concern that you want to be heard, that you want what you say be taken seriously.

Sometimes, however, your emotional reactions are intensified because what is happening in the present echoes a similar moment in your earlier life. For instance, suppose your partner is late coming home from work and you feel intense panic and anger. Odds are that you are tapping into a lode of times when another person has disappointed you. Perhaps in a previous relationship, or in your parents' marriage, lateness indicated infidelity. In these cases, when your emotional response seems surprisingly strong, out of proportion to the situation you are facing, your emotions offer a vehicle for exploring your deeper underlying concerns.

What are core concerns?

Core concerns are these that are deeply rooted in family-of-origin experiences and that recur frequently in the present. *Transference* refers to the process by which strong feelings from one's childhood keep coming up again in adult life. These feelings particularly tend to resurface vis-à-vis family members such as a spouse or children. Researcher Lester Luborsky (1986) has studied the phenomenon of transference, noting that most people have a few sensitive themes that evoke particularly strong feelings, and that these issues are the hot spots that easily and frequently cause tensions to erupt in their lives.

Someone who was either ignored or especially favored by his or her parents, for instance, may tend to be supersensitive to being ignored in adulthood. A person who received too much criticism may experience supersensitivity to criticism as a core concern. Someone who was abandoned by a parent who died or left the family may feel wary of trusting that loved ones will stay in the relationship; for this person, security of commitment may be a core concern. A person whose parents held what felt like a tight rein on them might be especially sensitive to any signs of feeling controlled by a mate.

Luborsky calls these deeply felt and oft-evoked sensitivities *core conceptual themes*. Integrating his concept with conflict-resolution terminology, I call them *core concerns*. Most spouses have recurring core concerns that can be tripped fairly easily by day-to-day circumstances.

> *Tanner would quickly experience anger when he felt at the mercy of other people's agendas and unable to bring his to the fore. When Kate was making summer vacation plans, Tanner reacted as he used to with his mother, squelching his own desires and agreeing to all her suggestions. By acting overly compliantly toward his wife, as he had toward his mother as a child, Tanner inadvertently was setting up a situation in which his wife would appear to dominate him as his mother had. When he suddenly became aware that their summer schedule allowed no room for his own objectives, a volcano erupted within him. The underlying concern "What about what I want?" was his core concern, a holdover from his family of origin.*

Psychologist Paul Wachtel (1977) points out that, like Tanner, without realizing it couples often participate inadvertently in recreating situations that trigger longstanding core concerns. One of the payoffs of getting to know yourself and your partner intimately is you can then become adept at identifying these core concerns. Once you can identify them, you can sort out what you are doing and what in the present situation feels the same as in your earlier experiences. You then can add to this information by taking a fresh look at your present circumstances to see what is now different.

Often we choose a partner who is in a deep way familiar to us, so the mate we choose may act like the people in our early lives, in our old family drama. Kate, for instance, was a strong, take-charge woman who didn't necessarily ask explicitly what Tanner wanted on their summer agenda. This made it much easier for Tanner to comingle his wife and his mother in his mind and react as if the two were one and the same. These partial similarities between your partner and a parent makes it all the more likely that the two of you will find yourselves replaying old scenarios.

On the other hand, this tendency to pick a partner with some similarities to a parent gives you a second chance, an opportunity to put new endings to the old stories.

> *Merry had a father who was domineering and controlling. She married Gil, a generous and kind man. Gil also, however, took his responsibilities as head of household very seriously. Without realizing it, in a subtle way he gradually took on the role of Merry's father by making decisions for his wife, such as when and where she worked outside the home (see Chapter 7).*

Once they understood the way their relationship had recapitulated an old theme, Gil and Merry felt liberated, free to choose new ways. Gil could use support-talk skills instead of making decisions for his wife, and they could make shared decisions instead of his having to bear full responsibility for family choices.

Alternatively, you may find you are reenacting the relationship you observed between your parents, replaying their dramas again and again. Think about your spats with your spouse. Did your parents ever argue in a similar style or about similar issues?

Kate used to get irritated when Tanner would come home and drop his jacket on a living room chair. "Hang it up," she pleaded again and again. Suddenly she realized that picking up after her husband had been a major issue for her mother, who frequently used to complain of her husband's tendency to leave a trail of clothes and other objects in his wake.

Once they realized that this was an inherited battle, Kate and Tanner could laugh. "That's one less battle I need to fight!" Kate smiled. "I prefer a house with a place for everything and everything in its place, but I'd rather have jackets on chairs than arguments. And overall I'm lucky to have married a guy who's neat—in more ways than one."

Understanding the roots of his wife's irritation, Tanner experienced a change of heart. Instead of feeling controlled by his wife and resisting change, he suggested, "How about if we buy more hangers and clear out some of the extra coats from the front hall closet? I would be more likely to hang my jacket if finding a hanger and space were less of a struggle."

Fortunately, history is not destiny. You can use your skills—fix-it talk, cleanup talk, shared decision making, conflict resolution—to choreograph more satisfying patterns for all the situations that currently frustrate either of you. If you can recognize your core concerns, you can map new solutions, new ways to meet these concerns in more satisfying ways. Understanding each other intimately, with a deep understanding of the sources of each of your core concerns, speeds up these sensitive dialogues.

Victoria and Austin often felt irritated at each other. To their relief, they gradually discovered that in almost every instance when either or both of them became irritated, standard underlying concerns had recurred. Victoria almost invariably was concerned about whether she was appreciated and loved. This scenario, she realized, echoed her mother's relationship with her father, and her own relationship with her father as well. Both she and her mother regarded her father as king and continuously sought his approval. The deal had been, "If you will adore me, I will serve you." Victoria was serving Austin, but expected in return an adoration that Austin hadn't understood he was supposed to give.

Austin's parents had been quite distant from each other. His father tended to be wary of his mother's attempts to connect, experiencing them as attempts to control him. Austin's concerns virtually always centered on power issues. He felt irritated if he thought he was not acting as an autonomous person but was submitting unwillingly to what he thought Victoria wanted of him—as his father had felt subservient to his mother.

The new relationship Victoria and Austin choreographed was one of intimacy with equal power, of connection between two strongly independent spouses. By concentrating on the cooperative communication basics—eliminating crossovers and saying instead of hinting when they wanted something—they developed a mutually appreciative relationship free of controlling or feeling controlled by the other.

Accessing Deeper Concerns

Psychologist John Norcross (1986) explains that the term deeper in psychological terminology describes thoughts and feelings that are either less accessible to conscious awareness or that originated early in life. Deeper concerns thus would refer either to unconscious desires or to desires that stem from early childhood experiences.

 ## Take a depth dive

Identifying these deeper concerns may take more than ordinary talking about a problem. A depth dive into subconscious, family-of-origin sources of current strong feelings can be helpful. It also can be very emotional, so proceed with care.

To explore these intimate inner thoughts and feelings, both of you need to be *certain* that you are highly skilled at all the communication basics. There is no room for toxicity, crossovers, or negative listening in this kind of intimate exploration.

To enter the depths and be sure you come back up safely, you might want to keep the following list nearby to guide the process.

1. *Identify an emotional moment*— Note a particularly strong feeling, especially one that tends to recur or that has been persisting.

2. *Recall a similar feeling in a past experience*— Close your eyes and allow an image to arise of an earlier moment in your life when you experienced a similar feeling.

3. *What's the same?*— What do you notice that feels the same in this earlier situation as in the current one?

4. *What's different?*— What elements of the present situation differ from the past situation?

5. *Find new options*— How can these differences open up new options for you in the present dilemma that were not available in the original situation?

The following example shows how Aaron and Donna used these techniques to understand what was happening when one of them felt unaccountably strong feelings emerging. A depth dive is appropriate when a couple notices a feeling that has been stronger than seems to make sense in the current situation.

1. Close your eyes and focus on the feeling

"When we were out with Pam and Joe in the park this afternoon and you went into quiet mode, I felt furious," Aaron said.

"Want to close your eyes, focus on the feeling, and see what images it brings up?" Donna asked.

Aaron, eyes closed, related, "I was furious because I wanted you to realize that I feel terribly alone when I'm the only one having a good time. I felt like I was the only one having a good time. And I had been really up, frolicking around the picnic grounds. I was mad though, because I felt like no one else wanted to have fun. That thought infuriates me, the thought that I have to maintain myself and everyone else."

2. Recall a similar feeling in a past experience

"Where does that idea come from?" Donna asked.

Aaron, his eyes still closed, answered, "That's my mother and my brother. Whenever I was in a good mood, they were overwhelmingly negative. I can still hear my brother's putdowns: 'Folks, look at him. He's an Irish setter. He's a nut. What's his problem?' They could turn my happiness into humiliation in no time."

3. What's the same?

"When you were quiet, I figured you were saying the same kind of thing to yourself."

4. What's different?

Donna continued, "Sounds like that's what felt the same, that happiness leads to feeling humiliated. What's different now from then?"

Aaron opened his eyes, smiling, "I sure am glad you like my happy side. And that we can have fun together."

5. Find new options

"I just have to remind myself," he continued, "that your silences don't mean you're thinking critical thoughts about me, and that I can ask you what you're thinking about instead of assuming the worst."
"Sounds better to me!" Donna grinned.

If it feels too risky to have this kind of deeply intimate dialogue with your partner, listen to those voices of caution. There are no trophies for diving too deeply or in unsafe conditions.

Interlocking core concerns

Often a situation will trigger not one but two overreactions—one from each partner. In the following example, interlocking core concerns trigger intense emotional reactions in both Aaron and Donna.

Donna was feeling lonely. She was beginning to make friends in their new community in the mountains, but she didn't feel close to anyone yet. That evening, she tried describing her feelings of loneliness to Aaron.
Aaron erupted angrily, "Why are you complaining so much? Can't you just enjoy life?"
After they both had calmed, Donna realized her two core concerns had both been triggered. One was loneliness. As a child she had lived in an isolated setting where she had longed for playmates. Her second core concern was to be able to express feelings and have them received with empathy. "Can't I have needs and feelings? Is anyone there for me? When is it my turn to be heard or nurtured?" she thought to herself.
Donna's second concern interlocked with one of Aaron's concerns—feeling like a failure if Donna was unhappy. When Aaron heard Donna express vulnerable feelings, he suddenly felt inadequate. To cover his feeling of guilt, his sense of responsibility for Donna's distress, and his shame at not knowing how to respond helpfully, Aaron reacted to Donna as his parents had to his tender feelings and as Donna's mother had to Donna's. He angrily criticized her.
Again, Aaron and Donna realized something complex was happening beneath the surface of this incident. They talked it through, each seeking to understand the roots of their strong reactions. As they figured it out, they decided to redo the conversation.
In their second-draft attempt, Donna received empathy for her loneliness, and Aaron felt terrific about his new supportive listening skills.

Through understanding their interlocking core concerns, Aaron and Donna converted their moments of distress into opportunities for intimacy and personal growth.

These are happy stories. Though they involve moments of anguish, they have happy endings. The distressful incidents in each case lead to sympathetic new understandings that enable the couples to discover liberating new ways of handling the dilemmas of living together.

Sexual Intimacy

Sexual intimacy is one of the unique features of married life. A marriage manual I saw recently from the 1970s focused primarily on sexual how-tos. There still is validity to this focus. Regular mutually satisfying sexual activity is generally a cornerstone of a good marriage.

While it is not essential, and some individuals and couples do manage with very little, sexual intimacy is like good nutrition and regular exercise in that it is decidedly healthy for you. Sexual release has potent physiological impacts. The more relaxed mood you may sense in yourself and in your mate after satisfying sexual fulfillment is a well-documented biochemical reality. Sexual activity also has potent effects on your relationship, reassuring you both of your shared affection. Like sunlight and water for plants, sexual intimacies keep your emotional connection nourished and healthy.

Practice smart sex

Ignorance is not bliss. Knowledge is power. Just as talking may come naturally to people but skills for handling the various kinds of dialogue in marriage must be learned, sexual acts come naturally but additional information can be very helpful. Libraries and bookstores now carry many books that give the how-tos of sexual functioning that are analogous to the how-tos of verbal communication in this book.

Be sensitive to frequency and fidelity

Sexual distress often involves disagreements about the frequency of sex and difficult healing of wounds from infidelity.

Sexual activity does not need to be frequent, but it does need to be in proportion to the degree of interest of both partners. People's rates of arousal vary widely, although in mid-marriage several times a week is fairly typical. In Lois Leiderman Davitz's (1988) study of exceptionally happy versus adequately satisfied couples, more than 84 percent of couples who felt particularly positive about their marriages enjoyed sex twice a week or more. Of couples who felt that their marriages were adequate but not great, a similar percentage, about 84 percent, had sex one to three times a month or less. In another study that covered a wider age range, 65 percent of the couples had sex one to three times a week, with younger couples tending toward higher frequencies and older couples tapering off. When partners have different desires concerning frequency, the skills of shared decision making become essential.

Fidelity is a central feature in most marriage contracts. Infidelity can shatter the marriage bond. While the majority of marriages do survive a single incident of infidelity, trust is difficult to restore.

Naïveté increases the risk of infidelity. Too many marriages end because one partner naïvely falls into a situation that results in sexual interest in a new person. Most unfaithful spouses that I have worked with in my practice did not set out intending to have an affair. More often, violations of a monogamous relationship seem to occur because of naïveté about the following several realities.

- Most sexual infidelity begins with someone becoming intimate socially with someone other than their mate. Talking about private matters invites sexual arousal, which may be why women typically want to connect emotionally by talking before sexual contact.

- Time alone with someone other than your partner in a private place, with the door closed, adds to the risk.

- Allowing your marriage to become malnourished because the two of you spend too little quality time together adds to the risks.

- Allowing your marital sexual relationship to atrophy invites vulnerability to sexual interest in others.

- Exposure to a new sexual partner heightens sexual interest.
  Laboratory rats show this pattern. Copulation rates are high when a male and female rat are initially put together in a cage. Over time they settle into a somewhat less frequent routine. If the rats are then separated and each put into a different cage with a new partner, their sexual frequency will temporarily zoom up, and then with familiarity again drop to more moderate rates. This phenomenon poses risks for marriage. Amorous arousal in someone other than your mate will be almost guaranteed to be more intense than with your more familiar partner. This intensity is a factor of newness, not love. This misunderstanding particularly frequently leads to divorce.

- The intensity difference with a new partner is primarily in the rapidity of initial arousal. The full sexual act itself is often more satisfying with a familiar partner. If you have been listening well to each other, you know best one another's pleasures and rhythms.

For practical as well as health, ethical, and religious reasons, marriage offers a safe zone for sexual enjoyment. Sex is an art form that lends itself to perfection over time. Married lovers who let themselves be creative and well informed can combine the excitement of novelty with the potency of knowing one another's mysteries. Add in the power of genuine love and you have a recipe for longstanding sexual satisfaction, free from guilt or fear, and open to enjoyment whenever and wherever.

Intimacy is communication

What do couples need to know to use their power of two toward enjoyment of a sexual life that is especially powerful and loving? Sexual and verbal intercourse bear a number of resemblances. The principles of sensitive attunement to one another and of symmetrical attention to the satisfaction of each of you, for instance, apply in both intimate realms. In fact, the basics of cooperative dialogue are fundamental to all intimate connecting, verbal and sexual.

- *Say it*— Intimacy begins with expressing your thoughts, feelings, and sensual impulses.

- *No polluting*— The more your connecting is criticism-free, the more your freedom of emotional and sexual expression can flourish.

- *Listen bilaterally*— Intimacy involves being both closely attuned to your partner and listening to your own physical sensations.

- *Use Symmetry*— Balancing sexual giving and receiving means that both of you matter.

- *Use climate controls*— The warmth of shared physical passion solidifies your bond.

Come live with me and be my love,
And all the pleasures prove.

—Christopher Marlowe,
The Passionate we will Shepherd to His Love

Chapter 13

Making Your House a Loving Home

Can Marlowe's romantic image of living together be a reality in today's world? Many people feel chronically busy and most "leisure" time is occupied with tedious chores. Are happy marriages just a TV fiction? Absolutely not.

Healthy couples don't just get along. They actively enjoy their ordinary time together. They laugh. They tease each other. They play together, even as they are busy with the work of living. And they love each other.

The pressures of time, money, and all the rest of life's challenges will always be there, but while you fix leaky faucets and wipe babies' bottoms you can enjoy affection, humor, and companionship.

Joy is a choice

Joy in being together, like a sense of joy at being alive, comes partly from temperament, partly from how you spend your days, and partly from attitude, which can be chosen. Fortunately, biological temperament alone does not determine destiny. As psychologist Jerome Kagan has observed, temperament does cause children to begin their lives as more shy, solemn, resilient, or energetic (Kagan, Reznick, and Snidman 1988). Over time, however, only a portion of the children born shy, for instance, remain withdrawn throughout their lives. The majority learn to expand their emotional bandwidth.

You and your partner both have initial temperamental tendencies. Nonetheless, you each can moderate your temperament by deciding, say, to smile, not scowl, when you greet each other each morning. You can express appreciation for the particularly tasty dinner your spouse has cooked rather than eating it without comment. You can wash the dishes feeling burdened and grumpy, or turn on the radio, sing aloud, and even put the suds aside for a moment and dance.

Sharing and Separateness

A good marriage is that in which each appoints the other guardian of his solitude.

—Ranier Maria Rilke, *Letters*

Joy in a marriage partnership generally signals that two emotionally healthy individuals are succeeding in creating a vibrant and robust shared life. But what is "emotional health"? Psychologist Andras Angyal (1965) defines emotional health as having two components. On the one hand, you need to feel good about who you are and what you are doing with your life as an autonomous individual; on the other hand, you need a sense of connection with others, of belonging.

Similarly, a healthy marriage gives the partners both ample space to be separate and consistent ways to connect as a couple. Both partners feel the freedom to live the life they choose as individuals. At the same time, they enjoy a strong sense of togetherness.

Too much separation can leave you feeling unattached. Too much connection can lead to claustrophobic interference in each other's lives. Family therapists label a marriage with insufficient connection *disengaged;* a marriage with too much connecting is called an *enmeshed* marriage.

Is time together really important in a marriage? Psychologists Jacobson, Waldron, and Moore (1980) studied what makes partners in happy marriages more pleased with their marriage on some days than on others. On fifteen consecutive evenings participants filled out checklists, including daily satisfaction ratings. For both men and women in these happy marriages, sharing positive activities and talking together markedly increased their satisfaction ratings. For men, doing joint activities was the most important—sitting and reading together, taking a walk, going out together for a meal. For women, talking together was the most significant. When husbands asked how the day had gone, showed interest in what their wives said by agreeing or asking relevant questions, talked about personal feelings, or even apologized for something that had not gone well, these communications led wives to increase that day's satisfaction rating.

In addition, affectionate behavior and family activities such as doing dishes and playing with the children contributed positively to both husbands' and wives' satisfaction ratings. Men especially loved receiving affectionate behavior of any kind—loving words, embraces, or sexual attention—from their wives. In general, however, the shared activities and pleasing conversation had the strongest impacts on how enthusiastically spouses rated their marriage.

As important as together time may be, time spent alone also has a revitalizing effect for many people and needs to be valued. Marriage does not mandate that all time and pleasures be mutual. Reading, daydreaming, individual sports, cards, basketball, a book group with friends, and a myriad of other activities enhance life and needn't be given up with marriage. Limiting yourself solely to activities that you and your partner share can stifle who you are and who you can become.

Children

The fullest challenge of the power of two may be when the two of you, in loving each other, decide to grow another human being. Nurturing children from infancy through to adulthood involves teamwork of the highest degree. While each of you needs a separate relationship with each of your offspring, you also need to accomplish the parenting project together.

The stakes are high if you and your mate disagree with regard to how to handle parenting and lack adequate skills for conflict resolution. Unless you are able to talk such dilemmas through to consensus you are likely to render each other ineffective. The skills of shared decision making and conflict resolution become essential in this arena. If you persist in disagreeing, your children will pay the price, and your marriage will feel like you are working against each other instead of helping each other.

A general rule in conflict resolution is that getting more information is one of the keys to finding solutions. With regard to child-rearing dilemmas, this strategy is often the most useful, and is certainly far preferable to fighting over who is right and who is wrong. Parenting, like conflict resolution and smart sex, takes major skills for which few couples have received adequate training.

Work—at home and abroad

Marriage is a commitment to partnership in the business of keeping alive. There's lots of work to be done in this project—earning and investing, cooking and cleaning, childcare and grocery shopping. It's no wonder then, that if you or your mate does not perform the roles you have taken on, marital satisfaction may dip. Mates who perceive that their partner is failing to keep up their agreed-upon household responsibilities tend to experience more marital dissatisfaction (Zeitlow & Sillars, 1988). By contrast, when couples feel that they are sharing tasks, their satisfaction with the relationship and feelings of commitment to the marriage increase.

Doing your part seems to be not just a matter of getting the work done. Sharing tasks symbolizes your cooperation and your interdependence (Canary & Stafford, 1992). Each time you do your fair share or more for the family, each time you join in willingly when there's work to be done, and reliably accomplish the tasks you have taken on, you raise by yet another notch the satisfaction level in your marriage.

Freud highly valued the contribution of work well done to a healthy life. He described a healthy person as one who is able to work and to love. This formula could be extended to couples by saying that a healthy couple is one that is able to accomplish the work of a couple and to be able to enjoy loving each other.

 ## Dividing the labor

As suggested at the outset of this book, the work of a couple involves multiple elements:

- providing financially and otherwise so that the family has the necessities to sustain life, such as food, clothing, and shelter
- providing for the ongoing maintenance of the household with accomplishment of shopping, cooking and meal cleanup, house cleaning and laundry, and home decorating and maintenance
- providing for the care and upbringing of children

A healthy couple is able to accomplish a clear division of labor so that these tasks of ordinary life can be accomplished in a way that seems fair to both and in accord with what each member of a couple most enjoys doing. Gender no longer determines who will do what in most households. Division of labor is usually necessary instead.

Division-of-labor discussions do best when they follow the guidelines for shared decision making. Each person is responsible for voicing his or her own concerns and preferences and for offering what he or she is willing to do in the way of solutions.

Especially when it comes to deciding who will do which household chores, volunteering and requests work well. That is, each person offers to do what he or she prefers to do, and asks when there is something he or she would like the other to do. Tasks that neither partner wants to do then get divided in whatever system feels fair to both parties.

Gina and Gerald both work outside the home. Every so often they set aside time to rethink how to divide up the tasks of running their household. "So let's take a fresh look at how to divvy up the housework." Gina said.

> *"I can handle the day-to-day housekeeping, keeping the house picked up, and all the cooking. Grocery shopping gets to be a burden though, because it's so hard to do with the kids. Would you be willing to do the shopping on your way home from work?"*
>
> *"On the way home from work I'm usually too tired," replied Gerald, "but I would be willing to go out after supper to shop once or twice a week. I'd much rather do that than do the dinner dishes like I have been. As to keeping the house clean, vacuuming is my specialty."*
>
> *Gina and Gerald continue to sort through the work of running a household until it has all been accounted for.*

Several dialogue fundamentals make Gina and Gerald's division of labor talk flow relatively easily:

- Both partners are willing to say what they want, putting their cards on the table instead of hinting or speaking in *don't wants.*

- Both speak about their own feelings or ask about the other's preferences without crossovers or trespassing—saying what they think the other would like to do or should do.

Love

> *Some pray to marry the man they love,*
> *My prayer will somewhat vary*
> *I humbly pray to Heaven above*
> *That I love the man I marry.*
>
> —Rose Pastor Stokes, "My Prayer"

Love is an activity, something you can choose to do, a stance you can take. As one divorced woman told me when her ex-husband suddenly died, "I was so busy trying to change, and correct, and control him, I didn't understand back then that to love is to cherish." To love your spouse takes active commitment to cherish his or her presence, to appreciate his or her contributions, to negotiate respectfully when there are differences, and to care in every way for his or her being.

Love also sometimes provokes emotion, a feeling that may surge up at surprising times, ebbing and flowing depending on how relaxed or busy we feel, how much we are focused on our loved one, how open we ourselves are to receiving love, or how secure or threatened each of us feels. The emotion can fill us at different times with potent inner excitement, contentment, playfulness, or peace.

Like a diamond, love sometimes sparkles, sometimes sits blankly like plain glass. Like a diamond, love has multiple facets. To conclude this book, here are a few additional practical thoughts on more of love's many aspects.

❤ To be loved, be likeable

One facet of loving is liking. Fortunately, what makes people likable needn't remain a secret. We feel attracted toward people who emanate positive feelings. We desire to back away from people who emanate negative feelings. And we feel neutral toward people who give forth very little feeling.

As I have reiterated many times in this book, a dominating personal style, habitual disagreement, commands, complaints, and irritability are unpleasant and erode the quality of a marriage (Markman & Hahlweg, 1993; Jacobson, Waldron, & Moore, 1980). Even in the first years of marriage, the honeymoon period, hostility and abrasiveness rapidly lower spouses' ratings of their marriage (Newton & Kiecolt-Glaser, 1993). The negative power of two then comes into play. If the receiver is high in what psychology researchers call *negative reactivity* and reacts with matching unpleasantness, negative cycles of criticism and countercriticism can sweep a couple into a hopelessly unpleasant vortex of distasteful interactions (Margolin & Wampold, 1981).

By contrast, positivity draws us in. Communicating in cheerful, optimistic, and uncritical ways invites your partner to mirror back equally positive banter (Canary & Stafford, 1992). The more positive appreciation and good humor you show your mate, the more of it you will receive in return. Your styles may differ. One of you may be a teaser, the other a toucher. One of you may bake cookies; the other may buy chocolates. Feeling loved, however, you will find yourself giving off more and more warm affection. This kind of positivity cycle heralds a happy home.

For a more loving relationship, therefore, conduct a personal inventory. When and how often are you critical, judgmental, grumpy or unpleasant? Any negative emanations are reason to reassess your contributions. How often do you emanate caring affection, willingness to do your share and more, compassionate understanding in difficult times, and joy?

❤ Love is an aesthetic experience

Human beings are drawn toward beauty. Neatness, cleanliness, and an artistic or colorful appearance draw people closer, while a disheveled or chaotic appearance puts people off.

Aesthetics doesn't mean that you need to spend hours applying makeup or a lot of money buying fashionable clothing. It does mean that a few moments in front of a mirror to look relatively more rather than less attractive may have significant payoff in the moment-to-moment love quotient in your home.

Loving is seeing what is there

Loving can be as simple as watching appreciatively the one you treasure. This kind of appreciation requires that you focus on each other, away from distractions like television or the commotion of too much to do and too little time to do it.

Toward your spouse, enjoyment can arise in response to almost anything. You can appreciate how your partner looks, the telltale dimple when he or she is about to tease you, or the intense look of concentration when he or she is thinking through a challenging problem. You can appreciate something your partner has done—an especially well-prepared meal, a room that has been artfully rearranged, a business deal that will bring in extra income. Enjoyment can come simply from the fact that your mate is there, by your side, a partner augmenting and enhancing your life.

Appreciation can be especially meaningful when you notice the accomplishments that your partner particularly values or that he or she has put extra effort into for you. For instance, appreciation for the long hours of a dedicated breadwinner, of the creative skills of a partner who takes pride in parenting, or for the ingenuity of a mate who has fixed a stubbornly leaky faucet turns the accomplishment into a shared source of goodwill. Like the heartfelt expression of the words "I love you," appreciation for ordinary actions can be reiterated over and over and yet continually casts a warm glow.

How is appreciation expressed? First, it needs to be felt, allowed as a joy within you. Then it needs to be communicated. Words, though sometimes helpful and almost always welcome, are not essential. A playful grin, a warm smile, shared laughter, the meeting of eyes, an affectionate hug— these are the ultimate glue with power to hold the two of you together forever.

Love equals passion plus compassion

True love has not only passion but also compassion. Caring in this compassionate way includes the ability to see your mate's mistakes as problems, as problematic actions that, while mistaken, are well meant, simply human, or signs of a handicap. With compassionate love, you can see your mate's frailties as a part of a whole person for whose well-being you deeply care. With compassion, you can understand that even if yours is a match made in heaven, neither of you is an angel.

Love is warmth

Love may begin as hot romance and potent sexual attraction. Romance certainly brings pleasure. Over the years of a marriage, however, the temperature of love changes. It goes from a consuming and sometimes dangerous heat—a flame that can flare but also flicker out—to a sustaining and enduring warmth.

Love is listening

Love in its hot phase feels like a compelling desire to attach permanently to another person, to become a part of them or to subsume them into your own world. Love then needs to evolve with the recognition that your partner is a separate person.

Differences inevitably arise when two maturely distinct autonomous individuals build a partnership. Your mate is not your clone, nor your puppet. Love rests on the profound understanding that even in the worst of times, even and especially when you differ, *both* of you have legitimate and different concerns. Longstanding love then requires that you grow together *with* your differences, not fight against each other's uniqueness.

When you want an object to sit on a couch, you just put it there. Not so with two separate individuals. You can ask, you can explain why you would like your partner to take that seat, but you cannot make your mate do what you want and still have a loving connection. For love, you need to listen. As you listen, your world is augmented by taking in a second point of view.

Love is enjoying

People are attracted to others with whom they have enjoyable interactions (Burleson & Denton, 1992). This chapter began with a description of joy in marriage. The more joy, the more love, and the more desire to spend time together. These interactions are all positive synergies; that is, each enhances the others. If you wake up in the morning and greet your partner with joy at seeing him or her right there in your very own bed, then your mate will feel loved and is likely to mirror love back. With all that love and joy going on between you, of course you desire to spend time together. Time together adds again to your overall sense of delight in your marriage, making it easy to wake up the next morning delighted to greet your mate yet again. Just as negative cycles of anger, controlling, criticizing, feeling hurt, and striking back characterize marriage in its most unhappy modes, positive synergies characterize marriage at its best.

Starting these positive cycles can be the tricky part, especially if you have not been in the habit of giving each other friendly, appreciative, kindly, or playful gestures.

> *Jim and Tina had learned not to fight, but something still was missing in their marriage. While they were no longer giving each other a hard time, they weren't giving each other many positives either.*

I gave Jim and Tina each ten poker chips, white ones to him and blue to her. Their assignment was to exchange all the chips, every day, one at a time. With each one they were to give something positive, in words or actions. This meant that each of them would initiate at least ten positive interactions every day.

Even with the first chip, the tone of their talking brightened. "Jim, I'm sorry I've been grumpy a lot lately, because I really do love you," Tina began, handing a chip to Jim with her affectionate apology.

"I have my bad times, too," Jim acknowledged, adding shyly, "Anyway, I do like hearing those 'I love you' words." Jim handed Tina a chip for sharing intimate feelings.

"And thanks for helping me with the dishes last night," Tina continued, smiling tentatively as she handed Jim an appreciation chip.

"Here, let me get you a tissue," Jim offered, seeing a tear of relief roll down Tina's cheek. He gave her a chip for affectionate helpfulness.

"Thanks," Tina grinned. "I'd better start using it, too, or else you'll have to learn how to swim. We might drown in all this good stuff."

The poker chips helped Jim and Tina consciously focus on enjoying each other. With or without poker chips, if you pay attention to how many positive exchanges you initiate each day with your mate, you will have a good measure of how actively love abounds in your shared life space.

Best of all, the more you express love, the more you will feel it. William James, the great nineteenth-century psychologist, said the act of running from danger actually makes us feel more scared. Similarly, when we talk and act lovingly, we feel feelings of love. While not every moment in married life can be an expression of love—sometimes you just want to sit down to get the bills paid, or you need to cook dinner—you may be amazed at how much enjoyment and affection you can infuse into everyday living.

Love is how you talk

Love is more than liking, more than appreciating, more than warm feelings, compassion, and positive synergies. Love also is a set of habits.

- To love is to be in the habit of taking care that when you open your mouth to talk, it is to speak with insight and consideration, not to cross boundaries or spew toxicity.

- To love is to be in the habit of listening with your ears open to learn, not to criticize. Love, in short, is using the secrets you have been learning in this book to build a marriage that is a blessing to you both.

Love gives you the power of two

Two are better than one, since they have a good reward for their labor.

For if one falls, the other will lift him up; but if one falls alone, there is no second to lift him up.

When two lie together, they warm each other; but one alone, how can he keep warm?

If one is attacked, both can stand up against him; and a threefold cord cannot be quickly broken.

—Kohelet (Ecclesiastes) translation by Bruce Heitler

Bibliography

Angyal, A. 1965. *Neurosis and Treatment: A Holistic Theory.* New York: John Wiley & Sons.

Bograd, M. 1988. How battered women and abusive men account for domestic violence: Excuses, justifications, or explanations? In *Coping with Family Violence: Research and Policy Perspectives,* edited by G. T. Hotaling, D. Finkelhor, J. T. Kirkpatrick, and M. A. Strus. Newbury Park, Calif: Sage.

Burleson, B. R., & W. H. Denton. 1992. A new look at similarity and attraction in marriage: Similarities in social-cognitive and communication skills as predictors of attraction and satisfaction. *Communication Monographs. 59* (September).

Burman, B., & G. Margolin. 1992. Analysis of the association between marital relationships and health problems: An interactional perspective. *Psychology Bulletin.* 112:39-63.

Canary, D. J., & L. Stafford. 1992. Relational maintenance strategies and equity in marriage. *Communication Monographs. 59:* (September).

Carnevale, P. J. D., & A. M. Isen. 1986. The influence of positive affect and visual access on the discovery of integrative solutions in bilateral negotiation. *Organizational Behavior and Human Decision Processes,* 37:1–13.

Carter, E., & M. McGoldrick. 1989. *The Changing Family Life Cycle: A Framework for Family Therapy.* Boston: Allyn & Bacon.

Davitz, L. L. 1988. Seven secrets of a super solid marriage. *New Woman.* August.

Eicher, D. 1982. Marriage: Sex figures in many unhappy unions. *Sunday Denver Post.* October 17.

Fisher, R., & W. Ury. 1981. *Getting to Yes.* Boston: Houghton Miflin.

Freud, S., 1917. *Standard Edition of the Complete Psychological Works of Sigmund Freud,* J. Strachey translator and editor. New York: Norton.

Ginott, H. 1965. *Between Parent and Child.* New York: Macmillian.

Gottman, J. 1994. *Why Marriages Succeed or Fail.* New York: Simon and Schuster.

Gray, J. 1992. *Men Are From Mars, Women Are From Venus.* New York: Harper Collins.

Greenberg, L. 1984. A task analysis of interpersonal conflict resolution. In *Patterns of Change,* edited by L. Rice and L. Greenberg. New York: Guilford.

Hamel, J. M. 1995. Doctoral dissertation on transformational marriages. at Fielding University.

Harlow, H. F. 1958. The nature of love. *American Psychologist.* 13:673–85.

Heitler, S. 1993. *From Conflict to Resolution.* New York: Norton.

Holtzworth-Monroe T., & A. Anglin. 1990. The competency of responses given by maritally violent versus non-violent men to problematic marriage situations. Paper presented at the meeting for the Association for the Advancement of Behavior Therapy, San Francisco, November.

Jacobson, N. S., H. Waldron, and D. Moore. 1980. Toward a Behavioral Profile of Marital Distress. *Journal of Consulting and Clinical Psychology.* 48(6):696–703.

Jacobson, N. S., J. M. Gottman, J. Waltz, R. Rushe, et al. 1994. Affect, verbal content, and psychophysiology in the arguments of couples with violent husband. *Journal of Consulting and Clinical Psychology.* Oct. 62(5):982–88.

Kagan, J., J. S. Reznick, & N. Snidman. 1988. Biological basis of childhood shyness. *Science.* 240:167–71.

Kohelet (Ecclesiastes). Unpublished translation by Bruce Heitler.

Kurdek, L. A. 1993. Predicting marital dissolution: A five-year prospective longitudinal study of newlywed couples. *Journal of Personality and Social Psychology.* 64:221–42.

Lehman et al. 1986. As reported in *Journal of Social and Personal Relationships,* 1988. Listener response strategies to a distressed other, by C. I. Notarius and L. R. Herrick. 5:97–108.

Lerner, H. G. 1990. *The Dance of Intimacy.* New York: Harper & Row.

Lewis, S., & W. Fry. 1977. Effects of visual access and orientation on the discovery of integrative bargaining alternatives. *Organizational Behavior and Human Performance.* 20:75–92.

Luborsky, L., P. Crits-Christoph, & J. Mellon. 1986. Advent of objective measures of the transference concept. *Journal of Consulting and Clinical Psychology.* 54:39–47.

Margolin, G., & B. E. Wampold. 1981. Sequential analysis of conflict and accord in distressed and nondistressed marital partners. *Journal of Consulting and Clinical Psychology.* 49(4):554–67.

Markman, H. 1979. Application of a behavioral model of marriage in predicting relationship satisfaction of couples planning marriage. *Journal of Consulting and Clinical Psychology.* 47(4):743–49.

Markman, H. J., & K. Hahlweg. 1993. The prediction and prevention of marital distress: An international perspective. *Clinical Psychology Review.* 13:29–43.

McKay, M., P. D. Rogers, & J. McKay. 1989. *When Anger Hurts: Quieting the Storm Within.* Oakland, Calif: New Harbinger Publications.

Medved, D. 1990. *The Case Against Divorce.* New York: Ballantine.

Newton, T. L., & J. K. Kiecolt-Glaser. 1995. Hostility and erosion of marital quality during early marriage. *Journal of Behavioral Medicine.* 18(6).

Norcross, J. 1986. Levels of change. In Integrative dimensions for psychotherapy, edited by J.O. Prochaska. *International Journal of Eclectic Psychotherapy.* 5(3):256–74.

Notarius, C. I., & L. R. Herrick. 1988. Listener response strategies to a distressed other. *Journal of Social and Personal Relationships.* 5:97–108.

Notarius, C., & H. Markman. 1993. *We Can Work It Out.* New York: Perigee, Berkley Publishing Group.

Pruitt, D. G. 1981. *Negotiation Behavior.* New York: Academic Press.

Schwartz, V. 1995. On a biological regulation of aggression. *American Journal of Psychiatry.* 152(11):1698–99.

Shapiro, J. 1992. *Men, A Translation for Women.* New York: Dutton.

Tannen, D. 1994. *Talking from Nine to Five.* New York: William Morrow and Company.

Wachtel, P. 1977. *Psychoanalysis and Behavior Therapy: Toward an Integration.* New York: Basic Books.

Zeitlow, P. H., & A. L. Sillars. 1988. Life-stage differences in communication during marital conflicts. *Journal of Social and Personal Relationships.* 5:223–45.

Some Other
New Harbinger Titles